With Heads Held High

By Peter Haworth

© Peter Haworth 2015

All rights reserved. No part of this publication may be reproduced, stored in a retrieval system or transmitted by any means, electronic, mechanical, photocopying or otherwise without the prior consent of the author.

DEDICATION

Once again I am indebted to my wife Julie who has had to endure the roller coaster emotions engendered during the course of compiling this diary. From the highs of promotion to the depths of relegation she has been a constant source of calm and reason. Never slow to offer her opinions, on anything ranging from football, politics, the NHS, the Banks, and my driving technique, once again she has been my inspiration!

ACKNOWLEDGEMENTS

Firstly my thanks must go to my old work colleague and friend Ed Skingsley (PNE ED). To have to proofread a diary of a Premier League season for a neighbouring rival club cannot have been easy. To read of the excitement and elation that comes with success can only be something that he dreams of. Seriously many thanks for the numerous corrections and alterations made to make the book more readable. He will note that some of the amendments which he attempted to 'sneak in under the wire' do not feature. Nice try Ed!

Special thanks also to Colin Waldron for writing the foreword. Colin on who being approached said "I don't have to read it do I?" has done me proud.

I would also like to mention the part played by fellow Dotcom Walker Brian Higginson (Scouse Brian) who first got me interested in the idea of digitally printing the book, and mentored me throughout the process with great enthusiasm. Brian's genuine desire to see all the North West clubs do well does him great credit. It is a pity he is associated by accident of birth with Liverpool FC, one day we will convert him.

To John and Judy W, and John G for being my fellow Claret diehards and pre match beer connoisseurs. Sitting outside a pub in the middle of winter drinking beer in thermals and with gloves on just wouldn't be the same without them.

To my walking pals in the Lancashire Dotcom Walkers group, and the Burnley Contingent, who over the last few years have provided many hilarious moments. The countryside of Lancashire and The Yorkshire Dales, and the good companionship enjoyed on our rambles is priceless.

Finally once again above all to the manager, backroom and playing staff at Burnley FC for providing a fantastic couple of seasons. I never once thought that I would see the Clarets play Premier League football. To have seen it happen twice within the space of five years is nothing short of unbelievable.

A special thanks must go to my mate of many years (and beers) Steve Calderbank. His technical wizardry in converting this book from digital to print format has been outstanding. No monetary reward could be deemed anywhere near adequate. So there will be none!

(Well there's a surprise then…….Steve C)

TABLE OF CONTENTS

DEDICATION	3
ACKNOWLEDGEMENTS	4
FOREWORD	7
INTRODUCTION	9
THE JOURNEY BEGINS	13
MAY/JUNE	41
JULY	56
AUGUST	68
SEPTEMBER	89
OCTOBER	106
NOVEMBER	124
DECEMBER	148
JANUARY	174
FEBRUARY	199
MARCH	223
APRIL	239
MAY	263
REVIEW	282

FOREWORD

I was pleased to be invited to write the foreword to this book, clearly written by a man in love with his local football club, as I too have been touched by a love of Claret and Blue since Jimmy Adamson signed me from Chelsea.

It didn't take long for my BFC affair to begin and many similarities between then and now remain today. A small town population recorded as 76,489 (1971 census), down to 73,021 (2001 census). About that number now regularly file into Old Trafford on match days. A limited ground capacity, today about 22,000 bums on seats. In my playing days attendances of 30/40,000 for the visits of the 'big teams', with the majority standing were not unusual. No rich oil Sheiks or Oligarchs on the board at the Turf. There's a few in Bacup, but they tend to watch cricket! Often the lowest player budget in the league, and nearly always the bookies favourites for relegation. The 2013/14 season where we claimed promotion for the second time in 5 years, had once again seen us start as short odds relegation candidates.

So the recurring question continues. How the hell do they do it?

Ironically the same winning philosophy has transpired through many generations of Burnley teams over the last fifty years plus. It goes something like this:

"We might not be the most skilful, or the most expensive team today, but we will all show more effort, determination and heart than you. If you don't match us in these areas, we'll win."

On occasions some of the multi-millionaire entertainers who visit Turf Moor mistakenly leave these three components on the car park.

Peter covers this simple Burnley psychology very well in this book. He probably explains it better than I as he evaluates the 2014/15 season in his own distinctive way.

I was proud to be Burnley Captain and that pride stays with me today. I still remember the old metaphor that I was told by Jimmy Adamson when I signed for the club, he said:

"Remember Colin, it's not the size of the dog in the fight that matters, it's the size of the fight in the dog!"

Enjoy the read.

Colin Waldron

Burnley FC 1967-76, Captain 1968, 1974

INTRODUCTION

In 2010, hoping but not really expecting, I made the rash statement on the back cover of my first book, "A Season in the Sun", that on our return to the big time I would once again attempt to capture the thrills and spills of another season in the top flight. The incredible events outlined in the next few pages are what fellow Clarets, lead us to exactly where we are now.

Relegation from the Premier League in 2010 was a bitter pill to swallow after the excellent home form at the start of the campaign. The defection of our then manager Owen Coyle to near rivals and fellow relegation battlers Bolton Wanderers ripped the heart out of both team and fans alike. The appointment of Brian Laws was never popular with the fans and the season fizzled out in disappointing fashion. The Directors - having appointed Laws and backed him with cash - felt obliged to give him fair crack of the whip at reviving our fortunes. However by Christmas 2011 it was obvious the team was going nowhere and the fans were becoming even more disgruntled. Laws' demise was inevitable and the board looked to young, upcoming Bournemouth manager, Eddie Howe.

Eddie, a rising star after having saved a financially crippled Bournemouth from Football League extinction, had then masterminded their promotion to League 1. His ability to manage on a shoestring budget obviously fitted the profile for any prospective Burnley manager, and his attractive attacking style of play made him a natural fit for the Clarets.

Unfortunately Eddie was unable to bring any consistency to the Clarets. Scoring goals didn't seem to be too much of a problem but stopping them was a different matter. Games where we scored two or three times often saw the opposition repeat or better the feat and Eddie seemed at a loss to get to grips with defending. A guy who had spent his entire career on the South Coast appeared unsettled in his new Northern surroundings. When in 2012 Bournemouth, now backed with Russian money came-a-calling, Eddie was unable to resist the lure of the sunny south and we were again looking for a manager.

Unexpectedly the position went to Sean Dyche who, with limited managerial experience, had unfortunately lost the Watford job after a relatively successful season running a club with poor gates and little money (sounds familiar doesn't it)? Immediately Dyche set about stiffening up the defence and almost immediately the goals against started to dry up, unfortunately so did the goals for! The second half of the 2012/13 season saw some dire performances and the side sliding towards a very congested bottom end of the table. A late rally to the season left the Clarets in mid table safety and ironically above free spending and bitter local rivals Blackburn Rovers, who by this time had become something of a laughing stock, (as opposed to a chicken stock)!

I think it is fair to say that before the 2013/14 season got underway the level of scepticism among Clarets fans hit an unprecedented high. Many fans were highly critical of the football played under Dyche, long serving players were leaving the club and once again we seemed to be in financial meltdown. Senior players such as Lee Grant, Martin Paterson, and even Chris McCann, a product of our own youth system all declined the offer of new contracts and left for pastures new. Speculation regarding the free scoring Charlie Austin, very much the fans "darling" continued throughout the summer. Charlie in fact seemed to have landed his dream move to the Premier League with newly promoted Hull City, only for the deal to fall through due to a failed medical.

This was not only a personal disaster for Charlie but also for the club. They had seen their prize asset devalued substantially overnight and the source of potential revenue to fund incoming transfers disappear. As players left one by one through the summer the dearth of incoming signings alarmed the supporters greatly. However through it all Dyche and his staff maintained a calm resolve, seemingly unruffled by all the doom and gloom.

A major problem area for the team was the goalkeeping department, Grant having left for Derby County and with both Brian Jensen and Jon Stewart released, it left the club without a keeper. Dyche moved swiftly to land Tom Heaton from relegated Championship rivals Bristol City. Tom came with a good pedigree having previous experience with Manchester United and Cardiff City, and was to prove an inspirational signing.

Many players came in to the club in the pre-season period on trial but only two were initially offered contracts, Scott Arfield - a midfielder, once rumoured to be a target for Coyle whilst at Burnley, and now released by Huddersfield, and a young striker, Ryan Noble also released, by Sunderland.

The most protracted signing was that of midfielder David Jones released by Wigan. Jones went on to play in the bulk of the pre-season friendlies but with no sign of a contract being drawn up. It transpired that he was unable, due to contractual obligations with Wigan, to sign until August -

which he duly did much to the relief of the long suffering supporters.

Again it's fair to say that in the eyes of most of the fans the 2013 summer transfer ins and outs had left the club in a weaker state than at the end of 2012/13. This allied to the dismal performances often served up during the latter half of that season, left many fans fearing a relegation battle, a view shared by the Bookmaking fraternity.

Then, the final straw. Almost on the eve of the new season Charlie Austin departed to 'moneybags' Queens Park Rangers, newly relegated from the Premier League. Austin, whilst not getting his move to the 'big league' joined a club who, due to the wealth of their owners would surely be challenging again for honours.

What a disaster for the Clarets. Although not totally unexpected, their Talisman was gone. Where would the goals come from now? Charlie had virtually carried that responsibility on his shoulders for most of the previous season. Still, the manager and the club appeared calm - although it was not so easy for the fans and they were far from happy.

THE JOURNEY BEGINS

First game up was a rerun of last season's opener with a home game against Bolton Wanderers. Although Coyle was no longer with our opponents having been sacked in the previous season, their proximity would ensure a lively atmosphere and decent crowd. As part of the 125th Anniversary celebrations of the Football League, Sky television decided to screen the game live and we were back to the days of lunchtime kick offs.

As often happens when we fear the worst, the performance turned out to be much better than we had expected. The Clarets came out of a hard fought draw probably feeling a little unlucky not to have bagged all three points. Midweek saw a thumping 4-0 away win at York City in the Capital One Cup (Cocup) and the following Saturday another away win in the Championship at Sheffield Wednesday.

August turned out to be a highly satisfactory start to the campaign with seven games played, five won, and a solitary defeat at Brighton where new keeper Tom Heaton was controversially sent off. Of the seven played, five were in the league and the Clarets followed up the Cocup win at York with a home victory over near neighbours Preston North End. Disappointing, but not totally expected were the low attendances at Turf Moor for the league games. Only 12,919 turned up for the Bolton game although the attendance was probably affected by live coverage on TV and fans still on holiday. The Yeovil match attracted 10,085 with very few opposition fans making the long journey from deepest Somerset. Thus the month ended with Burnley sitting third in the league, a position we could only have dreamt of before the start of the new campaign.

The end of August saw the closure of the summer transfer window, and Clarets fans had patiently waited all month to see where the Charlie Austin money would be spent. In typical Burnley fashion, it wouldn't! Despite consistent rumours that striker Ashley Barnes from Brighton was about to sign, the window closed with just the last minute signing of another winger, Michael Kightly on a season long loan from Premier league Stoke City. Kightly, a player with a decent pedigree and known previously to Sean Dyche, had injury problems at Stoke and was looking to get 'game time' and his career back on track.

There seemed to be parallels between the 2008/09 season developing, in that we had an unfancied, small but tightly knit squad, and were hopefully at the start of another successful League (Cocup) run. However we were certainly better placed this season compared to then.

September saw the good early season form continue with three wins and a draw in the league and another Cocup victory at home over Nottingham Forest. The league wins coming at home to Birmingham and Charlton, and a very pleasing away win at Leeds. The only disappointment was a 1-1 home draw with Blackburn Rovers, due to a late equaliser. Danny Ings clean through, was denied a winning goal by a professional foul from the Rovers sub Williamson who was duly red carded. At the end of the month we had not only maintained our league position but bettered it moving up to second.

Notable in the team's success was the developing partnership between Danny Ings and Sam Vokes. Ings was duly fulfilling the promise that was always evident but thwarted by serious injuries in his early time at the Turf. Now fully recovered he was scoring goals for fun, as was his much maligned strike partner Vokes. The sale of Austin had given Big Sam a chance to establish himself and getting regular games had seen his confidence grow immeasurably. The two strikers were forming an intuitive partnership likened by Clarets Legend, David Eyres as being akin to Toshack and Keegan in their Liverpool glory days.

What a fantastic week for the Clarets in early October. Firstly we went top of the league following a Tuesday night away win at Doncaster. This was followed by an England Under 21 call up for Danny Ings. On Friday 4th October Sean Dyche was named Championship Manager of the Month for September. To cap off a perfect week, the Clarets convincingly beat much fancied Reading at the Turf to stay Championship leaders, the goals again coming from Ings and Vokes. Heady times! The feelgood factor was returning to Turf Moor and the fans were beginning to once again "Dare to Dream".

Another away victory this time at Ipswich saw the Clarets go two points clear at the top as the end of October approached. The win gave the Clarets their first win at Ipswich in 43 years and their best start to a season since 1897. Last game of the month would be at home to Queens Park Rangers....and the return of Charlie Austin! Surely a decent crowd for this one with Clarets fans experiencing a mixture of euphoria and disbelief at the way the season was panning out.

Sure enough the Clarets run had rekindled the enthusiasm in the town, and a much improved attendance of 16,074 saw the Clarets despatch QPR 2-0 and go three points clear at the top. Once again the Ings/Vokes partnership paid dividends with both goals going to the former. The game also bizarrely had mascot Bertie Bee sent off, and pantomime villain Joey Barton hit on the head by a plastic Coke bottle launched from the James Hargreaves stand! Austin got a good reception from the crowd on his return but was then 'pocketed' by the Burnley defence and suffered a very quiet afternoon.

One black cloud on the horizon was the threat of gathering injury problems to an already paper thin squad. Missing from the QPR game was Scott Arfield - injured in training, and also influential midfielder Dean Marney was unable to complete the game. Kieran Trippier had taken a number of solid whacks in recent games and with the Cocup tie against West Ham coming up quickly after QPR, it was maybe time for some team changes.

The Clarets made four changes for the Hammers cup tie, David Jones was suspended after already picking up five bookings, Kightly and Duff were rested, and Marney still unfit. Despite the changes, the Clarets made a good showing against the Premier league side but were eventually undone by two penalty decisions, the first decidedly questionable!

As feared, injuries and suspensions were now starting to impact on the small squad. What a pity that the defeat to West Ham blotted a perfect copybook for October. However, the Clarets finished the month top of the Championship, clear by three points and with a positive goal difference of 17. Free scoring Burnley had 24 goals from 13 Championship fixtures and their miserly defence had conceded only seven.

The good early season form continued into November with a fighting comeback from a two goal deficit at Millwall to take a point.

The first and only home game of the month saw Eddie Howe's promoted Bournemouth as visitors, with much speculation as to what sort of reception Eddie would receive. The Clarets were boosted ahead of the game by a second consecutive Manager of the Month award for Sean Dyche. Further good news came with another selection of Danny Ings for the England Under 21 squad, and he was also named Skybet Championship Player of the Month for October.

The crowd resurgence for the QPR game had quickly ebbed away and we were back down to something over 12K with a decent away following considering the distance involved. For the second consecutive week the Clarets went behind, this time shortly after half time to a goal in a lifetime effort from Bournemouth's Rantie. Once again the team showed its fighting spirit as Ings levelled with six minutes to play. A pretty neutral reception for Eddie Howe confirmed that we had moved on and he will occupy a very brief chapter in the history of the Clarets.

After a welcome two week break for International friendlies - England having successfully qualified for the World Cup finals in Brazil 2014 - the Clarets were back in action at highly fancied Nottingham Forest. The result was a hard earned point after being under the cosh for lengthy periods. Goalkeeper Heaton was barely troubled, thanks to the solidity of a now very reliable defence. The point was sufficient to keep us in top spot but now only on goal difference as QPR and Leicester maintained their good early season momentum.

With the November loan window about to close speculation was rife that there would be additions to the squad to cover the hectic December schedule before January's return to open season in the transfer market. Frustratingly Dyche was unable to bring in new recruits for a variety of reasons. Players were allegedly reluctant to sign because they felt they would not be automatic choices due to the success of the regular starting eleven. Some leading Championship teams were unwilling to loan us players as they didn't want to help a potential promotion rival. Players that may have fit the bill from Premier League teams were too expensive for our meagre budget. On top of that the Manager's desire not to bring in players, who may be disruptive to the excellent team spirit, meant we entered the festive period with a threadbare squad, praying to avoid injuries and suspensions.

November ended with an away fixture at Huddersfield and with Dean Marney missing again through injury, we were once again stretched. The first half performance was poor and worse was to follow as we went two goals down early in the second period. Despite a late Ings goal the Clarets suffered their second defeat of the campaign in their seventeenth match. The situation was further aggravated by a sending off for Michael Duff at the end of the game, and the 'reward' of a one match suspension to follow.

November had not been a good month and Leicester's win at home to Millwall took them three points clear of the Clarets at the top of the division. QPR were tucked in behind us on goal difference. No wins, three draws, and one defeat was a poor return but we had played only one league game at the Turf in that run and hopes were high of a return to form as December started with two home fixtures.

The first December game a Tuesday night fixture against Watford, who were among the pre-season favourites for promotion after making the play offs last time round. This season they had made a stuttering start and currently sat mid table. The Clarets lost Marney and Ings to injury and with Duff suspended the small squad was stretched to breaking point. In a game of few chances we managed a fairly comfortable 0-0 draw, but a win for QPR dropped us to third. Ironically Leicester lost on their travels and we moved a point closer to the top now trailing by two points.

Next up was lowly Barnsley at the Turf who, having had a disastrous start to their season, had sacked their manager and were currently in the hands of caretaker, and ex Claret, Micky Mellon . As often happens, Mellon's first game in charge resulted in an unlikely away win at Brighton in midweek and they came to the Turf in determined fashion. The game is won for us midway through the second half with a peach of a left foot shot from Michael Kightly. The Venky Boys of Blackburn do us a favour taking a point at QPR and Leicester lost away for the second time in a week. This combination of results sent us back to the top on goal difference from QPR and one point ahead of Leicester. Hopefully this win would put us back on track after a disappointing sequence of draws and the defeat at Huddersfield. Next on the agenda was a massive test away at Leicester in a televised early kick off game.

Burnley were back at full strength for this game but the early exchanges had Leicester on top and ahead from another contentious penalty decision. Needless to say the penalty was "potted" by the Clarets nemesis, David Nugent. Ings saw a header hit the post but at the interval we trailed to the single goal. The half time team talk certainly did the trick and within 90 seconds of the restart we levelled as Ings controlled a Trippier cross and fired home from close range for his sixteenth goal of the season. Now we looked more like the table toppers and probably should have led when a terrible back pass by De Laet let in Vokes who was foiled by a save from Kaspar Schmeichel that his dad would have been proud of. Despite late pressure from the hosts we earned a very creditable draw and remained at least for a few hours top of the league. Unfortunately later in the day QPR's win at Blackpool took them above us by two points, whilst an impressive six game winning run by Derby County saw them close to within three points. With other sides in the play-off zone also winning the pressure was starting to mount ahead of a busy Christmas schedule that would take us to the season's half way point.

The first festive fixture was Blackpool at the Turf on Saturday the 21st and with our visitors enjoying a depressing run of three defeats on the bounce we were hopeful but not over confident of the three points. Derby games by their nature are often unpredictable affairs where form can be turned on its head. After 20 games in the league we had still lost only twice and despite a recent run containing more draws than wins, a 40 point return was no mean feat.

A high tempo first half ended 1-1 but within a couple of minutes of the restart, a superb curling strike from the edge of the box by Scott Arfield gave Gilks in the 'Pool goal no chance. A goal worthy of winning any game is what it proved to be in this one despite chances at both ends. A very enjoyable game; fiercely contested and with no shortage of skill, added another three points to the total. With other results going our way we returned to the top of the tree and were Championship leaders at Christmas.

Boxing day brought an away fixture at Middlesbrough. Having survived a torrid opening we fell behind midway through the half to a long range effort, and despite going close through Ings were probably lucky to reach half time only one goal down. A better second half performance was unable to bring a goal and we slipped to a 1-0 defeat and conceded top spot to Leicester City.

Following closely on the heels of the Boxing Day game was another away fixture, this time at Wigan Athletic. The hosts were unbeaten since appointing Uwe Rosler as manager following the dismissal of Owen Who? and another tough test was anticipated. A game of few chances and neither side were unable to break the deadlock and the game ended goalless.

The end of the Wigan game marked the half way point in the season, with Leicester and Derby both winning we now stood third in the table on goal difference. Leicester lead with 48 points with Derby and ourselves on 44, QPR on 43, with Nottingham Forest on 39, and Ipswich 35 occupying the final play off places.

There was no doubt that results were starting to tail off and wins, particularly away from home were becoming hard to come by. The defence continued in miserly fashion conceding only 16 goals in 23 fixtures, bettered only by QPR with 13. The first half season performance of 12 wins, eight draws, and only three defeats was incredible and totally unexpected by the vast majority of fans.

The problem now was how to replicate the first half season and the demands on such a small squad were already beginning to show. January saw the reopening of the transfer window and everybody was praying that Dyche would be provided with the funds to attempt to strengthen the team. Several of our more affluent opponents had certainly started to gather momentum. An additional striker to provide cover and options was high on everyone's wish list and similarly a centre midfielder would have been most welcome. Time would tell, however the first priority was the New Year's Day home game with Huddersfield. We definitely owed this lot one, having gone down to them in the away fixture in November, and lost twice to them last season.

The New Year got off to the perfect start with a 3-2 win and a return to second place in the table as Derby lost at home to Wigan.

The first Saturday in January is traditionally FA Cup 3rd round day and this season we were drawn away to high flying Premier Leaguers Southampton. It was a game with special significance as it brought us face to face for the first time since his departure with "One of our Own" - Jay Rodriguez. I suppose for us the FA Cup was a bit of a distraction and in view of the league position we probably would not mind unduly if we went out at this stage.

At half time and trailing 2-0 a confidence sapping heavy defeat looked on the cards, but whatever Sean Dyche put in the half time tea certainly seemed to do the trick. By 57 minutes the scores were level with goals from the dynamic duo, Vokes and Ings. The pair went close again in what was now a pulsating cup tie before Rodriguez on as a substitute, and his England colleague Lallana, put the hosts 4-2 up. Kevin Long pulled one back three minutes from time and the Saints just about managed to hold out. Television pundits praised our efforts and we emerged from a classic cup tie with pride intact. Now it was back to the serious business.

Great news ahead of the trip to Yeovil! The Clarets managed to secure the signing of long term target Ashley Barnes from Brighton & Hove Albion. Dyche had pursued the player since being rebuffed in the summer and it was hoped that the striker would give the team more options and depth as we tackled the second half of the campaign.

New signing Barnes had to settle for a place on the bench for the first away league game of 2014. Once again it was déjà vu for the 'Burnley Hitmen' as a screamer from Ings gave the Clarets a first half lead, and a tap in from Vokes doubled it in the second. Despite a better second half showing from the struggling hosts and a late goal and nervy last ten minutes, the Clarets held out for an invaluable away win and remained in second place.

Next up Sheffield Wednesday at the Turf. The Owls had turned into something of a bogey side for us at home and on the back of a thumping 6-0 victory over Leeds and some impressive recent form, they would be no pushover. That's exactly how the game turned out, despite taking a lead through Sam Vokes we were unable to hold on to it for more than a couple of minutes. The Clarets put in a creditable performance but due to some inspired goalkeeping by Kirkland between the Owls posts we were unable to grab a winner. With the other three teams in the top four all winning we dropped out of the automatic promotion places and now occupied third, one point behind QPR, and six behind leaders Leicester who had now won six on the bounce.

No game on the next Saturday as it was FA Cup 4th round day and our scheduled opponents Bolton were still in the competition. The Clarets took advantage of a blank week and headed off for Spain for a few days warm weather training in Alicante.

With us taking the Saturday off Leicester took full advantage by winning again to go nine points clear as we stayed in third place, a big gap starting to open there as the division started to take shape for the run in to the winning post. Three points were urgently needed from the next game at home to Brighton.

This match saw me enjoying for the first time the hospitality package in the 1882 lounge, more of that in the next chapter. My daughter and I and four friends took our padded seats in the 100 Club section of the Bob Lord stand and I was struck by how different the view was to that afforded by my usual seat in the James Hargreaves Upper. Being almost directly behind Sean Dyche as he prowled the technical area I almost felt tempted to give him the 'benefit' of my tactical nous……..

Unfortunately a bit of a nothing game ended with a nothing score and we headed back to the lounge for a few consolation beers awaiting the outcome of the "Guess the time of the first goal competition", it could have been a long night! Once again our single point was poor reward as our nearest rivals, Leicester, QPR, and Derby all won again. Leicester's lead over us was now 11 points, with us still having a game in hand, whilst we were now three points behind QPR who by chance were our next opponents at Loftus Road. Derby in fourth closed to within one point of us albeit having played one game more. The feeling among the fans seemed to be that the two automatic places were slipping from our grasp and a play-off place was now most likely barring any disastrous run of form.

January therefore saw four league games resulting in two wins and two draws, quite a respectable tally of eight points from a possible twelve. However due to the red hot form of Leicester and good points returns by QPR, Derby and

Nottingham Forest the chase for automatic promotion places had become increasingly difficult.

February kicked off with the divisions' 'Game of the Day' - the away fixture at second placed QPR. As the January transfer window closed at 11.00 pm on Friday 31st the Clarets not unexpectedly had added no further signings to that of Ashley Barnes. Thankfully though, they had managed to retain their major assets in Ings and Trippier who at least now were here till the end of the season. In contrast big spending 'Arry' Redknapp at QPR added five players to an already bulging squad on deadline day. Ironically 'Arry's plunge into the market was prompted by an injury to our old hero Charlie Austin who since his arrival at QPR had provided most of the goals for their promotion push. Poor Charlie had once again suffered a shoulder injury that dogged him in his time at the Turf and now looked set to miss the remainder of the season.

The game was screened live by Sky TV with a 12.15 pm kick off and it was not long before one of Redknapp's new signings, Kevin Doyle, headed the hosts in front from a corner. We feared the worst but the Clarets weathered the early pressure and started to get back into the game. On 25 minutes Ings volleyed Burnley level in typical fashion but not for long as veteran Richard Dunne fired QPR ahead again from a poorly defended corner. Half time and trailing 2-1, we were down but not out. Again Sean Dyche worked the half time magic and the team came out firing on all cylinders. A lovely cross from Kightly and near post finish by Sam Vokes levelled it on 54 minutes. Better was to come as Ings dispossessed the QPR full back to set up a tap in for Vokes and it was 3-2 to the Clarets on 62 minutes. A long half hour ahead we thought, and so it proved as another deadline day signing Maiga saved a point for the hosts with about 10 minutes to go. Substitute Junior Stanislas almost nicked it in the dying minute but his shot goes narrowly wide and we had to settle for the point.

A great result from a great game, but somehow we felt slightly disappointed. This was an indication of how far this team had come, before the season started we would have expected a heavy defeat at Loftus Road against the promotion favourites, now we are disappointed to have only drawn with them! Unfortunately Leicester won with a debatable late goal away at Bournemouth and whilst we remained in third place we now trailed the leaders by 13 points. Derby leading 3-1 away at Birmingham late in the game contrived to concede twice and could only draw leaving them a point behind us in fourth, whilst Forest won their fifth consecutive home game to close to within 3 points of the Clarets. Hotting up indeed!

A comfortable home win over struggling Millwall in the next match saw the Clarets regain second place as QPR were without a game on the Saturday. The Lions managed to snatch a first half lead but could only hold it for two minutes before Danny Ings levelled. It was all the Clarets now and though Ings missed a penalty, we still led at half time courtesy of a crisp Dean Marney drive. The second half produced no real scares and a further Ings goal wrapped up the points.

QPR lost at Derby on the following Monday evening to leave the Clarets in second spot on goal difference.

Next up in a busy week was a Tuesday night fixture at near neighbours Bolton Wanderers, not such "Mighty Whites" this season as they struggled at the wrong end of the table. Still as with all 'derby' matches a hard fought encounter was on the cards. The Clarets fielded an unchanged side again and despite a below par first half performance got in all square at half time. Normal service was restored on 58 minutes with a Sam Vokes goal from close range and we ran out one goal winners. The result took us three points clear of QPR in third place and Leicester's lead at the top was cut to eight points following our second win in the week. Could we make it a hat trick of victories at Eddie Howe's Bournemouth on Saturday?

In the event Burnley gave a below par performance, but a goal from substitute Keith Treacy saved a point for the Clarets at the Goldsands Stadium. Despite being not at our best we still avoided defeat and came home with something. Three defeats in 31 league games confirmed we are not an easy side to beat, a quality which would prove vital in the run in.

The value of the point gained at Bournemouth was highlighted by QPR's result on the following Sunday. At home to fellow play off challengers Reading they went down 3-1 and were roundly booed from the pitch. Since Charlie Austin's injury they had collected only one point from a possible nine. Our return of seven from the last nine strengthened our position in second, four points clear of QPR who now had one game in hand. Our superior goal difference effectively meant we were two wins to the good on them. Derby won at Sheffield Wednesday in midweek to push QPR down to fourth and they closed to within 2 points of us.

The next game was home to Nottingham Forest who had a difficult midweek fixture at home to leaders Leicester before our meeting. It was another vital game for us but we approached it in confident mood.

Forest and Leicester fought out a 2-2 draw on the Wednesday night which was probably the best result for us. Forest now were on a 14 match unbeaten run and so two teams in top form went head to head at the Turf. What happened in the first 45 mins was almost unbelievable for Clarets fans as Forest were totally blown away. A very impressive opening half saw the Clarets in at half time 3-0 up and it really could have been more. Scott Arfield started the scoring and two more from the almost unplayable Sam Vokes had the fans ecstatic. Predictably the half time break changed the flow of the game and Forest with nothing to lose tried to mount a fight back. Chances came and went at both ends and the visitors went home with just a consolation penalty, scored on the rebound after Tom Heaton saved the initial attempt.

A magnificent victory for the Clarets and a huge confidence booster for both the team and the fans. This win brought to an end a highly successful February that left us second in the table, 8 points behind Leicester, two ahead of Derby, and seven to the good over QPR who still had a game in hand. Three wins and two draws brought a very respectable 11 points from a possible 15 and we were riding high entering March with just 14 games to play.

Saturday 1st March brought another major challenge as third placed and in form Derby County visited Turf Moor. A win in this game would take us five points clear of our nearest rivals for second spot, a defeat would catapult Derby above us. In what was becoming typical Burnley style, whilst not at their best the Clarets won the game fairly comfortably 2-0. No goals for the prolific strikers this game, both coming from central midfielders Jones and Marney. As a large contingent from Derby swelled the crowd to a much more respectable 17,000 plus, there was a growing conviction around the town that automatic promotion was now a realistic goal.

Expectation levels went through the roof as the Clarets ended 35 years of hurt winning the next game at Ewood, against bitter enemies Blackburn Rovers. Again the Clarets not hitting top note but coming back from a goal down at half time to win 2-1 with goals from Shackell and Ings. The mood of joy in town was unconfined and Sean Dyche, aka 'Ginger Mourinho', would probably be given the freedom of the borough! This result coupled with an unexpected home defeat for Derby opened up an eight point gap between us in second and Derby in third, with QPR now nine behind with 12 games to play. March had started exactly where February ended and what a crucial time to put such a good string of results together.

Close on the heels of the long awaited and much celebrated victory at Ewood came another series of midweek fixtures. Tuesday evening saw Derby only manage a home draw, whilst QPR went down 2-0 at Brighton. Wednesday took the Clarets on their travels again, this time to struggling Birmingham City.

After a first half of Burnley dominance we led 1-0 at half time thanks to a close range Dean Marney header. Radio Lancs first credited the goal to Vokes and then at half time to Danny Ings. Three scorers for only one goal! No indication though in the first forty five minutes of the drama that was to follow. On 64 minutes with the Clarets seemingly in control, there was a sudden outbreak of goals. Firstly the Brummies equalised through their on loan Manchester United substitute Macheda, only for Michael Duff to restore our lead on 67 minutes. This was short lived and on 69 minutes Birmingham levelled again through on loan Manchester City youngster Huws. A much more open game now twisted again in our favour as Sam Vokes put us ahead for the third time with only four minutes remaining. Surely another three points in the promotion bag, but no, four minutes into the five of additional time, Macheda equalised again, this time with more than a strong suspicion of handball.

We felt robbed and desperately disappointed that we came away with only the one point instead of all three. We were now going away from home and expecting wins where for many years we would have been happy to avoid defeats. The result maintained the eight point gap between us and Derby, and stretched it to ten for QPR, and with crucially now one game less to play. Leicester's win at Barnsley on the Tuesday night now moved them seven points ahead of us with a game in hand.

Somewhat worryingly in this game Danny Ings limped off with an ankle injury and there was a collective prayer among all concerned with the club that this would not prove to be serious.

Leeds at the Turf were the next opponents and with a big away following, circa 3,500, a crowd of 18,000 created the usual hostile atmosphere that accompanies this fixture. As expected, Ings sat this one out with news that he was to see a specialist on the following Wednesday. Not great news this but it would be only the second game he had missed this campaign, and gave Ashley Barnes a chance to make his first start for the Clarets.

A slow start by the team saw us fortunate not to go behind early in the game, Dave Jones presenting a gilt edged opportunity to the Championship's top scorer Ross McCormack, who hits the post. Our luck doesn't hold and on 26 minutes McCormack nods home powerfully to give the away side the lead. Not for long though, on 38 minutes

Marney finds Trippier with an exquisite pass and the full back's hard low cross is bundled in for an own goal under pressure from Vokes. A scrappy first half ended 1-1 but a much improved second period saw Arfield give us maximum points converting his chance with a second bite at the cherry.

What a week! Victories over arch local rivals Leeds and Blackburn, with an away point at Birmingham thrown in as well, it didn't get much better than this. QPR beat lowly Yeovil to stay 10 points adrift, and third placed Derby could only draw at Reading to also fall the same margin behind. A strong run by Wigan now saw them 15 points away from us but with two games in hand and a visit to the Turf still to come; a possible threat?

A great weekend is complete as Danny Ings was crowned Championship Player Of The Year at the awards ceremony on Sunday 16th March having been voted for by the majority of managers. A fine achievement and thoroughly deserved. Now we hoped the injury news would be good ahead of Saturday's visit to struggling Charlton Athletic.

Unfortunately the news was not good, Ings following a midweek visit to a specialist was ruled out for a couple of weeks. Then on Thursday came further concern as Kieran Trippier was reported struggling with a hamstring injury. Dyche moved swiftly and brought in the currently out of contract experienced Northern Ireland International Chris Baird. The player signed on a short term contract until the end of the season, as cover in defence and midfield. Ahead of the game Clarets fans nerves started to jangle as they heard Derby had beaten Nottingham Forest in the lunchtime kick off 5-0. This result not only narrowed the gap to seven points but considerably improved Derby's goal difference.

However, there was no need to worry as we continued our magnificent run of form in 2014. Baird came in for Trippier, and Barnes started for Ings for the second time. On a very poor pitch not really conducive to our passing game we started cautiously before Barnes opened his Clarets account with the opener on 38 minutes. He was denied shortly after by a brilliant close range stop by the home keeper. Further second half goals from a Vokes penalty, and an extra time Kightly effort completed a comprehensive victory. All the chasing pack recorded victories bar Forest but the 10 point gap to third remained as another game was eaten up. The unbeaten league form since the Boxing Day defeat at Middlesbrough now read, Won 10, Drawn 5, what a magnificent effort in 2014, and now it was nine to go.

Tuesday 25th March saw a full Championship programme and we were home to struggling Doncaster Rovers, Derby had a tricky away fixture at Ipswich, while QPR and Wigan met at Loftus Rd. Leaders Leicester had on paper at least, an easy task at home to Yeovil.

The Clarets were again without Ings and Trippier, and in front of a strangely nervous Turf Moor crowd were on top in the first half but went in goalless. The crowd's edginess was I think prompted by the closeness of the finish line and the desperation to get over it before we could be caught. Derby led at Ipswich and QPR were ahead of Wigan with Leicester surprisingly trailing to lowly Yeovil. Meanwhile, back at the Turf, normal service was resumed in the first minute of the second half as we won what looked a soft penalty… which was promptly dispatched by Vokes. The crowd relaxed and we took charge of the game, Stanislas added a second from a flowing counter attack and we were home and dry for the night. The only downside being a late booking for Marney which triggered a two match suspension, starting with the home game against Leicester.

Ipswich did us proud by coming from behind to beat Derby, QPR went into third place, beating Wigan by one goal, and Leicester were fortunate to equalise in extra time. Eight games to go and now three points behind Leicester who had a game in hand, 10 ahead of QPR, 13 above Derby and Wigan 17 adrift. Surely this meant only QPR could now threaten our ever strengthening position! Indeed we now started to harbour thoughts of going up as Champions if we could see off Leicester at the Turf on the coming Saturday, March 29th.

The Sky TV publicity vehicle was in overdrive. Allotted the early Saturday kick off spot, this game had been widely advertised by the broadcaster as, "The Championship Decider" – and as if to reinforce the point, they had even arranged for the Championship trophy to be displayed in all its glory on the pitch.

We all hoped they were not getting a little ahead of themselves! If indeed it was the 'decider' then unfortunately the trophy was headed for the Midlands as the Foxes ran out comfortable 2-0 winners. Burnley, severely handicapped by the loss of the injured Ings and Trippier, and the suspended Marney, were completely derailed after four minutes. On the Bob Lord stand touchline big Sam Vokes crumpled to the floor unchallenged and our chances in this game were as good as over. Unable to continue and with no recognised striker on the bench, Dyche was forced to change the 4-4-2 system that had served us magnificently all season and opted for Edgar in midfield as the replacement. We now went 4-3-3 or 4-5-1 depending on your perspective.

Leicester whilst posing no real threat began to control the game and on 34 minutes our perennial "Thorn in the Side", David Nugent gave the visitors the lead with a well taken effort. With Barnes manfully ploughing a lonely furrow up front, there was precious little attacking threat as the wingers failed to support and the absence of Trippier seriously affected the offensive options. 1-0 down at half time but still in the game. This almost became two down as a fierce shot from Knockaert rebounded off the Burnley crossbar early in the second period. The last hope of any reward disappeared as Schmeichel saved from Arfield, and it was effectively game over on 77 minutes as Wood completed the scoring for Leicester to send their fans into delirium.

Results elsewhere were generally favourable as Blackpool managed a surprise draw at QPR leaving the Londoners still nine points adrift. Derby were the only winners which took them to 10 points shy of the Clarets with seven games to play. Once again we ended the month in second place, and still with a healthy breathing space over the chasing pack.

What a pity that the hardest game of the season came when the small squad was at its weakest. With the various transfer windows all now closed we could only hope that a further weeks rest would see some of the injured players returning for the next game away at Watford. Without doubt the lack of cover in various areas had left us severely exposed in recent games and once again the fans nerves were jangling. During the long unbeaten run from Boxing Day, Burnley had built an air of invincibility about themselves, and we hoped this feeling could soon be recovered.

Terrible news followed early in the week as Sam Vokes injury was confirmed as a ruptured anterior cruciate ligament and that was Sam out for not only the rest of the season but also more than likely into the next campaign. With Ings still not fit this left the squad with only one recognised senior striker in Ashley Barnes.

Team news for the game at Watford was not good as neither Ings nor Trippier made the squad, with Vokes out and Marney serving his second match suspension, Burnley were again without four key players. The game started poorly for us as we trailed after only nine minutes to a well hit shot from distance, going in one down at half time.

However, once again this side showed its tremendous fighting spirit in the face of adversity. On 86 minutes Arfield scored an extremely vital equaliser. QPR and Derby went down at Bournemouth and Middlesbrough respectively, thereby extending the gap between us and third to 10 points with only 6 games to play. The results this weekend meant Leicester City could not be caught by anybody but the Clarets, and were therefore promoted and almost certainly as Champions.

Whilst Sean Dyche's oft repeated mantra was that "We take it one game at a time", the fans despite their extreme caution were now beginning to believe that we were unbelievably almost there. Even QPR manager Harry Redknapp conceded, admitting *'It is almost impossible now, to be fair. Nobody is going to catch Burnley now, are they?* Midweek games followed the Watford fixture with all three contenders again away from home, the Clarets at Barnsley and QPR and Derby at our Lancashire neighbours Blackburn and Blackpool.

Never thought I'd see the day when I would be praying for a Rovers victory!

Tuesday 8th April saw euphoria levels amongst Clarets fans reach uncharted heights. An Ashley Barnes seventh minute header gave the Clarets maximum points from the trip to Barnsley in a game in which the hosts barely troubled the Clarets. The Rovers duly obliged by beating QPR 2-0 and Wigan lost at home to lowly Millwall. The only fly in the ointment was Derby who overturned Blackpool by the seaside despite trailing after 20 seconds. The game at Barnsley had also marked the return of Danny Ings after missing five games and Kieran Trippier returned to the bench. Dean Marney also returned after serving his suspension - and thankfully once again the squad numbers seemed much healthier.

The results of the midweek fixtures now left Derby as our nearest challengers for automatic promotion as they trailed us by 11 points with 15 to play for. QPR were a further point behind with nobody else in touching distance. The majority of fans believed we were there, but Dyche and senior players still quite rightly urged caution. The plain facts were however, that if the Clarets beat Middlesbrough at the Turf on Saturday 12th, and Derby failed to beat Huddersfield at home, promotion was ours!

QPR were the televised lunchtime kick off and with the score at 2-2 against Forest going into the last ten minutes it was looking good for us. Then bad news 'number one' for the day as QPR went wild and ran in three late goals. Derby were at home to Huddersfield and went 1-0 down early in the game, good start Terriers. Then bad news 'number two', Derby equalised and went ahead as the Huddersfield keeper palmed a tame effort into his own net! The Yorkshiremen then ensured they had no chance as they had two men red carded and conceded a third.

At the Turf Trippier returned to the line-up and the Clarets were virtually at full strength. A strong opening half with some flowing football failed to produce a goal despite a looping Kightly header hitting the bar. Middlesbrough were no mugs and tested Heaton on a couple of occasions from range. Then early in the second half, disaster struck as we were caught on the break and Boro went one up. Despite numerous attempts on goal and frantic pressure their 'keeper kept them ahead and for the second successive home game we were beaten. The gap was now eight points to Derby, and nine to QPR, with twelve points to play for. It was going to be an interesting Easter weekend coming up!

A lovely sunny Good Friday had the Clarets at the seaside for a 5.15 kick off against near neighbours Blackpool in another game televised by Sky Sports. Sky had a Championship double bill lined up as they also were due to feature Doncaster v Derby following at 7.30. A win for Burnley and anything but that for Derby would see us promoted.

The Clarets fulfilled their part of the bargain emerging one goal winners in a typical derby battle against rivals now deeply embroiled in a relegation battle. Not a classic game, but a classic goal by Michael Kightly was the decider, in what was a thoroughly professional performance. Now come on Doncaster do your bit!

Unfortunately Donny, also involved in the relegation dogfight, were not up to delivering their part of the deal and went down 0-2. These results left Derby as the only side now capable of stopping the Clarets gaining second spot and automatic promotion. With three games left for each team the Clarets still led by eight points with only nine to play for. Derby had to win their remaining three fixtures which in their current good form was not impossible, however if Burnley gained two points from their last three games all Derby's efforts would count for nothing.

So with Claret's fans nerves in tatters once again we went into the Easter Monday games with ourselves at home to the in-form play-off contenders Wigan, and Derby at home to another of the relegation strugglers, Barnsley.

At last, on Monday 21st April 2014 the Clarets clinched their promotion back to the Premier League with a 2-0 home victory over Wigan. Two magnificent goals from Barnes and Kightly and a typical chasing and pressing performance saw the Clarets home in style. Ecstatic crowd scenes at the conclusion marked a truly miraculous achievement by this bunch of players and the management team. Derby also managed a win but the three points for Burnley meant it was all in vain and they must ride their luck in the play-off lottery. It was, however a great effort by Derby who pushed us all the way. An unbelievable promotion sealed and with two games still to play. What an incredible season!

On Easter Monday we found ourselves back in the Premier League for the second time in five years. The success in 2009 was very much built on the slogan "Dare to Dream" but Dyche's achievement this time was built on a much more solid platform of "Belief". Our success was once again proof that, in football at least, miracles can and do happen.

After Monday's events the last home game had a very strangely relaxed feel about it. Once again Sky had selected the game for early kick off screening. The visitors Ipswich had an outside chance of making the play offs but needed a victory. From the outset that was never really on the cards. There must have been a temptation to take the foot of the gas with the job already done, but not from one of Dyche's teams. Burnley resisting the opportunity to make changes fielded the full strength line up and once ahead from Kightly early in the second half were rarely troubled. A comfortable 1-0 victory, and then the presentation of the Runners Up medals, and a lap of honour. How thoroughly deserved was that!

Ahead of the last game of a truly momentous season, Sean Dyche was once again crowned Championship Manager of the Month for the third time in the campaign. Surely Manager of the Season would be a more appropriate title! For the ninth time this season a Burnley game is selected for live TV, this time at Reading. Yet another record in a record breaking season.

On Saturday 3rd May this magnificent Clarets team closed the season with a 2-2 draw against their playoff hopeful hosts. Despite going one down they once again rose to the challenge to lead 2-1 at half time. The desperate Royals levelled with a tremendous volley and seemed to have done enough to clinch the final play off place, until a goal in added time for Brighton away at Nottingham Forest cruelly denied them. What a heartbreaker football can be!

It's difficult to find words to adequately express what an absolutely outstanding season this had been for those of the Claret and Blue persuasion, but I think the season's statistics reveal the true scope of this unbelievable effort. From 46 Championship games played, 26 were won, 15 drawn, and only five lost. This resulted in a points total of 93, again a record haul for a team finishing runners up in the

Championship. It was also the most points ever recorded in a season by the Clarets since three points for a win was introduced. This team rattled in 72 goals whilst only conceding 37 to emerge with the best defensive record in the division. From the doom and gloom of July and August to this was absolutely magnificent!

So we find ourselves with the exciting prospect of another tilt at the Premier League, the Land of Milk and Honey. I am besieged by my readers, well my Arsenal supporting nephew, demanding a second book. I feel duty bound to take up this challenge and once again record my personal highs and lows of the season. Who knows how it will turn out, many of you, well one person, and my wife, have asked for this book to be written in a more "bodice ripping" style. The only bodice ripping I can recall is Andre Bikey in the Play Off Semi Final against Reading in 2009 as he attempted to remove his shirt on being red carded! We certainly don't want a repeat of that. No, I can't promise any action of a 'steamy' nature but it will be one hell of a ride. Hold on to your hats!

MAY/JUNE

Well I have to say that of all the many seasons I have supported the Clarets, 2013/14 has got to be one of, if not **the best**. A great team effort from everybody concerned with the club, the Manager and coaching and backroom staff, the players, and of course the fans. There was a terrific vibe which developed throughout the season and such a unity of purpose that failure had become almost unthinkable. However as one fantastic season ends, the preparation for the next has to start with hardly any time to savour the moment.

Even before the season ends football journalists in the national press are already linking us to players whom they seem to feel we may have an interest in. Notable among the early runners are Craig Gardner and David Bardsley of Sunderland, both of whom are coming out of contract. Also mentioned is prolific Championship marksman Troy Deeney of Watford, a player known to Sean Dyche from his time at that club. Another linked is the young Everton centre back, Shane Duffy who has previously had a short uneventful loan spell with Burnley during Eddie Howe's reign.

Equally as important as to who is coming in, is who is going out. Will the club be able to persuade key players such as Danny Ings and Kieran Trippier to commit their future to longer contracts at the club? If not will the club be forced to cash in on these two vital cogs and start to search for replacements?

Then there are a number of players who have played supporting roles in the past season who are now coming out of contract. Which of these will be released and which retained? Notable in this group are Junior Stanislas, David Edgar, Keith Treacy, Danny Lafferty, Luke O'Neill, and Brian Stock. Finally there is the situation regarding long term servant Michael Duff who is coming to the end of a one year contract but who has played a major part in our great season. Duff now 36 surely deserves another year and a last fling in the Premier League.

A major influence on the promotion season was also Michael Kightly who came on a one year loan from Stoke City. He has made it quite clear that he would like to stay, will he be given that chance? Chris Baird also joined on a short term contract and made a vital contribution when covering for Trippier's injury in the later stages of the season. What will the future hold for him?

By the miracle of modern social media *Twitter* the answer to one of these posers comes as early as May 5th. Brian Stock tweets *"Wanna say a big thanks to all the players staff and fans of Burnley FC for making my 2 years here a memory I will never forget Great club"*.

This is followed shortly afterwards by the Lancashire Telegraph announcing the release of Stock, Edgar, and Treacy. They also add that contract negotiations are taking place with Stanislas and Lafferty.

The situation seems to be slightly confused regarding Keith Treacy, although he is definitely released there appears to be some kind of option to return pending a trial in the summer. It looks like Sean Dyche, who has gone a long way towards rehabilitating the sometimes wayward Keith, is leaving the door open for him if he can convince him of his ongoing commitment in terms of fitness.

In an online article BT Sport columnist Mike Calvin is asked to nominate his top five managers of the year. In reverse order he goes for Russell Slade (Leyton Orient), Kenny Jackett (Wolves), Brendan Rogers (Liverpool), Tony Pulis (Crystal Palace), and top of the pile, good old Ginger Mourinho himself! He writes, *"Scandalously sacked by Watford, a club subsequently enslaved by speculative Italian owners, Dyche has defied budgetary limitations at Burnley to reach the Premier League. That tends to be a dangerous achievement for upwardly mobile managers, but he is a progressive, intelligent individual who will surely receive the support he deserves, whatever next season brings. Don't rule him out overseeing another modern miracle, of survival. Number one, without a bullet"*.

The budgetary limitations were certainly reflected in Sean's post match comments after promotion was clinched against Wigan. He said, *"What we have done is historic. The challenge of the Championship is getting harder and harder. Clubs who are relegated are getting richer while other clubs have got wealthy backers behind them. We have a very low budget in the grand scheme of this division and we have come this far using just 22 players. That is incredible. It is a marker in history to do that and I'm not sure we will ever see it done again"*.

Writing in his column in the Daily Mail, Martin Samuels questioned the impact that Financial Fair Play (FFP) rules were having on the gap between rich and poor. Burnley had not been promoted 30 minutes when a major bookmaker was offering odds of 8/15 to be relegated and 1/33 to finish outside the Premier League top 10. He wrote, *"What a horrid failure of a competition that represents. Going up, Burnley should have fabulous momentum from this season, but the cynics conclude it will count for nothing, As a small, efficiently run club, unable to spend big, logic suggests they are doomed. Just finishing in the top half is considered an equivalent feat to Algeria winning their World*

Cup group. So what exactly has financial fair play and all its pale imitators achieved? Surely this canyon-like gap between rich and poor is what UEFA and its allies should be trying to address. Instead the reams of red tape have done nothing to better allow a promoted club to survive their first season, let alone thrive. These FFP boys have all the answers, but never to the right questions".

What Samuels says about FFP is certainly true and I believe most supporters of small clubs like ourselves believe that the "big shots" will ride roughshod over any attempts to curb them. It is doubtful that it will address the deep division between the haves and have nots.

This is precisely why for us promotion to the Premier League is so important. Promotion if managed correctly not only ensures our financial survival but also maintains our competitiveness. If as many believe we again fail at the first hurdle at least the parachute money cushions the blow for the short term future. At best we may yo-yo between Premier League and Championship, but this is infinitely preferable to a slow lingering decline on ever decreasing revenue.

Mid May sees the return of season ticket sales suspended since the end of the discount period at the end of March. Many supporters took advantage during this period to buy tickets for 2014/15 at 2013/14 prices. With the team going so strongly through February and March it was no surprise that an estimated 13,000 tickets were snapped up in the period. With the segregation policy dictating the Cricket Field stand for away supporters only, and other ground improvements necessary to comply with Premier League regulations reducing capacity, this left possibly only in the region of a further 3000 seats to sell.

Obviously with promotion gained an increase in the ticket price was generally expected. However it came as a real shock when it was announced that tickets that had been renewed at £455 in the discount period would now be priced at £685 for new purchasers! It transpired that the actual price would be £585 but with a "retainer" of a further £100 which would be discounted off tickets subsequently bought for the 2015/16 season. Uproar on the fans forums is the only way to describe the reaction. Even Claret Tony editor of the Claretsmad website, and generally regarded as a fair minded supporter of the Board was outraged. The club had been quick to promote the slogan "Our Town, Our Turf" but Tony's article on Claretsmad was headed "Our Town, Our Turf, Their Prices".

Certainly the message board superheated for days after the announcement of the price hike. Had the Board underestimated the strength of feeling particularly regarding the "retainer"? It would be interesting to see what the take up on the outstanding tickets would now be. Would the furore die down in a few days and fans keen to see Premier League football bite the bullet and cough up? The Board it could be said were generous in their offer of frozen prices in the discount period. However it looked like they now intended to maximise revenue from those who had not taken advantage of the early bird offer.

The scale of the financial boost that the club will receive as a result of promotion is highlighted in a newspaper article detailing TV money earnings for the just completed Premier League season. Cardiff come bottom of the earnings table, as well as the Premier League, but their total is a staggering £62,082,302. This is made up of the equal share of TV money £52.2m, money for extra games shown £8.6m (minimum guaranteed), and money for finishing position £1.2m. This of course does not include any revenue from gate receipts. So it looks as though we will receive at least this sum even finishing bottom. Of course we could end up with the £97,544,366 received by Liverpool who were pipped for the title by Manchester City, but still came out tops cash wise by virtue of being televised in more live games. The bean counters at the Turf must be rubbing their hands with glee!

Meanwhile speculation continues as to possible transfer targets with the popular press certainly having a field day. Along with the previously mentioned we have in addition:

Chris Eagles (Bolton Wanderers)

Ludovic Sylvestre (Blackpool)

Alfred Finnbogason (Herrenveen)

Charlie Austin (Queens Park Rangers)

John Guidettii (Manchester City)

Emyr Huws (Manchester City)

Steven Cauker (Cardiff)

Britt Assombalonga (Peterborough United)

David Ngog (Swansea)

James Wilson (Manchester United)

Jordan Rhodes (Blackburn Rovers)

Harry Kane (Tottenham Hotspur)

Mike Williamson (Newcastle United)

Ben Hamer (Charlton Athletic)

Steve Cook (Bournemouth)

Steven Reid (West Bromwich Albion)

James Mcarthur (Wigan Athletic)

Josh Brownhill (Preston North End)

.....to name but a few! Definitely some wild imagination involved in some of that lot. I particularly like the sound of Finnbogason, about time we got some exotically named players.

Its Mid May and with a dearth of hard news coming from the club, it's probably a good time to update readers of my first Clarets diary, A Season In The Sun, with a few details of what has happened to me on a personal level since May 2010. As you may recall I had spent the best part of the last 38 years toiling in the weaving industry. This came to an abrupt end on July 4th 2011 when three days short of my 60th birthday I joined many of my former colleagues on the employment scrapheap. Yes redundancy had finally nabbed me, but in all honesty it came as something of a relief. Work had once been a place I looked forward to going, and the camaraderie and thought that I was contributing to something, made it feel worthwhile. Over the last few years with the decline of the business and the subsequent loss of many long serving comrades this was no longer the case. Whilst I was a little apprehensive of the financial implications I was looking forward to getting my life back!

Then, a "sliding door" moment, on leaving the bank after depositing my meagre redundancy payment, I walked slap bang into a guy with whom my wife and I had spent many happy Saturday nights in the alehouses of Burnley. This man, a colossus of the local teaching scene, or so he never stops telling me, was to open up a whole new chapter in my life. I am sure many of my readers will have been acquainted with him at some time in their lives so in an attempt to preserve his anonymity, I will refer to him only as Geoff Ashworth of Barden School! I think in the last 25 years I had probably only come across Geoff on one or two occasions but it was fate that made our paths cross on that day.

It soon transpired that Geoff was also recently retired and that he now spent much of his time rambling, something that many of us think he has always done. Here I refer to rambling of the walking variety. Geoff knowing that I too had often rambled, duly invited me to come along and join a walking group which met every Tuesday. This group, known as Lancashire Dotcom Walkers, mainly consisting at the time of retired teachers, was primarily Preston and South Ribble based and Geoff was then the only Burnley participant. Geoff not being a man to miss an opportunity to get somebody to share travel costs thereby hit on me. My wife concerned that I would miss the contact with people now that I was no longer working, and knowing Geoff had a wicked sense of humour, readily encouraged me to go along.

Suffice it to say that joining up with this merry band was one of the best moves I have ever made. A day walking whatever the weather, with good company, and usually with a pub thrown in somewhere takes some beating. From a group of around a dozen in September 2011, numbers have swelled to the point where now in May 2014 we are regularly around thirty walkers per outing which brings its own logistics problems. The "Burnley Contingent" as we are now known is regularly in excess of a dozen, and most of these directly recruited by our friend Geoff. We periodically participate in various challenges within the group billed as Burnley v The Rest of the World. How appropriate that we are also winning most of these challenges. Many of the Burnley Contingent have also taken to regularly Thursday walking so not much chance of boredom here.

Amongst this group are football fans of many persuasions. Needless to say quite a few are North Enders, whilst we also have followers of Liverpool, Manchester United, Derby County, Oldham Athletic, and last but certainly least Blackburn Rovers. Poor old Blackburn John as he is affectionately known, has often over the last three years been eagerly sought out on a Tuesday walk as the Rovers have careered steadily downhill. I have known people go to some lengths to avoid a ribbing but surely booking a trip to Vietnam and Cambodia ahead of this seasons Ewood encounter was going a bit far, literally! Did him no good we were still waiting for him on his return. Hopefully there will be more tales to recall of this fine body of men, and women of course, as this diary progresses.

Saturday 24th May saw the final promotion place clinched by QPR in the Championship Play Off Final at a packed Wembley stadium. What a disaster for Derby and Steve McLaren, totally in charge for most of the game and with the opposition reduced to ten men after an hour, they succumb to a last minute goal by Zamora. How cruel after what had been a magnificent season for them after McLaren's appointment following Nigel Clough's departure from the club. How glad I was that we had not had to go through the torture of the play off lottery. There are some good players at Derby and perhaps a chance for us to do a bit of cherry picking. I personally would not be averse to a move for Chris Martin to add to our striking options.

On Wednesday 28th May Danny Lafferty becomes the first of the out of contract players to be offered terms to sign on the dotted line. He puts pen to paper on a three year deal, which is an astonishing show of faith from Sean Dyche offering such a long contract to a player not regularly in the starting eleven. Perhaps it is a reward for the player's patience and willingness to be a part of the squad without displaying the petulance and tantrums often shown by players on the fringe. Let's hope that Danny can repay the manager's confidence in the coming seasons.

The world has gone mad! It's the 29th May and as I drive into Burnley on Colne road I am greeted by an illuminated road sign asking, ARE YOU PREPARED FOR WINTER? It goes on to suggest that I should contact lancashire.gov.uk for advice. Now forgive me but is May not in Spring? Is Spring not followed by Summer and Autumn before we get back to Winter? What a waste of time, effort, and money! Lancashire.gov.uk I can only assume must be anticipating one hell of a winter.

Still it makes a change from the sign instructing me to, THINK BIKE. I have been thinking bike for several months now but can only come up with a two wheeled structure with pedals. My imagination is perhaps not as good as it once was. Perhaps it should read, THINK BACK, then it would remind us of what winter was like and we would ask ourselves if we are prepared for it.

OK, rant over. Whoever decided to install those signs needs to have along hard look at exactly what is the point of them. In this era of austerity, this is surely Nanny state lunacy yet again.

May ends with the best possible news for all Clarets, Kieran Trippier signs a new deal extending his stay till the end of the 2016/17 season. The undisputed best full back in the Championship has committed himself for a further two seasons ensuring that even if he is sold it will not be on a decreasing valuation. I'm sure Sean Dyche would not have wanted the headache of having to try and replace 'Tripps' ahead of the Premier League campaign. Now come on Danny Ings!

June begins as May ends, quietly. Despite increasing numbers of players being linked to us, many of which are pure invention by journalists with column inches to fill, there are still no signs of incoming transfer activity.

With the World cup in Brazil now only days away interest now switches in that direction. England warm up with a comfortable if unconvincing 3-0 Wembley victory over Peru. This is followed by a 2-2 draw with Ecuador in the heat of Miami. For this game England field what is mainly a second string and I can only hope that we do not need to call on this defence when we get down to the serious business. Some of these guys would be nowhere near an England shirt if they weren't playing for "Big 4" clubs. The round of warm up games ends with another game in Miami this time a 0-0 draw with Honduras. The only memorable thing about this game is the fact that it was stopped for approximately 40 minutes due to electrical storm activity. It's hard to recall a single shot on goal from either side and even when Honduras are reduced to 10 men we are still bereft of attacking ideas and goal threat.

Not the most auspicious start to the World Cup campaign and on this showing an early exit beckons.

For my own part I am currently involved in GCE Exam invigilating to earn a bit of cash to boost my meagre pensions. So far having officiated in 15 exams I am experiencing serious mental exhaustion as the tedium of it takes its toll. Fortunately only three more to go before I escape on my fourteen night cruise of the western Mediterranean. Bliss!

June 10th and still precious little news coming out of Turf Moor so time for a little aside here. My daughter Stephanie who some may remember from Book 1, had been suggesting we bought a bird feeder to encourage our small feathered friends into the garden. For the past few weeks we had been visited by Blue Tits, Coal Tits, and Robins. Encouraged by the prospect of enticing more Tits into the garden I invested in a seed feeder and deluxe seed mix which indicated I would soon be overwhelmed by them.

What has happened since.... **Nothing!** In fact literally not a dicky bird! My garden has become a bird free zone. Where have they all gone? Are they being held hostage? Have I been sold a pup? Still, having made the investment I will persevere and hope to bring better news shortly.

Suddenly a thought came to me. Where is the best place to get advice on virtually any topic? Why the Claretsmad messageboard of course, an expert for every day of the week! So I posted the following, "In an attempt to entice Tits into my garden I have invested in a seed feeder and seed mix. Previous to this I have been regularly visited by small birds, now nothing! What has happened? Where have they gone? Any ornithologists out there?"

Needless to say responses were much quicker at coming than the birds. Dibranchio opined that the post was *"loaded with double entendres and will hopefully lead to a fun filled thread"*. What could he possibly mean. Thankfully the majority of replies were of a more serious nature and contained some very useful tips. However perhaps the most unusual suggestion came from Elbarad who posted, *"I'd hang some fashionable shoes from a tree and post a sign offering shoes for half price in the front of the house. That ought to draw them in."* Similarly Alp posted, *"Give em a bath too, water draws em in and it is nice to see tits in the bath."*

Suffice it to say that the oracle that is Claretsmad certainly worked the trick and that very same evening my feeding station was visited by a pair of humble sparrows! They have broken the ice and I now eagerly await some more exotic species.

Thursday 12th June saw the opening game of the World Cup between Brazil and Croatia. The Croats, very much the underdogs surprisingly and deservedly took an early lead, and I wondered if an upset was in store. Now this was clearly not in the script and the referee contrived by means of one of the most abysmal and home biased performances I have seen to ensure the host nation started with a 3-1 victory. The whole thing left a sour taste and the cynical cheating and diving by the Brazilians sullied the great reputation of this famous footballing nation. Almost every challenge deemed a foul was followed by attempts by both Brazilian players and manager to get the offender carded. The pressure put on a weak referee by 200 million home supporters was such that a fair contest was never going to be the case. It looks as though we might as well hand them the trophy now and save the bother of the rest of the tournament. Having watched this I fear for what

England will have to face from past masters of the dark arts such as Italy, and win at all costs Uruguay.

On Sunday 15th June my wife and I set sail from Southampton on P&O's Azura for 2 weeks cruising the Western Med. My trip down to Southampton necessitates an early morning start which means I miss England's World Cup opener against Italy. I am not at all surprised to learn that despite once again a brave effort, we have lost! At dinner onboard ship I find myself sat with a Derby County fan, however I decide not to gloat as he is very complimentary about the Clarets and says we deserved it.

Three days into the cruise on returning from a trip to Seville I find three texts waiting on my phone from people telling me Chelsea at home is the first game of our second Premier League adventure. This is followed by an away game at Swansea, then home to Manchester United. What a cracking start! I always think it's best to meet the best sides early before they have settled into a rhythm so those two home games will do nicely. The same day also brings news that Sean Dyche and his backroom staff have signed improved contracts. Excellent news!

The 19th June signals England's exit from the World Cup. I watch the bulk of the game with many other England fans in Brodie's Bar on the ship and can only feel extreme disappointment at how tame has been our effort. Isn't it bloody marvellous that the goals to put us out are scored by Balotelli for Italy (ex Manchester City) and Suarez for Uruguay (currently Liverpool). These are two players who have milked the English Premier League for millions whilst showing no respect for it. How fitting they should bring about our downfall. It's about time the English clubs started to play some home grown talent and leave these mercenaries to pick up their fortunes at somebody else's expense.

I couldn't work up the enthusiasm to watch the final group game, a lifeless 0-0 draw with Costa Rica who go onto qualify for the knockout stages along with Uruguay. World Cup holders Spain and former winners Italy join us in an early and inglorious return.

Whilst still afloat Sky Sports News are reporting bids of £750K for Derby's Craig Bryson, and £1m for Craig Dawson of West Bromwich Albion, both apparently rejected. Dawson is reported to have submitted a transfer request. My Derby pal on the ship is unhappy about the link with Bryson and feels he wouldn't leave to come to Burnley. We will see! By the end of the last week in June, despite numerous rumours, the only signing is as expected Kightly from Stoke City for an undisclosed fee.

On his way out of Turf Moor is Junior Stanislas who having been offered a contract has declined the offer. On Thursday 26th June confirmation is received that he will be rejoining Eddie Howe at Bournemouth on a three year deal. Junior will always be fondly remembered for his goal against Blackburn Rovers at Turf Moor in the promotion season which so nearly gave us our long awaited win over the enemy. It's doubtful that he would have been a regular starter in the Premier League so we wish him well in his new start.

That just leaves Michael Duff and Luke O' Neill of the out of contract players still to have their futures confirmed.

JULY

As we enter July it's not only the weather that is heating up. As expected, with the return to pre-season training scheduled for Thursday 3rd July, and the majority of many players contracts ending in June, transfer activity is also starting to simmer.

First bit of firm news comes on the opening day of the month with the re-signing of long term servant Michael Duff, again on a one year contract. A loyal club servant "Mickey" has been with the club since 2004 and the contract is no more than he deserves following a fantastic season. A popular player both in the dressing room and with the fans, his vast experience and calming influence will be vital to our Premier League hopes.

This news is followed on the 2nd by the signing of Scottish international goalkeeper Matt Gilks who despite being offered a new contract at Blackpool decides to join the Clarets. Gilks should provide some experienced cover for Tom Heaton but I can't help wondering where this leaves Alex Cisak. On the same day the media are reporting a record breaking bid for Watford striker, Troy Deeney. Deeney has been prolific in the last two Championship seasons and the bid of reportedly £5m is quickly rejected. There are rumours of interest by several other clubs including Norwich, West Bromwich, Swansea, and Aston Villa. This one looks like it may need a substantially increased bid to get it over the line.

As the team return to training there is further disappointment as red hot target Craig Bryson decides to sign a new contract with Derby County despite apparently having agreed terms to join us. Obviously Derby not wanting to lose the player have pushed the boat out and matched our terms with the added bonus of a five year contract! So my new found Derby County friend aboard ship turned out to be right. It's doubtful that we would be offering that length of contract to any player at 27 years of age. So unfortunately this will mean a rethink for Sean with hopefully a plan B already in place.

Better news on the 4th with the announcement of the double signings of striker Marvin Sordell from Bolton, and experienced midfielder/defender Matt Taylor who is out of contract at West Ham. Sordell is a player known to Dyche from his time at Watford. After a promising spell at Watford he was snapped up by then Premier League Bolton for a fee of £3.5m. Unfortunately his spell at our neighbours has not turned out to be a happy one and we are rumoured to have picked him up for a fee in the region of £500/750K. Still only 23 years of age this will represent very shrewd business if Sean can develop the potential he obviously sees in him.

Taylor is also an ex Wanderer, but more recently with West Ham. He also has Premier League experience with Portsmouth. He is a left sided midfielder or full back and at 32, and with lots of top level games under his belt, will hopefully provide some necessary know how to a team that will need to learn fast. He is also something of a dead ball expert as Clarets fans will testify following his goal against us at Turf Moor in our last Premier campaign. To further rub salt in the wound he also scored a penalty against us for West Ham in last season's Capital One cup tie. At least he won't be doing that again!

It's Monday July 7th, my birthday. Amongst the number of presents awaiting opening is one that I have been intrigued by for some time. It has sat in our spare bedroom for many weeks since our long standing friends of many years sold their house in Burnley and departed for pastures new in Lincolnshire. The gift whilst in a cardboard box comes also in a Clarets Store bag and I have with great willpower resisted the temptation to open it till the appointed day. Now the time has come and as I remove it from its box, joy of joys! It is none other than a Clarets garden gnome replete in claret and blue kit about to kick a little black and white football. How thoughtful of my friends, and no doubt at no little expense knowing club shop prices. My wife immediately declares that he is far too good to go out in the garden and he takes up residence in the conservatory. She quickly decides that he should be named Sean in honour of our illustrious manager and so Sean the Gnome becomes a member of the Haworth household. Now some may think this tacky but I can only assume these are rather shallow people and we will endeavour to give Sean a good home for the rest of his natural. Mind you if he turns out to be unlucky and we lose a few I might banish him to the garden.

Sean the Gnome is not the only new Claret to appear on the 7th July, following on shortly is the announcement of a fifth signing for the Clarets, Steven Reid released by West Bromwich Albion. Reid a former team mate of Sean Dyche at Millwall can play at right back or midfield and brings with him a wealth of top flight experience. On the downside is his age and dodgy injury history. At 33 Reid joins on a one year contract, after previous spells with Millwall, Blackburn Rovers (spit), and West Bromwich Albion. I would expect that he will be mainly employed as back up for Kieran Trippier and may not actually see much game time.

It is becoming quite clear that Sean, Dyche not the gnome, is employing a different policy regarding new recruits to that of Coyle (spit again) after our previous promotion. Where Coyle favoured untried youngsters such as Eckersley, Easton, Edgar and Guerrero, Sean has leant much more heavily on age and experience with the signings of Kightly, Gilks, Matt Taylor and Reid. Whilst none of these new recruits could be described as exciting new additions it is essential that following the departure of the likes of Stock, Edgar, Stanislas, and Treacy, that we continue to build on what was already a small squad.

On the 8th July out of contract defender Luke O'Neill signs on for a further two years. O'Neill has had precious little first team action with us since his signing from Mansfield and last season had two spells on loan at York and Southend, the latter cut short by injury. Sean obviously sees something in the lad and it may be that once again he will be loaned out to get more first team action, hopefully at a reasonable level.

On Monday 14th July the squad are scheduled to fly out to Austria for a pre-season training camp incorporating one friendly fixture against an Austrian side. Despite continuing rumours over the previous weekend of possible new additions it looks as though none are as yet forthcoming. Strongly linked, in fact in some quarters reported as a done deal, is the signing of Middlesbrough striker Lukas Jutkiewicz. The most favoured potential striker signing according to the fans forum on Claretsmad is undoubtedly Troy Deeney. However with a suggested bid of £5m already rejected, and Watford's determination to hold on to their prize asset, it looks as though we may well be switching targets. Jutkiewicz was believed to be heading to near neighbours Bolton but suggestions are that we have scuppered that deal. The message board as usual is split between posters who think that Jutkiewicz is not good enough for the Premier League and those who feel if Dyche wants him then he can be improved to that level. The usual argument develops as always going round and round in circles with increasing acrimony between the two factions. Other recently suggested targets include Callum McManaman (Wigan Athletic), Henri Lansbury (Nottingham Forest), and some Mexican who is allegedly joining up with us in Austria for a trial!

There may or may not be any truth in these rumours but one thing for sure is that Burnley will not be spending big in the transfer market. This is made patently clear in an article by journalist Joe Bernstein in The Mail on Sunday of 13th July. In an interview with Dyche, Sean reveals that agents have been bombarding him with phone calls, emails, and faxes, believing he has money to burn. Sean goes on *'One agent sent me a message to tell me his player was available at 15 million Euros and wanted £45,000-a-week salary, net. My reply was two words:"Wrong club." 'I was thinking, at least do your homework. It's not going to happen at that level at Burnley. I'm not stupid and I know we've got to be competitive but would I do that and rip the heart out of the club? No, it's not my style.'*

Bernstein continues by saying that most importantly Dyche will not allow the squad to feel any fear about the second Premier league adventure. Sean is quoted as saying *'We are leaving Burnley-world and going into the reality of Premier league-world but it's not scary.' I know if you catch some of those top boys like Aguero and Sanchez when they are on a hot day, you can get badly hurt. But without being disrespectful, they are still human. They have ups and downs, no player no matter how valuable can be a magician every single week. We are built on a real group mentality rather than individuals. If we bought one big star you'd get this weird thing in the camp. You'd have baggage of all the players who have done well for you whose contracts are nowhere near that of the signing you have just made. It would hurt us so, if my chairman came to me and said "Look. We will buy that £20m player", I would say I don't think it is appropriate for this club at this time. It would harm the group and unquestionably we have talent here already.'*

One of my pet hates of the last Premier league season was the switching of kick off times to suit our lords and masters at Sky. Today 14th July, sees the announcement of the TV companies early season games to be screened live. As I expected our opener with Chelsea is one selected and we now have to wait till Monday 18th August for our first action. Bloody Hell we will be playing catch up after the first games!

Also moving but staying on the same date is the second home game against Manchester United which is chosen by BT Sport. This game will now kick off at 12.45 on Saturday 30th August. A further two games, away at West Bromwich, and home to Everton are switched to Sunday kick offs, at 16.00 and 13.30 respectively. In all four changes for TV before October is even out. This situation will become further aggravated by the fact that we will have to move to Sunday games to accommodate the clubs playing in the Europa League where fixtures are scheduled for Thursday evenings. So much for my long awaited couple of pints with friends in the pub before a traditional 15.00 kick off on a Saturday. I am going to have to get used to drinking at anti social hours, probably out of a brown paper bag.

Tuesday 15th July is a big day in the Lancashire Dotcom Walkers' calendar. Today is the 2nd annual Bowls challenge, The Burnley Contingent v The Rest of the World, at Bretherton Village Institute's Bowling green. Once again I note that for us it is an away game following last year's inaugural match at

Longridge. Dotcom leader Bob Clare (Ex Barden school teacher) I think summed the mood of the contest up excellently in his report. I quote *'There was a high turnout for this event which is always marked by animosity, unpleasantness, and vicious gamesmanship.'*

The tone for the contest had already been set from the previous week with a prominent member of the Rest of the World (ROW), Sat Nav Dave, suggesting that the result of last year's contest, a 3-3 draw, had been influenced by biased refereeing by Nigel Hext (also ex Barden PE teacher). He went on to suggest a couple of other possible referees, not surprisingly both from the Rest of the World team. I quickly pointed out to him that it was highly unlikely that Nigel would be biased towards Burnley, given that he lives in Mellor, within spitting distance of Blackburn, and has a thicker Cockney accent than Chas & Dave. Furthermore he is an Oldham Athletic fan!

Having duly assembled at Bretherton it was quickly apparent that we were slightly outnumbered, by twenty to eight! It was then decided that six ROW players would transfer to us. Now cast your mind back to school games lessons when the two captain's got to pick their teams each having an alternate selection. Not a bad way of ensuring fairly evenly balanced teams. Did that happen here, NO! We were given Blackburn John and Stuart from Mellor, Andy (Derby County fan) and his wife Anne (a Burnley lass, born and bred). The final two making up our numbers were the aforementioned Nigel and Bob Clare by dint of the fact that they had taught in Burnley. Forgive me thinking it but could the Blackburn pair have been planted on us with instructions to lose their end? Would a Derby fan be going all out for the Clarets after pipping them for promotion? Could Nigel and

Bob who were also doubling as referees be seen to favour us with any decisions in light of the previous accusations? The whole affair had the whiff of a fix about it.

This was further confirmed on commencement of the first round of four matches. It quickly became apparent that the pairing of Jean/Jim from the ROW were certainly no slouches at the game and could have passed as professionals. Similarly, joint Dotcom leader John and his wife Dianne paired in one of the other games were also regular bowlers. It came as no surprise that after the first round we trailed 4-1 with three to play. Despite a valiant effort by Nigel and myself which completely overwhelmed our opponents, Scouse Brian and Eileen, the other couples could not match our performance. The final match score of 5-2 to the ROW, was a bitter pill to swallow. It was however made a little sweeter by the excellent, all you can eat hot buffet for £4.99 at the Blue Anchor, Bretherton. Pints of beer also assisted in the lifting of the mood, and after a short walk on a lovely sunny day, it was all smiles in the car park.

On reflection we had been stitched up and this was the first ever defeat for the Burnley Contingent in any challenge. Next time we will be ready for them and the gloves will be off!

Also on the 15th the Clarets confirm the sixth pre-season signing, the strongly rumoured Lukas Jutkiewicz. The 25 year old striker signs on a three year deal from Middlesbrough after finishing the season in good form on loan at Bolton. Not a popular signing with many Claretsmad posters but he is deemed good enough, and of the right character by Sean. Dyche said of his signing *'I still think there is development in Lukas, he's 25 and has been around a little bit now and he finished last season very strongly. I feel there is even more to come and he'll be hungry for that. He'll be working with a good group who are all hungry to not only achieve things but to keep pushing themselves as individuals. That's a big part of our mentality and he'll fit into that very nicely. He's a physical presence who can hold the ball up very well and link play. We think that there are goals in him and it is very similar to the Sam Vokes story where he's always done well and we're looking for him to build on what he's done. There is a nice demand now in that area of the pitch as all the players offer something different to the team so we're happy with how that is developing.'* With Ings, Barnes, Jutkiewicz, Sordell, and Vokes when fit, further striker signings now look unlikely.

The Austrian training camp is rounded off on Sunday 20th July with a resounding victory in a friendly against a Styria Select XI. The Clarets run out 8-0 winners with goals from Barnes (2), Sordell (2), Jutkiewicz (2), Arfield, and the youngster Gilchrist. Good to see the strikers getting off the mark in a friendly some described as akin to playing a team of waiters! At the end of the day you can only play what's put in front of you. The game as usual was marked with multiple substitutions in order to give most players a run out in what was no more than a training exercise.

Apparently we are now being quoted at odds of 7500/1 to win the Premier League, now that's worth a tenner of anybody's money! Can see the bookies taking a real caning there! At the same time the odds for staying up are 11/8, and 4/7 for going down. Think I'll take the first bet not much money to be made on the others.

Recently a thought has crossed my mind, perhaps sparked by the 7500/1 odds to be Champions, that in Sean Dyche we may have discovered the modern day Brian Clough. Cloughie could turn relatively unknown players seemingly into world beaters and create teams at both Derby and Nottingham Forest that achieved far more success than could possibly have been dreamed off. Players such as Hector, O'Hare, McGovern, and Robertson would never have been the first players on the list for the big city clubs of the time. Clough's teams were based around teamwork and work rate, ring any bells? They were also noted for their attacking nature and fair play ethic, sound familiar? Perhaps it comes as no surprise that both Dyche, and Ian Woan, his assistant have both experienced playing for the man dubbed the greatest manager England never had. Early days yet but it will be interesting to see how Sean's career develops. If he can reproduce a fraction of Clough's successes for the Clarets he will indeed be a true Claret Legend to rank alongside the greatest.

The first friendly on home soil is an away fixture at Accrington Stanley, our nearest neighbours. Bit cheeky of our pals from the lower regions of League 2 to charge £15 for a meaningless friendly, but I suppose it may be their biggest pay day of the season. No shocks here, the usual early friendly scenario of multiple changes, with the Clarets using 23 players. Again featuring prominently are a number of the Development squad youngsters, and the game is won 1-0 by a goal from one such lad, Jason Gilchrist. That's Jason's second in two games and he even gets his picture in the Mail on Sunday Sports section!

Quickly following this one is Preston North End away, a result I will either be relishing or dreading as I do battle with the Dotcom walkers PNE brigade.

Well wouldn't you just credit it, after leading through a Jutkiewicz goal early in the game we are pegged back and finally beaten by a 35 yard free kick in the dying minutes. Why does it always happen when I have been winding up opposition fans? Why could it not have happened at Accy? I don't know any Accy fans, are there any? Sean says in his after match comments that is just exactly what we need pre-season, well that may be so, but I can tell you it's not the kind of result I need! One or two regular starters were again missing but nine of the team got a full ninety minute run out as we build the fitness levels. Blackpool away next up on Saturday, at the last count they have managed to muster 12 players but still no goalkeeper. I suggest long range shooting should be the order of the day. With regards the PNE fans I will just have to trot out the old meaningless friendly line, and it's about fitness not results at this stage. That should keep them quiet; alternatively I will switch off my phone and shut down email.

A bit of good news on 30th July as Ben Mee signs a new contract committing him to the end of the 2016/2017 season. That means we now have nine players signed till that date and contributes greatly to our squad stability.

Following close behind on July 31st comes the announcement that goalkeeper Tom Heaton has also signed giving him another three years on contract. Still no commitment from Danny Ings though, should a tempting offer come our way it may be hard to resist. The problem then of course is that he has to be replaced, and as we enter August there is only one month left in the transfer window.

As anticipated the flak coming from the Dotcom Walkers Nob End fraternity is not long in coming. The accursed 'Flatlanders' as we affectionately refer to them seem to be waging a concerted battle of words with me via all communication channels. Even my long lost adversary PNE Ed (of book 1 fame) has bizarrely started texting me pictures of his grape vines in Longton! How weird, he is referring to it as the Lancashire Med, I think he means Lancashire Mud. Hopefully I may have silenced them by telling them I am now looking forward to the opener against Mourinho's Chelsea and asking them who have they got? In fact it is a home game against Notts County, followed by away fixtures at Rochdale (league Cup) and Scunthorpe, WOW!

AUGUST

August begins with a weekend trip to Hawes for my wife and myself for some serious boozing and a little light walking. Predictably the weather, glorious for most of July, has decided to turn nasty for this weekend, well at least according to the forecast.

Can't argue with the forecast Saturday. I decided to make a bit of a journey south to Buckden and do one of my favourite circular walks, Buckden-Cray-Yockenthwaite-Hubberholme-Buckden. After a pleasant interchange on the car park with a Liverpool fan who was very complimentary to the Clarets, we set off in fine but overcast warm weather. It's not long before its coats off and down to T-shirts. As usual that is the signal for a shower so its coats back on by Cray. Approaching Scar House we meet a couple of fellow walkers eating lunch in the middle of nowhere. Engaging them in conversation we are staggered when they reveal themselves as fellow Burnleyites, small world isn't it! We suggest to them a little addition to their stroll which will take them the same route as us. We then continue our walk in pleasant enough conditions till we hit the penultimate stretch Yockenthwaite to Hubberholme at which point the heavens open. Sheltering, to no avail, under a tree by the River Wharfe, who should come along but our new found friends, soaked to the skin. If they hadn't followed my advice they would have been back in the pub in the dry! Still like true Burnleyites they smiled in the face of adversity and carried on with us back to base. If you ever read this, Tony Doyle of Worsthorne, sorry!

On arrival back in Hawes, of course by now sunshining, I try to ascertain the score from Blackpool via the internet on my mobile phone. I can only assume the internet in North Yorkshire is powered by clockwork. Each page loads so slowly I am in danger of running out of battery power. However, I eventually learn that we have beaten our hosts, who include more trialists than Burnley Magistrates court, by a solitary Marvin Sordell strike. Still at least it's back to winning ways and starts August in a manner we hope will continue.

Tuesday 5th August marks my Clarets debut this season for the home friendly against Celta Vigo. During the day I am pondering trying my new kit out for the game, highly expensive Clarets Polo Shirt, with Claret (well Burgundy) trousers. I will of course take my usual good luck charms of Claret and Blue Worry beads, although these are now in a rather dilapidated condition following a mid season collapse last year (shoddy Greek workmanship), and the 'More Than 90 Minutes' wristband of book one fame. Probably best to assess the powers of this kit ahead of the Chelsea game and perhaps make any necessary adjustments for the Verona match as a final trial.

I wonder if our visitors from Spain are referred to as Celta Vegans, but think it unlikely as reports are filtering through that their tackling in previous friendlies has been of a more carnivorous nature!

Well it turned out to be a game of two halves, or two sides in the case of Celta Vigo, the visitors opting to field a different team in each half. They had embarked on a pretty hectic schedule of warm up games having played at Norwich on Friday, Wolverhampton on Saturday, the Clarets Tuesday, and Everton Wednesday. For our part we opted for pretty much the Championship line up. Heaton returned in goal for his first pre-season action, the defence was as usual, as was midfield with the exception of Wallace for the still absent Kightly. Up front was the pairing of Barnes and Jutkiewicz, with no place in the squad for Danny Ings.

Our visitors were out in the ring like Spanish bullfighters but were floored by an opener for the Clarets within three minutes. An excellent ball slid through by Wallace found Jutkiewicz beating the offside trap and scoring with style. The Spaniards clearly not treating this game as an easy warm up, continued to enjoy much possession but a well drilled Clarets formation held them comfortably. In contrast we were looking far more dangerous on the break and the impressive Jutkiewicz almost doubled the lead holding off the defence before hitting the post. Some meaty exchanges followed as half time drew near with a mass melee resulting in the booking of one of the Spaniards. Half time arrived with the lead intact.

Vigo switched the teams at half time with the possible exception of the keeper and once again started the second half with attacking intent. We were lucky to survive as a cracking shot cannoned off the bar to safety with Heaton beaten. Not for long though as a slick move saw the visitors level with a very tidy goal. Their joy was short lived as Ben Mee found Ashley Barnes with a quick throw in, the ball was quickly delivered into the box where Jutkiewicz finished convincingly. More blood and thunder challenges ensued and a second Spaniard fell foul of the referee's notebook. Could we hold on? Unfortunately not as another well worked and finished goal from our energetic visitors saw the game finish all square.

As the players trooped off for a plate of Paella and Chips, washed down with Sangria and Moorhouse's Pride of Pendle, the crowd I think well satisfied, headed for home. It was certainly a game played at full pace and with no holds barred in the challenges, definitely a step up in the quest for match sharpness ahead of the season's opener. Next up is the last friendly against our Pasta and Pizza guzzling friends from Verona. Let's see what they make of playing after a lunch of Holland's Meat & Potato Pies.

In terms of my match kit, I opted for Blue trousers in preference to the Claret ones and perhaps that was what allowed Vigo back in the game. Perhaps some minor adjustments required for Saturday's game.

Ahead of the Verona friendly I find in the Daily Mail a quote, 'indispensable' 12-page guide, for the upcoming Premier League season. It's always interesting to read what the sports journos make of our chances and I confidently expect each one to be forecasting a season of doom and gloom ending in relegation. Interesting then to find that out of their ten regular columnists six are as predicted but four are 'believers'. I certainly didn't expect that. Furthermore none other than that font of soccer wisdom and part time modeller of M&S Suits, Jamie Redknapp, is tipping Danny Ings and Kieran Trippier to breakthrough into the England side. Martin Keown, the former uncompromising Arsenal centre back, tips Danny Ings as our key man. He then goes on to say of the Clarets, *"Their home form is their big hope. Turf Moor has always been a difficult place to go, with a sloped pitch and the fans create a febrile atmosphere. Dyche has real confidence too but his players have to match him."*

Sloped pitch? Where has that come from? Has Keown ever been to the Turf? Anyway let's hope he is right and I am sure that 'febrile' atmosphere will be evident come the appearance of Chelsea.

After reading that and a couple of pre match pints sat in the sun outside the Talbot I am ready for the second European challenge, Hellas Verona. The game produces a fairly even first half at not quite the same ferocity as the Celta Vigo game. Verona, in front of probably a couple of hundred of their colourful, and certainly noisy fans, look a more than useful side. At half time its 0-0, but the game explodes on the restart as the Italians go ahead with a headed goal from their Greek midfielder whose name is too long and tortuous to even attempt to spell. No time for despondency as almost from the kick off we are level with a smart Matty Taylor finish from a Danny Ings pass. The Clarets are then ahead with a fine headed goal by Jutkiewicz, 'The Juke', who is certainly creating a big impression in the pre-season games. The game is wrapped up with a gem of a free kick from 25 yards, Ross Wallace giving the Verona keeper no chance at all with his perfect placement.

The visiting fans who could hardly be described as 'Gentlemen of Verona' spent the half time break in the JHU concourse throwing beer about and singing fascist songs accompanied by Nazi salutes and Swastika signs! They seemed to thoroughly enjoy their day in the Lancashire sun, singing and chanting continuously. Presumably they have now moved on to invade some other peaceful corner of Europe.

With regards to kit adjustments, following the draw with Celta Vigo, I decided to give the worry beads a rest. I have been a bit less confident in their abilities since the cord snapped coinciding with a poorish run of form last season, broken beads equating to broken spell. For this game I decided to ditch them, needless to say they will now stay at home for the Chelsea game. Anyway they are so last season!

We are now into the final week before the big kick off, and many fans myself included are looking forward to it with a mixture of great excitement and some trepidation. Last season has created a strong sense of belief in both team and fans and this is a valuable weapon. Nobody wants to see this shattered by a string of heavy defeats in the early stages of the season. I guess this was very much the feeling back in 2009 and whilst we took some batterings away from home, the early season form at the Turf was exceptional. I am praying that this will be the case this time but with some tighter defensive displays away from home. Still Chelsea and Manchester United for the first two home games is a tough ask and any points gleaned there will surely be a bonus.

For my own part I am determined to enjoy the season come what may. It is the reward for last season's magnificent effort, and we should all celebrate that fact. For me the most important thing that last season's achievement has brought is the financial stability that it guarantees the club. Estimated at worst to be in the region of £120m over the next five years, even if immediately relegated, this money, spent wisely, should keep the club competitive over at least that period.

Much has been made on the messageboards of the lack of 'big money' signings. Approaching Mid August and with the transfer window closing at the end of the month, even speculation about possible signings seems to have dried up. However, elsewhere the market seems to have gone mad with very average players being touted at exorbitant prices. I think our policy will be to ride out this monetary madness and concentrate on getting the maximum out of what we have. It is the Burnley way!

Thursday 14th August sees the Burnley Contingent walkers resume their conquest of the Ribble Way long distance walk. Ably led by Sherpa Walton we are proceeding downstream from Ribblehead in bite size chunks of approximately 7/8 miles. Today we are about to tackle leg 4 Wigglesworth to Gisburn, after a few weeks break from the trail due to walkers holidays. All assemble at the duly appointed time 13 people plus Button the Cockerpoo, who enjoys these walks more than anyone. On arrival at Wigglesworth I see our old Barden teacher friend who shall be referred to as Geoff A to preserve his anonymity, has come up with a new penny pinching idea.

Geoff due to what he describes as an old war injury is in the habit of using walking poles to assist his shattered Knees. Over the years he has developed his own inimitable walking style with the poles which is characterised by hitting the ground with them excessively hard. The result of this action is to destroy the rubber tips in a very short time. This means that when walking on hard surfaces Geoff makes an excessively irritating amount of noise, which I think he secretly enjoys. At least we always know where he is and there is no chance of him sneaking up on you. He has been likened to Blind Pugh and the Crocodile in Peter Pan that swallowed the alarm clock!

Today he has decided to take some action with the poles, mainly because the force of the metal ends hitting the ground is sending shock waves up to his shoulders, and he needs to absorb the impact. Deciding that 99p is too high a price to pay for new rubber tips, well noted for his thrift is our

Geoff, he has gone for a DIY option. He has found an old pair of pumps (plimsolls for the posh) and cut out small patches of the rubber soles which he has then bound with string and tape to the poles. Talk about Compo! Well suited with his endeavours he proudly shows them off to all and sundry and away we go. Needless to say after about 4 miles of Geoff's incessant poundings the 'new tips' are displaced and less than useless. Oh well Geoff back to the drawing board, and we all eagerly await the next reincarnation of the sticks!

Friday evening on the eve of the Premier League season, the Clarets spring a surprise announcing the signing of Wolverhampton Wanderers, Irish international left back, Stephen Ward. Ward who had spent last season on loan at Championship rivals Brighton was on the verge of signing for the south coast club when we intervened and snaffled him, reputedly whilst on his way for a medical at Brighton. A bit of a strange signing this as we already seem to be well covered in the Left Back area. It is being suggested that the player is a versatile performer and may actually be used in other roles, time will tell.

Saturday's initial Premier league games throw up an interesting result with new manager Louis Van Gaal's Manchester United losing at home to Swansea. Most of the other games go as expected, Leicester and QPR the other promoted teams with us manage a home draw and home defeat respectively. Our old pal Charlie Austin having a penalty saved in QPR's defeat! Worst thing about the opening day for me is the dire performance of my Fantasy Premier League team, 'Sean's Claret Aces.' Due to last minute injuries to Barkley (Everton) and withdrawal of Mertesacker (Arsenal), my injury hit squad earn me a paltry 8 points and on Sunday morning I am lying bottom of the 'Luis Suarez all you can eat invitational league!' A chance of some much needed points Sunday though with Sturridge, Sterling, and Coutinho for Liverpool, and Hart and Kompany for Manchester City, hopefully seeing off weak opposition.

Well the big day has finally arrived, it's over three and a half months since we wrapped up the promotion party, and now we are finally primed and ready to go again. As I write these notes at 11.20 a.m. I can already feel the nerves starting to jangle, God knows how the players must feel! I remain determined to enjoy the ride come what may, and am heartened to think that should the unthinkable happen and we lose, at least we will have the same points as Manchester United. I am further cheered by the performance of my Fantasy Football League guys from Liverpool and Manchester City whose efforts yesterday earned me a further 41 points. I have temporarily shot up the table from 18th (bottom) to ninth.

GAME 1 - Burnley v Chelsea, Monday 18th August, 20.00 hrs

I arrive at the ground in good time to allow for any parking difficulties and potential problems with the new swipe card turnstile arrangements. It's a fine sight to see the pitch in immaculate condition and the ground full. The packed away end is contributing to a lively atmosphere and the tension is mounting. As the teams emerge from the tunnel they are met by the message 'OUR TURF, BFC' spelt out by every member of the crowd in the Jimmy Mac stand holding aloft suitably coloured Claret and Blue cards. That's different!

We start the game confidently and are in control for the first three or four minutes before our illustrious visitors start to get into their stride. Then unbelievably we are ahead on 14 minutes with shades of the Robbie Blake goal against

Manchester United in 2010. Matty Taylor picks out Arfield just inside the right side of the penalty area, Scotty brings the ball down on his thigh then hits an unstoppable right footer past Courtois. What a dream come true for Scotty, not much more than 12 months ago released by Huddersfield and on trial with the Clarets. Beam me up Scotty!

Unfortunately the lead doesn't last for long as on 17 minutes a Fabregas back heel leads to an Ivanovic cross shot that hits the post rebounding to £32m debutant Diego Costa who fires home. Worse to come on 21 minutes as the impeccable Fabregas threads an impossible ball through the Clarets defence to the on running Schurlle who converts easily. A goal of true class and totally unstoppable. It's almost disaster time on 30 minutes as a horrific back pass lets in Costa who attempts to round Heaton who appears to bring him down. Not so according to the referee, to whom we are truly thankful, who promptly books the striker for simulation. However a now rampant Chelsea extend the lead on 34 minutes as a Fabregas corner picks out an unmarked Ivanovic who volleys home.

The Clarets are now looking edgy and struggling to get and hold the ball. Chelsea are in total control with their ability to retain possession, pass precisely, and killer movement. A Champions League team indeed. Fortunately we manage to get through to half time without further damage, but I can't help fearing the worst and hoping the game does not turn in to a rout. God knows what would have happened if the referee had given the penalty and reduced us to 10 men!

Thankfully Sean seems to have restored some composure in the interval and we are almost back in the game with another great Arfield effort brilliantly clawed away by the keeper. Trippier, after a quiet first half, is now finding his feet and getting forward effectively. Mee is also growing in stature as the Blues continue to retain possession well but don't carry the same bite. It's a much leveller second half but we never really threaten to get back into the game. I suspect that had we scored Chelsea would have gone up a gear. Jutkiewicz, who gave his all, and Ings who appeared to take a knock are replaced by Barnes and Sordell, whilst Kightly replaces Taylor. A much better second half performance but still with the odd nervous error at the back sees the game end 3-1.

It's probably a good thing to get this game out of the system. The team now know exactly what they are up against and to be fair did improve. Thankfully we won't meet a side as good as Chelsea every week. They were a very impressive outfit and considering the money spent, they bloody well should be. The Burnley crowd gave great backing to the team and they came off at the end to a good hand. It would have been nice to catch Chelsea on an off day, but instead we caught them very much on an on day. Hopefully some lessons will have been learnt, it was certainly a massive step up from the Championship. We had been beaten not by a few outstanding individuals but by a TEAM of outstanding individuals.

Result – Burnley 1 (Arfield 14) – 3 (Costa 17, Schurlle 21, Ivanovic 34) Chelsea

Burnley Team

Heaton, Trippier, Duff, Shackell, Mee, Arfield, Marney, Jones, Taylor (Kightly 70), Ings (Sordell 82), Jutkiewicz (Barnes 70)

Subs Not used – Gilks, Wallace, Long, Dummigan

Chelsea Team

Courtois, Ivanovic, Cahill, Terry, Azpilicueta, Fabregas, Matic, Schurrle (Willian 78), Oscar (Mikel 82), Hazard (Drogba 84), Diego Costa

Subs Not used – Cech, Filipe Luis, Zouma, Torres

Attendance – 20,699

Season Record – Played 1, Won 0, Drawn 0, Lost 1, Goals For 1, Goals Against 3, Points 0

League Position after Game 1 – 19th

Regarding my kit for the opening game, I stuck with the tried and tested outfit that brought success against Verona, however on arrival at the ground I was presented with a new natty Claret and Blue wristband. This was a gift from John & Judy W, whom you may remember from 'A Season In The Sun', who were recently returned from their 12 week tour of Europe. I have to say that after the result against Chelsea the jury is very much out on this particular 'lucky' charm. Still, Nil desperandum, let's give it another whorl. I noticed that changing it from left wrist to right at half time brought us a better second half result, that might be the key!

A new irritating feature that appeared on Monday night were the electronic advertising boards that ran the entire perimeter of the pitch. The garish colours and intensity which increased as the sky darkened I have to say were quite distracting. Thankfully we will only be subjected to these on the televised games, or will we?

There were some interesting team statistics published in The Daily Mail of 20th August, which may explain our defeat against Chelsea. It transpires that in terms of player's average height, Chelsea come joint top in the Premier league table at 6'1", Burnley come in at a mere 5'11". In terms of weight, Chelsea weigh in at 12st 4lb second only to QPR at 12st 7lb, whilst Burnley are a puny 11st, joint lightest with Arsenal (who are also the shortest). We are certainly living up (or perhaps down) to our tag of 'little Burnley'.

As August progresses rapidly the end of the transfer window looms large. We seem to have had a worrying number of transfer targets chased but few landed. As always the problem is one of money with the Clarets unable or unwilling to match club's asking prices, and the same applying to player's wages. Amongst many fans there is a growing sense of disappointment in the transfer dealings and a real fear that failure to bring in some quality new blood will ultimately lead to our demise. Still things are as they are and we just have to get on with it, so it's on to Swansea and game two.

GAME 2 - Swansea City v Burnley, Saturday 23rd August, 15.00hrs

A tricky looking fixture this, Swansea surprisingly predicted to be relegation candidates by a number of pundits (not by me), confounded the odds last Saturday with an opening day win at Manchester United. That result is sure to have given them confidence. The clubs have previously met in all tiers of the Football league but this is the first time in the Premier league.

The Clarets name an unchanged team from the Chelsea game but there are places on the bench for Steven Reid, and new signing Stephen Ward, who replace Kevin Long and Cameron Dummigan. Also a chance to see the new away strip of all black in action against the all white of Swansea.

We get off to a decent start without being under too much pressure but fall behind on 23 minutes to a goal from ex Clarets loanee Nathan Dyer. A ball played down the right flank eludes Ben Mee and leaves the pacy Dyer clear for a run into the box unchallenged. His shot appears to bounce ahead of Tom Heaton and although he gets a hand on it can't keep it out down by the post. Shortly after this point I realise I have forgotten the lucky charms and rectify that situation immediately. The Half time break comes with the score remaining at 1-0.

Sean's half time pep talk revolves around the fact that we are showing Swansea too much respect and asks for the team to respond with more freedom in their play. His chat seems to work as we get an improved second half performance with the Clarets in the ascendancy but unable to find a goal. Close things from a Jutkiewicz header, and an excellent move ending with the 'Juke' just failing to get on the end of a David Jones low cross shot are all we have to show for our efforts.

This game again illustrates the point that in Premier league football there are no margins for error. Defensive errors are nearly always punished and goal chances must be taken. For one day we hit the bottom of the table, but on Sunday QPR's thumping 4-0 at Tottenham lifts us off the bottom on goal difference. Well done Spurs!

As for the verdict on the 'lucky charms' performance, well we did improve after I remembered the wristbands, so I suppose some blame for the defeat could be attached to myself. However, at this rate 'Sean the Gnome' could be heading out of the comfort of the conservatory and in to the cold and wet of the garden!

Result – Swansea 1 (Dyer 23) – 0 Burnley

Burnley Team

Heaton, Trippier, Duff, Shackell, Mee, Arfield, Marney, Jones (Sordell 90+1), Taylor (Wallace 72), Ings, Jutkiewicz (Barnes 82)

Subs Not used – Gilks, Ward, Reid, Kightly

Swansea Team

Fabianski, Rangel, Williams, Amat, N.Taylor, Ki Sung-Yeung, Shelvey, Dyer (Montero 66), Sigurdsson, Routledge (Tiendalli 90), Bony (Gomis 64)

Subs Not used – Tremell, Bartley, Richards, Sheehan

Attendance – 20,565

Season Record – Played 2, Won 0, Drawn 0, Lost 2, Goals For 1, Goals Against 4, Points 0

League Position after Game 2 – 19th

A temporary reprieve from league action on Tuesday 26th August as we meet Sheffield Wednesday at the Turf in Capital Cup, Round 2, action. Will Sean take the opportunity to make changes and give a run out to some of the fringe players or will he go with the same in an attempt to build confidence? A difficult one to call with the impending visit of Manchester United now only a few days away.

Capital One Cup, Round 2 – Burnley v Sheffield Wednesday, Tuesday 26th August, 19.45hrs

The Owls are a team who over recent years I think it is fair to say have caused us problems at Turf Moor. This unfortunately was once again such an occasion.

The Clarets opted to take the opportunity to make multiple changes but still put out what on paper looked a respectable XI. Gilks came in for Heaton with Long, and Stephen Ward replacing Duff, and Mee in defence. Midfield saw Marney, and Taylor out, with Kightly, and Wallace taking the wide positions, Arfield moving to centre mid. Up front Ings, and Jutkiewicz were rested, for Sordell, and Barnes. Steven Reid once again took up position as bench warmer!

A game of few chances against a typically muscular Sheffield Wednesday side saw most fans leaving the ground thoroughly disgruntled after a 1-0 defeat courtesy of a late Owls penalty. There were very few if any positives to be taken from this game. Sordell and Barnes could make no impact first half, although both improved marginally in the second. Wallace was busy, but mostly ineffective. Ward made a quiet debut but was caught out of position as a move broke down in the midfield resulting in Shackell conceding the penalty that cost us the game. Arfield was nowhere near as effective in a central role compared to his contribution from wide positions.

Tactically we were disappointing, too often using the long ball to the strikers which was gobbled up by a robust Owls defence. This seems to be a feature of our play this season as we seem to be taking the easy option, perhaps down to lack of confidence. Three played, three lost, not the start we had hoped for.

Result – Burnley 0 – 1 (Nuhiu 78 pen) Sheffield Wednesday

Burnley Team

Gilks, Trippier, Long, Shackell, Ward, Wallace, Arfield, Jones (Taylor 60), Kightly (Ings 82), Sordell (Jutkiewicz 83), Barnes

<u>Subs Not used</u> – Heaton, Duff, Mee, Reid

Sheffield Wednesday Team

Kirkland, Palmer, Zayatte, Lees, Mattock, Maghoma (May 63), Coke, Semedo, Helan, Maguire (Nuhiu), Madine

<u>Subs Not used</u> – Westwood, Loovens, McCabe, Corry, Floro

Attendance – 4,979

So it's not the best preparation for another tough upcoming fixture against none less than Manchester United. United will be strengthened by this week's signings of Di Maria, and Rojo for a combined total in the region of £74m, but where are ours? Wednesday 27th sees another much rumoured target, Wigan's McArthur, apparently on his way to Leicester for a medical. Once again we seem to have been outbid and the Claretsmad messageboard is, not for the first time, approaching meltdown. Once again time is running out in the transfer window, and there is a fear that this will lead to panic buys at over inflated prices. We shall see.

Friday 29th August and reports come through that the McArthur deal to Leicester has fallen through, with Crystal Palace now believed to be showing an interest. Meanwhile strong rumours are circulating that the Clarets are pursuing

Derby centre back Richard Keogh. Also mentioned is the possibility of a double deal involving striker Chris Martin. Now he would be a decent capture but I think it's unlikely with Derby again riding high in the Championship. It smacks of another example of lazy journalism, or agents stirring the pot as both Keogh and Martin have just one year left on their contracts.

It's Saturday and the day of the big clash with Manchester United. The morning paper is full of the usual stuff about financial mismatches. On this occasion the Daily Mail goes with the story that one Angel Di Maria is the equivalent of 12 Burnley XI's in financial terms! Makes you wonder if we should even bother turning up. Once again we suffer kick off disruption time as the game is moved to a 12.45 kick off for live coverage by BT Sport.

GAME 3 - Burnley v Manchester United, Saturday 30th August, 12.45 hrs

After making the long walk to the ground, 2.43 miles in 39.05 minutes at an average walking speed of 3.74 mph, I am met by the sight of another full house at the Turf. The team comes out to a great ovation and the home crowd are clearly up for it. Sean has reverted after midweek to the usual starting eleven, whilst United field £60m new man Di Maria.

Playing towards the Cricket Field stand we start the game confidently and positively in contrast to our visitors who look decidedly edgy. Much has been made in the media of Van Gaal's liking for the three at the back formation and this is how they line up against us. Their slow start almost costs them as a tremendous Dave Jones free kick rattles the bar with the keeper rooted to the spot, only to rebound to safety. After about ten minutes United start to get to grips with the game as new signing Di Maria starts to influence proceedings. He is certainly looking to get on the ball as often as possible and looks a good player, if very one footed (left). One great through ball puts Van Persie clear of the defence but Tom Heaton makes an admirable stop from the one on one. There is a terrific atmosphere and the Clarets are giving as good as they get. United's defensive system is leaving large spaces between the flank defenders and the wide midfielders and we are looking to use this to our advantage. A tremendous first half has Scott Arfield the stand out player, unluckily being denied after comprehensively beating Tyler Blackett and seeing his shot deflected. What a revelation Arfield has been and he looks completely at home even in such exalted company. The sides go off at half time 0-0 but it's been anything but dull.

The second half starts with more of the same as the teams go toe to toe, the underdogs matching the superstars stride for stride. Still neither side can break the deadlock and as the game moves towards the final phase United start to get the upper hand. Di Maria exits around the 70 minutes mark as his influence fades and he is followed by Juan Mata with what looks like a hamstring injury. However, as witnessed on many occasions last season, the Clarets maintain their excellent defensive shape and there is no way through for the Reds. We are under pressure but there are no real close shaves. The game ends goalless and after a magnificent battling team effort we have our first Premier league point on the board. Who needs Di Maria, we have D Marney! Let's hope this stirring display can kick start our season. The team leave the stadium to another ovation and we are all 'Proud to be Clarets'.

I make the even longer walk home, 2.59 miles in 47.31 minutes at an average moving speed of 3.27 mph, a very happy man. For the eagle eyed who spotted the difference in mileage to and from the ground, I took a different route back and it was mostly uphill!

Result – Burnley 0 – 0 Manchester United

Burnley Team

Heaton, Trippier, Duff, Shackell, Mee, Arfield, Marney, Jones, Taylor (Reid 88), Ings (Barnes 78), Jutkiewicz

Subs Not used – Gilks, Wallace, Long, Sordell, Ward

Manchester United Team

De Gea, Evans, Jones, Blackett, Valencia, Mata (Januzaj 87), Fletcher, Di Maria (Anderson 70), Young, Rooney, Van Persie (Welbeck 73)

Subs Not used – Amos, Keane, James, Hernandez

Attendance – 21,099

Season Record – Played 3, Won 0, Drawn 1, Lost 2, Goals For 1, Goals Against 4, Points 1

League Position after Game 3 – 20th

Results at the weekend don't go kindly for us, a home win for QPR, and a late equaliser for Crystal Palace at Newcastle (3-3) conspire to leave us bottom of the table. However after such a heartening performance we are not dismayed, the only way is up! I think after initially seeing the opening fixtures this is where most fans thought we may be. An international break coming up now followed by a round of so called 'easier' fixtures will hopefully see the position improving.

SEPTEMBER

The opening day of September marks the closing day of the transfer window. Strong rumours have circulated since Saturday that the Hull City midfielder/striker George Boyd, was a serious target. This is confirmed early on the morning of deadline day as Boyd signs a three year deal for a reported £3m. More persistent rumours surrounding Bolton midfielder Mark Davies, turn out to be unfounded as by mid afternoon Boyd's signing is followed by that of Chelsea's Nathaniel Chalobah. At 19 years of age Chalobah has already had previous spells on loan at Championship level, one notably for Watford where he scored a beauty against us at Turf Moor. The England Under 21 international moves on a four month loan to get some Premier league experience. Cheers Mr Mourinho! Despite continuing rumours late into the evening linking various centre backs, that appears to be the extent of our business. However, at the very last moment in comes Manchester United and England Under 21 centre back, Michael Keane. The United youngster also signs on a four month loan deal. Boyd with full caps for Scotland, and the two young English lads should hopefully add some extra quality and depth to the squad for the forthcoming battles.

Chalobah and Keane join Danny Ings on England Under 21 duty during the International break. That should give Danny the opportunity to bring them up to speed with all things Claret.

It's now Monday 8th September and as I settle down to watch Switzerland v England in the Euro 2016 qualifier it strikes me how little I have thought about football in the last week. What was once an all consuming passion has become almost nonexistent. I did at the weekend have a moment of temporary madness when I contemplated going to Accrington Stanley but fortunately it soon passed. With hindsight perhaps I should have gone as Stanley came from behind to win 3-2 with two late goals and record their first win of the season. Am I becoming disinterested? Surely not after such a magnificent season as 2013/14. The problem with the Premier league is that the fixtures are quite sparse. International breaks seem to come frequently in early season making for prolonged gaps in the action. We have consequently only played three league matches and are already approaching mid September. Leagues 1 and 2 have already rattled up six, along with early entries into the Capital One Cup and Johnstone's Paint Trophy. Can England restore my passion? I'm not holding my breath!

The early minutes are disrupted by a visit to my front door by Jehovah's Witnesses. After a brief but entertaining chat they depart, but by half time, with the score at 0-0, I am wishing that they had stayed. The England build up as been akin to watching paint dry, slow, laboured, sideways, backwards and totally predictable. Nothing at all like a Premier league game where both sides go for each other's throats for ninety minutes. This England side has decent individuals but no cohesion with square pegs fitting into round holes. The only genuine wide man, the diminutive Raheem Sterling is played through the middle, where he is consistently bullied by the Swiss defence. I fear a repetition in the second half, then would you believe it, on 57 minutes a goal on the break for Welbeck. Beautiful in its simplicity with the speed of the counter attack started by Rooney and carried on by Sterling, this time out on the flank, leaving Welbeck to finish with a close range effort. Crucially not a sideways or backwards pass in sight. Normal service quickly resumes and we are fortunate to stay ahead thanks to a great stop by former Claret's loanee Gary Cahill. Welbeck adds a second, once again on the break, in added stoppage time and Euro qualification is off to a good start.

I recently came across a poem by a little known American poet of the late 19th/early 20th century by the name of Walter D Wintle, which may or may not be an alias. The poem is an inspirational text on the power of self belief and positive thinking. I decided to use it at the customary pub debriefing session after a Burnley contingent Thursday walk. The piece is called 'Thinking', or sometimes 'The Man Who Thinks He Can' and goes as follows:

> If you think you are beaten, you are;
> If you think you dare not, you don't.
> If you'd like to win, but think you can't,
> It's almost a cinch you won't.
>
>
> If you think you'll lose, you're lost,
> For out in the world we find.
> Success begins with a fellows will;
> It's all in the state of mind.
>
> If you think you're outclassed you are;
> You've got to think high to rise.
> You've got to be sure of yourself
> Before you can ever win a prize.
>
> Life's battles don't always go
> To the stronger or faster man;

But soon or late the man who wins
Is the one who thinks he can.

Now isn't that a valuable lesson and a powerful tool, and whose philosophy does that perfectly fit? On delivering my rendition, in true Churchillian fashion, I was promptly harangued by some of my more knowledgeable walking buddies and accused of 'nicking' the poem from Sean Dyche's office. It transpired that in a recent interview with Sean in the Daily Telegraph or Times, the above poem or part of it was prominently on display. Sean and myself certainly know a motivational piece when we see one and I have urged my wife, daughter, and my colleagues to adopt this henceforth as their mantra.

GAME 4 – Crystal Palace v Burnley, Saturday 13th September, 15.00 hrs

Our second away fixture sees us visiting Selhurst Park in South London for a game that has been targeted as winnable by many supporters. The concensus of opinion is that to stay up we must aim to take points from teams likely to be in the relegation dogfight and that anything picked up against the top teams is a bonus. Despite Palace finishing comfortably above the drop zone last season they are once again perceived as potential strugglers. One point from their first 3 games and the same goal difference as ourselves suggest there is little between the teams.

This indeed turns out to be the case as the sides battle out an entertaining 0-0 draw, and a valuable away point for the Clarets that so nearly was three. We show one change from the United game with new signing George Boyd coming in on the wide left of midfield in place of Matty Taylor. The other new signings Chalobah and Keane don't even make the squad but travel with the team. The omission of these two is not really surprising as due to Under 21 commitments they only join up with the team on Thursday lunch. For Palace, James McArthur a target for the Clarets in the last transfer window, makes his debut.

Palace have the better of the early exchanges, a header against the bar, and a shot cleared off the line have us feeling a little uncomfortable. Danny Ings picks up an early booking for 'diving' when TV replays suggest a penalty to the Clarets was perhaps the correct decision. As the half progresses our confidence grows and we start to take the game to our hosts. Then disaster on 39 minutes as the luckless Ings pulls up with what appears to be a hamstring injury. It's the end of his day and he limps off to be replaced by Marvin Sordell. Half time arrives with the scores tied level.

As the second half progresses we continue to grow in stature and are enjoying the balance of possession. Then on 84 minutes the chance to seal all three points and only our second ever Premier league away victory. Palace skipper, the Australian Jedinak, momentarily forgets what game he is playing, and wrestles Lukas Jutkiewicz to the ground in the box. It would have been a great tackle had we been playing Aussie rules, but referee Mike Dean is unsympathetic to our Antipodean friend and instantly awards the spot kick. Now the dilemma, with regular takers Vokes and Ings both absent who will take it. Up steps 'Man of the Season' to date, Scott Arfield. A firmly struck penalty to the keeper's right sees Speroni in the Palace goal pull off an excellent one handed save. Bugger! No time to feel sorry for ourselves and we continue to press the home team for the remainder of the game but unfortunately with no joy.

A precious point but once again the feeling that it could have been more. Radio Lancashire commentators, including summariser and former Clarets keeper Marlon Beresford, are of the opinion that it is an impressive performance. Once again we have maintained excellent shape throughout the game. Defensively we are looking the business with only four goals against in four games, three of which came in the first game against a rampant Chelsea who currently lead the table with a 100% record. However the concern is now the lack of goals, only one in four games, and with Ings likely to be out for some weeks someone needs to step up to the plate. One bit of good news, with results going our way we climb the table to a giddy 18th and almost out of the drop zone!

Result – Crystal Palace 0 – 0 Burnley

Burnley Team

Heaton, Trippier, Duff, Shackell, Mee, Arfield, Marney, Jones, Boyd, Ings (Sordell 42), Jutkiewicz

<u>Subs Not used</u> – Gilks, Wallace, Long, Reid, Barnes, Ward

Crystal Palace Team

Speroni, Marriapa, Dann, Delaney, Ward, Puncheon, Jedinak, McArthur (Bolassie 69), Zaha, Campbell (Williams 75), Gayle (Doyle 61),

<u>Subs Not used</u> – Hennessy, Fryers, Ledley, Kelly

Attendance – 23,929

Season Record – Played 4, Won 0, Drawn 2, Lost 2, Goals For 1, Goals Against 4, Points 2

League Position after Game 4 – 18th

It's Saturday 20th September and a big day in the Haworth household. Firstly in the morning my daughter is bridesmaid at the wedding of her friend Kirsty whom she has known since primary school. My wife and I attend the ceremony at the local church, St James, Briercliffe, and then for me it's a quick lunch and an afternoon at the Turf.

A big day for me also as I have foolishly volunteered to be Guest Reporter for the Claretsmad website at the Sunderland clash. Below find the uncut version of my report for that game.

GAME 5 – Burnley v Sunderland, Saturday 20th September, 15.00 hrs

Clarets can't Mackem have it!

Report of match Burnley v Sunderland from 20th September 2014

Reporter Peter Haworth

Why did I volunteer for this? My one and only previous experience of guest reporting was a horrific home game against Brighton in the Championship on 1st September 2012, resulting in a 1-3 reverse. Let's have none of that today I thought as I made my way to the game for a rare Saturday 3.00 kick off.

Our visitors, the 'Mackems' are apparently so called as a reference to the history of ship building on the River Wear, where the local inhabitants used to *make'em*. They are also known as the 'Black Cats', animals which are traditionally regarded as lucky! I can't say I've ever been convinced that anything about being a Sunderland fan could be considered lucky!

Arriving at the ground just in time for the teams coming out a quick look confirmed that the Clarets would make the one forced change, Sordell for Ings up front. That meant a home debut for George Boyd, a lookalike Chris Eagles with attitude!

A fairly lively opening saw us in the ascendancy with a few half chances but nothing to get over excited about. As the half progressed it developed into a fairly even contest with little goalmouth action. Sunderland probably having the bulk of possession but much of it consisting of a negative triangular passing movement between the Keeper and their centre backs. Jutkiewicz continued in his impressive early season form winning his fair share of aerial tussles, and his ability to turn a man causing problems. Boyd and Arfield were working hard on the flanks but Scotty was missing the magic touch of recent weeks. A half of few chances, and mostly long range shots ended goalless.

The second half started in similar vein and it had the feel that both sides were treating it like a game of cat and mouse. The teams were pawing at each other but not really going for the jugular. Around the hour mark Dyche replaced the largely ineffective Sordell with Ashley Barnes. Shortly after the visitors abandoned any suggestion of creative subtlety replacing wingers Johnson and Larsson, with the muscular Altidore who joined the equally beefy Wickham up front. This probably did us a favour as their play became more and more predictable. With the Clarets building momentum, the removal of Johnson allowing Trippier to get further forward, we started to get on top. On 68 minutes a strong penalty shout as the 'Juke' went down after breaking clear in the box, but nothing given. With the game rumbling to a conclusion a looping shot from Barnes rebounded off the Sunderland crossbar. At the other end we were mightily relieved to see a thundering long range shot hit the post rebounding onto Keeper Heaton's back and out. Could have gone anywhere that one. Wallace replaced the tiring Boyd, and Reid came on for the injured Dave Jones, but despite five minutes added time we couldn't conjure a winner.

Another good performance but with only the one point to show for it. Defensively this is as solid a unit as we have managed to turn out for many years. The worrying statistic is the goals for column where we are now by my calculations 436 minutes without scoring. It's clear that chances in the Premier league come at a premium, but we have to find a striking combination that will break the goalless streak, and quickly. Once again a great atmosphere in the ground created by two vocal and enthusiastic sets of fans. On a personal note, a big thank you to Tom Heaton and Kieran Trippier for the clean sheet and valuable Fantasy Football league points to my tally. Onwards and upwards!

Result – Burnley 0 – 0 Sunderland

Burnley Team

Heaton, Trippier, Duff, Shackell, Mee, Arfield, Marney, Jones (Reid 90+2) , Boyd (Wallace 86), Sordell (Barnes 63), Jutkiewicz

Subs Not used – Gilks, Keane, Ward, Kightly

Sunderland Team

Mannone, Vergini, O'Shea, Brown, van Aanholt, Cattermole, Johnson (Altidore 67), Larsson (Gomez 67), Rodwell, Giaccherini (Buckley 73), Wickham

<u>Subs Not used</u> – Pantilimon, Jones, Bridcutt, Graham

Attendance – 20,026

Season Record – Played 5, Won 0, Drawn 3, Lost 2, Goals For 1, Goals Against 4, Points 3

League Position after Game 5 – 19th

Just a word about the 'lucky wristbands' here. On Saturday, as a result of the dashing around caused by inconsiderate over running of the wedding in the morning, I completely forgot to wear them. Result? Exactly the same as the last two games. I am beginning to think this might be a load of superstitious nonsense. But dare I give them a miss next time?

On the Monday morning following the Sunderland game I am astonished to read that the London Metro has been running with a statement that *"Sean Dyche could be long gone by Christmas as Burnley appear well below the required top flight standard. The Clarets boss looks a spot of value to be next to go at 20/1"*.

What a bizarre statement and a prime example of how the remote southern press are out of touch with what is happening in 'little old Burnley'. I would imagine that Sean Dyche sits in one of the safest managerial seats in the Premier league. The achievement of last season in winning automatic promotion has given Sean untouchable status for the foreseeable future. Do they not realise that the vast bulk of the support for this club are aware of the massive imbalance in financial clout between the rest of the league and ourselves. Do they really think we expected to take this season by storm? If relegation it is to be then so be it, but I doubt we will see the ritual blood lust for the manager's head that is usually associated with that fate at Burnley.

Coming back to my Fantasy Football league adventure which had previously been going quite disastrously, it was not only Tom Heaton and Tripps making significant contributions in Game week five. It turned out to be a good week all round with a valuable contribution from my latest signing Ulloa of Leicester, who chipped in with two goals. A points haul of 71 for the week sees me climb to the dizzy heights of 14th (of 20) in the 'Luis Suarez all you can eat invitational league'. However injuries continue to plague my selections and I continuously have to plug gaps on a weekly basis with my single transfer allowance. It's not so easy this management game even with a transfer kitty of £100m to spend. Sean has my sympathy.

Tuesday was a walking day with the Lancashire Dotcom Walkers as we headed for Clougha Pike from Quernmore. It had been pretty quiet on the texts front from the Preston mob, I suspect as they were having a bit of a mixed start to the season. Paul, our sole United fan, is absent injured, conveniently so, otherwise he would have come under attack from all sides. That left Scouse Brian and his Liverpool team, who coincidentally at this stage of the season have lost more games than Burnley (three to two) as a prime target. Unfortunately as Brian is giving me invaluable advice on how to publish this tome, and whom I have appointed unpaid mentor, it seems a little churlish to upset him. There were the inevitable one or two wisecracks about our lack of goals along the lines of, *"Are they going to start training with goal posts soon"?* But of course these were treated with the contempt they deserved by the Burnley contingent.

No Saturday game for us on the last weekend in September, instead we are the only Sunday game as Sky TV select our trip to West Bromwich for live coverage at 16.00 hours. Unusually for the Clarets rumours of injured players start doing the rounds on Friday. Doubts are expressed about the fitness of Trippier, and the central midfield pairing of Jones and Marney. With Ings still out, and Vokes a long term absentee, the depth of the squad is about to be tested.

GAME 6 – West Bromwich Albion v Burnley, Sunday 28th September, 16.00 hrs

We knew there would be days especially away from home when we would get a bit of a mauling. WBA away was not meant to be one of these. Going into the game they sat two places and two points above us. This should have been another potentially 'winnable' fixture if we are to start climbing up the table.

Injury news turns out not to be good with only Trippier of the three doubts making the team. The loss of Marney and Jones leaves a gaping hole in the centre of midfield to fill and the job goes to Steven Reid returning to his previous club, and Scott Arfield. Marvin Sordell is also left out of the starting eleven from last week and that means a chance for Michael Kightly and Ross Wallace. This line up prompts a change in formation with Reid operating as a sitting midfielder behind Kightly, Arfield, Boyd, and Wallace, with Jutkiewicz as lone striker. I can't help feeling that this midfield looks a little lightweight and lacks bite. This turns out to be the case and after a slow start pressure starts to build on the Clarets as WBA start to find their feet.

How ironic that we go behind to a goal headed in from a corner around the half hour mark from long term summer target Craig Dawson. Even worse is to follow on the stroke of half time as we concede a second from another corner. A poor first half with no attacking threat and an isolated striker in Jutkiewicz means changes are inevitable for the second.

On for the second half come loanee Nathaniel Chalobah replacing Reid, and Ashley Barnes for Wallace. Chalobah's first action in Premier league football earns him a booking within two minutes of his appearance. Well at least a bit more bite there. Before we get chance to settle the new formation we fall further behind, and at 3-0 for a team that hasn't scored in over 490 minutes of league football, its game over. At least now in our more familiar formation of 4-4-2 we start to play some football and make some half chances. Sordell replaces the injured 'Juke' and begins to provide some forward threat with Barnes. Chalobah grows steadily in influence in the midfield and after his early booking can feel pleased with his Premier debut. On 90 minutes we concede the fourth and a bad day at the office is complete.

What can we conclude from this drubbing? Did Sean get the formation and tactics wrong initially? Should we have started with the inexperienced Chalobah rather than the veteran Reid? What will happen against the more powerful teams in the league?

A rather worrying defeat that sees us sink to the bottom of the table on goal difference and points dropped to potential relegation battlers. We have a clear week now before the next fixture away at Leicester, let's hope for better news on the injury front.

Result – WBA 4 (Dawson 30, Berahino 45+1, 56, Dorrans 90) – 0 Burnley

Burnley Team

Heaton, Trippier, Duff, Shackell, Mee, Arfield, Reid (Barnes 45), Wallace (Chalobah 45), Boyd, Kightly, Jutkiewicz (Sordell 68)

Subs Not used – Gilks, Keane, Ward, Long

West Bromwich Albion Team

Foster, Lescott, Dawson, Pocognoli (Gamboa 83), Wisdom, Dorrans, Morrison, Sessegnon (Samaras 74), Gardner (Yacob 87), Brunt, Berahino

Subs Not used – Myhill, Mulumbu, McAuley, Blanco

Attendance – 24,286

Season Record – Played 6, Won 0, Drawn 3, Lost 3, Goals For 1, Goals Against 8, Points 3

League Position after Game 6 – 20th

Well we were well and truly boing boinged by the Baggies and who could have seen that coming after three clean sheets. Obviously the disruption to the team through the loss of Ings, and now the engine room of Jones and Marney has been a major factor. Marney may have many detractors among the posters on Clarets forums but the energy he brings to the side should never be underestimated. The tactical change in formation never looked like working and showed that without doubt 4-4-2 works for us.

The important thing now is how we react to this mauling. Will it sap confidence or will we come out fighting?

From our experience of Mr Dyche I think that it is more likely to be the latter. The after match mood on the Claretsmad forum is one of as usual total over reaction. A heavy defeat always brings out the negativity and in some cases to absurd extremes. I hope the players have more sense than to read it or they might start to believe that after six matches we are already relegated. Pick yourselves up lads and go again!

Disaster on the Fantasy Football front, my boys had achieved a paltry total from Saturday's games and I was looking for Heaton and Tripps to come up trumps. Four goals conceded meant a return of zero points for both players and a pathetic 21 points for the week. That figure dropped me to 15th position out of 20, and with Stoke v Newcastle still to come on the Monday night I could plummet even further.

I suppose really the total disaster that was Sunday at the Hawthorns was all my fault. Adopting a cavalier approach to the wearing of the 'lucky wristbands' following my recent doubts over their efficacy, I decided to dispense with them altogether for this game. How foolish, I have incurred the wrath of the Gods. They have brought a plague of goals to rain down on us. Guess what, I think I will reinstate them for next week.

As expected Sean Dyche's post match comments were not too downbeat, although he was disappointed that for once we were not competitive which has become the hallmark of his teams. *"It's not a good afternoon that's for sure. We never got out of the blocks at all today, which is my main disappointment."* With regards to the missing players he felt, *"We have a squad, we've built a squad because we needed it and now you can see why. We want those players to come in and effect the game but that didn't quite work today. I thought Nathaniel was a positive because he wanted the ball and tried to play. We changed the shape, and obviously because of the changes because we've got injuries to Matt Taylor, Dave Jones, and Dean Marney. Of course they're three main midfielders for us but the performance level, the energy level, and the feel of the group wasn't quite there today and we need to learn from it. We've only had that once at Swansea when we looked unsure and today we looked super unsure of ourselves and we didn't deliver, it's as simple as that."*

Dotcom Walkers I guess are like any other group of people when it comes down to the understanding of modern technology. There are those who know what they are talking about, there are those who think they know what they are talking about, and there are those who haven't a clue what anybody is talking about! Without being unkind I would guess that Scouse Brian falls into the middle category. However he had not previously given any indication of being an avid fan of mobile telecommunication equipment. It was surprising therefore during an exchange of inter group hostilities to receive an email proclaiming **'sent from my iphone.'** Wow! Brian has decided not only to embrace the technology but has gone in at the top end.

Needless to say that resulted in a fair amount of ribbing when he showed up for the next walk, not only from the Burnley Contingent, but also from his allies, the Preston mob. Particularly unforgiving was PNE Chris, rapidly assuming the role of chief stirrer previously occupied by PNE Ed in 'A Season In The Sun'. Brian defended himself manfully but then generated further mirth by admitting that he had begun receiving odd messages through his device from beautiful Russian Ladies, who were very anxious to make his acquaintance! Chris pointed out to him that this would be as a result of him visiting dodgy websites. How surprising then that shortly afterwards I started receiving emails from PNE

Chris with the signature **'sent from my iphone'.** Now I know that Chris has recently had considerable success in renegotiating certain financial contracts, and can only assume that he has decided to invest his good fortune in researching the Internet dating scene in Moscow. He failed to show up with it on the next walk, claiming he didn't have a case. For his defence I presume he meant!

So September ends with the Clarets finishing it as they started it, bottom of the table. The month has proved to be winless and goalless for us albeit there have been only three fixtures. Two reasonable performances against Crystal Palace and Sunderland, and then a shocker at WBA. We enter October once again on our travels and if survival is to be achieved the wins and goals need to start coming now.

OCTOBER

The national press have obviously caught on to my concerns about our lack of goals, and as it's a quiet day for news they dispatch Daily Mail journalist Chris Wheeler to Burnley to get to the bottom of it. Under a banner headline 'FIRING BLANKS' he produces a list of chilling statistics about our lack of success in front of goal. I'm not going to repeat them here as I am sure anyone who is reading this is probably as well aware of our failings as I am. In his interview with Sean, the boss makes it clear that the loss of Vokes and Ings was bound to hurt but that provides the challenge for others to step up. Asked how he kept the players spirits up when the ball just won't go in, he responded.

"You look to reinforce their belief systems.' They're only human. Not everyone is super confident and some players sit on that knife edge."

"We reinforce the positive side of the game and the simplicity of it. Of course you hope for a goal because sometimes it alters mindsets and re-ignites confidence in people. You're waiting for the individuals to catch fire within that system and score. There are goals in people, it's just delivering it. I believe in the players we have at the club, otherwise I wouldn't have them here."

"We haven't gone obsessively into attacking but we've obviously tried to tweak things. We have to turn the screw and make sure those chances become goals. Can we make different types of chances than your stereotypical ones like a cross and a header? What kind of crosses, what kind of finishes, what kind of movement in the box?"

"We're getting into the right area but the hardest thing for coaches and managers to provide is that final touch into the net."

With those positive sentiments ringing in the player's ears, Leicester City just better watch out!

GAME 7 – Leicester City v Burnley, Saturday 4th October, 15.00 hrs

This game brings us face to face with our nemesis, namely David Nugent. How many times has this guy scored against us? And doesn't he just love it! To be fair he did also chip in with a few for us during our last foray in the Premier league whilst on loan from Portsmouth. Is today the day we break the Nugent Hoodoo as well as the goal drought?

Well there's some good news and there's some bad news. In a break with tradition we'll have the good news first, Nugent doesn't make the starting XI and has to settle for a seat on the bench. The bad news, neither Ings, Jones, nor Marney make it again, so it's an unusual looking midfield for the Clarets. Coming in for a Premier league debut for Burnley is Stephen Ward and he makes up a four with, Arfield, Boyd, and Kightly. Returning to our favoured 4-4-2 formation sees a start for Ashley Barnes up front alongside Jutkiewicz. Wallace drops to the bench and Reid disappears from the squad altogether following the defeat at WBA. Also missing is last week's second half debutant Chalobah who sustained an unusual but nasty windpipe injury in a midweek Premier Under 21 Cup tie.

Going into the game it appears that everybody in the national press has written off our chances and we may as well have stopped at home, we will see! After a bright opening few minutes where we are clearly demonstrating more attacking intent than in last week's disaster, Ward finds his way into the refs notebook on 7 minutes. We continue in a positive vein for the first quarter of the game but referee Phil Dowd is giving us nothing. Typically Barnes is pushed over on the edge of the Leicester box but Dowd gives a free kick to the Foxes as he falls onto the ball and handles. From the free kick play goes down the other end and we are behind as a cross from Mahrez is met with an excellent finish from Schlupp. I can't help getting that sinking feeling, here we go again.

However, would you bloody believe it on 39 minutes we are level, yes a GOAL for the Clarets after by my reckoning 565 minutes without one. It's a goal of classic simplicity as Arfield finds Jutkiewicz at the back post, his downward header back across goal is scrambled in by the sprawling Kightly. What was so difficult about that, why had it took so long in the making? The goal drought is ended!

The euphoria lasts for all of 60 seconds as Leicester regain the lead with a little good fortune. A cross from the left flicks off the retreating Jason Shackell straight onto the head of the incoming Mahrez who makes no mistake. How cruel was that? Half time arrives with no further action and we are again facing an uphill battle.

The Clarets continue to take the game to the hosts, and then just after the hour the arrival of the swaggering assassin, Nugent. The ineffective George Boyd makes way for Sordell as the Clarets continue to have plenty of possession but no real chances. The 2000+ Clarets fans are giving the team tremendous backing and can sense there is something to be had from this game. On 79 minutes it's Wallace on for Kightly to try and conjure up something different. Another bad blow on 86 minutes as Trippier sustains what looks like a possibly serious ankle injury and the game is stopped for six minutes whilst he is stretchered off. Tripps is replaced by another debutant, the on loan Michael Keane.

As the game runs into the sixth of seven minutes added time Arfield is brought down clumsily just outside the Leicester box. It's the perfect position for a left footed dead ball expert. Cometh the hour, cometh the man! Ross Wallace, slated for his performance last week at WBA and subbed at half time, turns instantly from villain to superhero. A classic free kick, up and over the defensive wall and arcing away from the keeper's clawing hand, nestles in the net. Now that's what you call an impact sub! Cue delirium among the travelling fans who had willed the team on so magnificently.

What a great effort following last week's tame surrender. News of our demise is a little premature, we are not dead yet!

Result – Leicester City 2 (Schlupp 33, Mahrez 40) – 2 Burnley (Kightly 39, Wallace 90)

Burnley Team

Heaton, Trippier (Keane 86), Duff, Shackell, Mee, Arfield, Kightly (Wallace 79), Ward, Boyd (Sordell 67), Barnes, Jutkiewicz

Subs Not used – Gilks, Hewitt, Lafferty, Long

Leicester City Team

Schmeichel, de Laet, Morgan, Moore, Konchesky, Mahrez, Drinkwater, Hammond (James 78), Schlupp (Knockaert 72), Ulloa (Nugent 63), Vardy

Subs Not used – Hamer, Wasilewski, King, Wood

Attendance – 31,448

Season Record – Played 7, Won 0, Drawn 4, Lost 3, Goals For 3, Goals Against 10, Points 4

League Position after Game 7 – 19th

Leicester manager Nigel Pearson was very ungracious towards the Clarets on local radio after the game. I guess they caught him at a bad time when he must have thought all the points were in the bag. Dyche understandably was over the moon and very appreciative of the superb Clarets crowd backing.

Unfortunately once again I feel I could have been the cause of another disaster. Initially after absentmindedly forgetting to don the 'lucky 'wristbands, I rectified the situation at half time and saved the day. God knows what would have happened if I had worn them all the game.

Queens Park Rangers 2-0 defeat at West Ham on Sunday 5th October saw us leapfrog above them on goal difference as we once again start to climb the table.

Tuesday 7th October sees the Dotcom Walkers heading for the far flung edge of the county at Silverdale, which I am informed is an AONB (Area of Outstanding Natural Beauty). The previous week's walk was from Padiham which some would claim is an AOLT (Area of Outstanding Local Thicknecks). Now this is not meant as a sleight on the local inhabitants but rather to the historical preponderance of people with thick necks in the area. This was caused by the high incidence of 'Goitres' in the Padiham area, which is a swelling of the thyroid gland causing a lump to develop in the front of the neck. This was as a result of a lack of Iodine in the local water supply before the days of 'iodised' table salt.

Needless to say the fact that the locals were known as Thicknecks produced much mirth among the 'flatlanders' from Preston and South Ribble.

During the course of a very pleasant stroll along the River Calder on a lovely sunny autumnal day, a challenge was thrown down by the aforementioned Preston mob. Retired policeman Jim Skipper (Skipper of the Yard) invited John W of the Burnley contingent to bet him £5 that Burnley and Preston would not be in the same league next season. Jim obviously buoyed by PNE's early season success, and obviously forgetting their characteristic trait of failing at the final hurdle, clearly expected a PNE promotion and a Clarets relegation. John W, well noted as a man not to take kindly to parting with money, declined the invitation, claiming 'he was not a betting man'. Unfortunately I could not allow the now baying Preston horde to get away with that and so have now heaped further pressure on the Clarets by taking on the bet. Still I can't see PNE going up anyway. Well maybe not....

Whilst walking next the sea at Silverdale I found myself in deep conversation with a number of the Preston mafia. We were discussing the merits of our magnificent comeback at Leicester. I meant to point out to them that as three of the next four games were at home, we would probably be pushing for a Champions league spot after that. Unfortunately it came out as pushing for a Championship spot after that, aargh! Cue great fun from the tormentors. Me and my big mouth, I am going to have be more careful whilst the Prestonians have their tails up, which hopefully won't be for long.

It's now Wednesday 15th October and it seems an eternity since the last game at Turf Moor. In fact there hasn't been a home game since September 20th, a break of four weeks, before Saturdays encounter with West Ham United. Unfortunately for me it will be a gap of five weeks before the next home game as this coming Friday we leave for a weeks holiday in Tenerife. Seven Premier League games played in two months since the start of the season, and of those only three at Turf Moor, mean many fans are suffering from soccer starvation.

Of course the dearth of games was once again due to the International break for Euro 2016 qualifying matches. England have been successful in the two game programme overcoming the hopelessly inept San Marino at Wembley, 5-0, and Estonia away by 1-0. This confirms their position at the head of the qualifying table. In such a weak group there should be no problem in making the final stages. However the victories whilst relatively easy were by no means convincing and a major improvement is still required to match the major forces in European football.

One plus point arising from the break is that it will have provided vital time for the recovery of our injured players. Hopefully Saturday will see the return of one or all of Ings, Marney, Jones, Chalobah, and Taylor. Vokes, still recovering from a cruciate ligament injury is still some way off.

More interesting statistics coming out of a survey into the cost of following a Premier League team, show that Burnley are joint top (or bottom if you prefer) of the league in relation to the price of tea, and pies. The most expensive cup of tea to be had is at Manchester United, Southampton, and Liverpool. They weigh in with a whopping £2.50 for a tea bag in a paper cup, whilst at Manchester City and Burnley the price is a miserly £1.80. City undo their good work in the pie chart by charging, along with Crystal Palace, and Southampton a staggering £4 for a 'growler'. At the Turf, and somewhat surprisingly at Chelsea, one can enjoy the crusted delicacy for a mere £2.50. We are certainly Champions League material when it comes to the cost of living essentials.

Also revealed in the same survey are the top prices for season tickets, and top match day tickets. Arsenal are champions with a season ticket price of £2013, and match day ticket at £97. Bottom of the league are West Brom at £449 and £39 respectively, whilst the Clarets are in a respectable 14th position with £685 and £42.

Friday 17th October sees me board the 'Flight to Hell' as I travel from Manchester to Tenerife on the 9.15, Jet 2, Boeing 757. Boarding in good time I am looking forward to a prompt departure. Unfortunately my hopes are dashed by, wait for it, birds on the runway! These feathery little blighters have successfully managed to cause a backlog of ten departures of which the pilot informs us we are last in line. Thirty minutes later we are airborne and it pretty soon becomes apparent that we are in for a rough ride. Dotted around the rear cabin of the plane are about eight sun lamp tanned, heavily muscled 'Boneheads', presumably on a weekend jaunt from their local gym to take in the cultural delights of Playa de Las Americas. Already pretty loud, these 'lads' quickly take the opportunity to top up their alcohol levels by pouring vodka from their duty free purchases into empty water bottles and quaffing merrily. Come the cabin attendant's drinks trolley and its more booze all round. Not an hour gone into a four and a half hour flight and some of these jokers are already 'ratarsed'. Suffice it to say for the rest of the flight we, and the cabin crew, are subjected to the clowns posturing and bellowing until gratefully the plane touches down in Tenerife. Now I remember why I hate flying!

Anyway enough of that and back to the main story that is:

GAME 8 – Burnley v West Ham United, Saturday 18th October, 15.00 hrs.

I am sat at a restaurant bar in Las Americas in stifling heat with my pint of Dorada and Tuna baguette, like the true Burnley fan I am, but my mind is many miles away across the sea at my beloved Turf Moor. Unable to attend this game I have instructed my old pal John W to text me goal updates, but only from the team in claret and blue. I am met with a deadly silence.

By half time I can stand no more and text him *"Where are the goals?"* The response goes as follows.

John W – Good ½ couple chances Juke slow to get on 1. Hammers noble & no 30 playing well (sic)

My daughter Stephanie then texts me from the Lake District informing me we are losing 1-0! Incredulous I am back to John W.

Me – Are we behind?

John W - George makes 1-2

John W – Danny misses a header

Me – What the Hell is going on? How did they get 2

John W – Bloody 3 now header corners (sic)

John W – Cole

Me – Did it finish 1-3? We are doomed

John W – 0-0 h/t we were best. 20 mins start scnd ½ they scored 2 looked great. Got 1 back briefly flattered. Set piece cole header 3-1. Fluttered a bit not really gonna get it back. Overall hit bar 2wice scored scrambly mess. Juke never gonna score works incessantly to no reward. Ings a bit meh! Scotty not centre mid missed marney big style. Chalobah prospect needs old hands to guide him. Heaton lost in box needs more commanding approach.(sic)

So that was one long standing fans concise report of the proceedings and very grateful I was to receive it, though not the result. I sank another pint of Dorada to compose myself. He later followed up with, *"Overall Dyche out bring on Pulis lump it long buy couple thugs in midfield – eg Nolan! Only kidding! Sean to stay Mckay out Haworth in! Its your fault man – who takes a holiday in the middle of the season?"(sic)* Who indeed?

Purchasing an extremely expensive copy of the Sunday Mirror (€2.20) allows me to put a bit more meat on the bones of John W's report. I note that the injury situation was much improved with Ings and Jones both returning, but still no Marney. As John had said we had the better of the first half, but the Mirror reported that the shift of the balance of the game was confirmed early in the second half. Mirror reporter Derick Allsop's verdict was, *"For all Burnley's composed football, they were ultimately out-paced and out-muscled by a West Ham team that looks capable of unsettling anyone."*

I think that Derick has hit the nail firmly on the head there, we are consistently being out-paced and out-muscled. These are the two stand out requirements in this league and unfortunately at the moment we are sadly lacking both.

Result – Burnley 1 (Boyd 60) – 3 West Ham United (Sakho 49, Valencia 54, Cole 70)

Burnley Team

Heaton, Trippier, Duff, Shackell, Mee, Arfield, Kightly (Sordell 83), Jones, Boyd, Ings (Chalobah 83), Jutkiewicz (Barnes 65)

<u>Subs Not used</u> – Gilks, Wallace, Ward, Long

West Ham United Team

Adrian, Jenkinson, Collins, Reid, Cresswell, Amaltifano, Song (Nolan 83), Noble, Downing, Sakho, Valencia (Cole 59)

<u>Subs Not used</u> – Jaaskelainen, Burke, Jarvis, Vaz Te, O'Brien

Attendance – 18,936

Season Record – Played 8, Won 0, Drawn 4, Lost 4, Goals For 4, Goals Against 13, Points 4

League Position after Game 8 – 19th

Of course another possible explanation for the poor result could be once again down to the absence of the, lucky wristbands'. I forgot them! To cap off the weekend on Sunday it decided to rain in monsoon proportions in Tenerife, just like home but with warm rain. A great day for the local shopkeepers who made a killing selling nylon ponchos for €4!

Feeling a bit down about the defeat but determined not to let it spoil my holiday I chanced across the perfect antidote. Near the Vulcano hotel in Las Americas is a 'strip' of bars which I am sure many readers will have visited. These include, The Corner Bar, Brahms & Liszt, Highland Paddy, Soul Train, The Highlander, The Bulls Head (with an excellent live band, The Vagabonds), and apologies to one or two more whose names I can't recall. Sandwiched in between this lot are also two Chinese restaurants.

If you ever want to experience a trip to Bedlam make a visit to this strip and take a seat outside one of the bars at anytime from 10.00pm. All these bars are involved in a fierce fight for custom, and all feature some sort of live music or karaoke. Beer prices are accordingly competitive and so is the volume of noise as each bar attempts to drown out its neighbour. Add into this mix the local street vendors consisting of two main varieties, Africans either dressed in traditional costume or designer sportswear, and rather dowdier Chinese, for some reason usually wearing illuminated umbrella hats on their heads. The Africans usually have a smooth line of patter for anybody that shows an interest in their varied assortment of 'designer goods'. This usually involves standard phrases such as, Asda Price, Buy one get one free, whist the Chinese tend to focus on illuminated novelties and are not such confident sellers. There is a constant stream of these guys and gals (in the case of the Chinese) so the customers senses are constantly assaulted by the volume of noise and the need to politely dismiss the would be purveyors. It's total madness! Like Las Vegas, it should be experienced once in life but once only. And for God's sake don't buy anything!

It was in The Highland Paddy that I heard the worst ever Karaoke rendition of the classic 'Any Dream Will Do' from Joseph's Amazing Technicolour Dreamcoat. The songstress, and I use that word in its loosest possible term, absolutely murdered the song in front of a packed bar. To be fair most of the customers did try not to laugh. Unfortunately they could resist no longer as at the end of the recital she decided to dedicate the song. In all seriousness she said, *"I have sung that song for my Dad"* (nice thought). *"He is not here"* (had he died?). *"He is in Scotland"* (wise man). *"He always said I sang it badly!"* Cue hysterical laughter and a good hand.

A last thing that struck me about these bars were some interesting notices. Firstly I came across 'No buggies in the bar after 9.00pm' and my favourite 'Tops must be worn in the bar at all times'. I will say no more.

All in all a great week in Tenerife, departing in temperatures of 35 degrees on Friday 24th October to enjoy a quieter return flight to a much cooler Manchester. Back in time for our next Premier League challenge at home to Everton.

GAME 9 – Burnley v Everton, Sunday 26th October, 13.30 hrs.

Another game switched to an early kick off for Sky TV and despite trying to remain positive I can't help an overwhelming feeling of foreboding. This is not helped by comments in the media by people such as Paul Merson (ex Arsenal) that he feels we are 'out of our depth in the Premier League'. The Mail on Sunday follows up with a header for the upcoming game. *"Everton's Ross Barkley suffered a head wound against Lille on Thursday and will be stitched up to face Burnley, whose season is falling apart at the seams."* Are we out of our depth? Is it falling apart at the seams? I don't know the answer but the longer we go without a victory the greater the loss of confidence and belief for both team and fans.

I decide on a walk to the ground in typical Burnley weather conditions, cloudy/blustery/sunny, and arrive in good time, for those who like statistics, covering a distance of

2.36 miles, in 38.49 minutes at an average moving speed of 3.65 mph, mainly downhill and flat. I notice as I am walking that I am wearing odd gloves, one grey and one black, is this a sign of oncoming dementia or an omen? This game I am taking no chances and am fully kitted out with both 'lucky wristbands'.

The team shows one change from last week with Stephen Ward replacing Ben Mee at left back. My pre match fears are quickly proved to be well founded as we go behind in four minutes. An impressive passing movement ends with Leighton Baines making for the line down the left flank and his superb cross is met with a powerful header by Samuel Eto'o who nets from close range. I am already fearing the worst as the Toffees look like they are going to take us apart with crisp passing and good movement, orchestrated by Gareth Barry.

We are battling gamely to stay in the contest and then on 20 minutes a lifeline. Everton striker Lukaku is guilty of a sloppy pass back to his defence, this is intercepted by 'The Juke' who feeds Danny Ings. Danny makes no mistake latching on to the through ball, rounding the keeper, and firing home. Tails up now and for a few minutes we are in the ascendancy. We are now looking a bit more like it and make one or two half chances.

Unfortunately it doesn't last and on 29 minutes we trail again as Lukaku finishes sloppily after enjoying a lucky break of the ball. It seems to be a feature of our games that the ball always runs kinder for the opposition than for us, or am I getting paranoid? That's it for the first half and the creeping doubts about our chances are intensifying.

The second half initially sees us with plenty of forward momentum but no cutting edge. There are a succession of balls into the box all of which are comfortably dealt with by the Everton defence. As the game enters the final phase the substitutions start. On for Everton comes Barkley for Lukaku, what a luxury to have a player such as him on the bench! Lukas Jutkiewicz is replaced by Ashley Barnes in a like-for-like switch. As we start to visibly tire Everton again take the upper hand. With 15 minutes to go Nathaniel Chalobah is warmed up and ready to come on but for some reason he doesn't get on till five minutes before the end of normal time.

By this time the game is up as Eto'o puts the game out of reach with a superb curling strike from outside the box. I can't help feel that our subs came much too late to have any impact on the game, and the third goal coming as we ran out of steam was the real killer. Everton are now coasting and Trippier's woeful backpass lets in Eto'o who just misses his hat trick as his shot across goal hits the far post and rolls back across the line into the hands of Heaton. The referee promptly signals the end and we are left to rue another defeat. We are the only team in the four divisions without a win, and have already lost as many league games as we did in the whole of our promotion season.

Result – Burnley 1 (Ings 20) – 3 Everton (Eto'o 4,85, Lukaku 29)

Burnley Team

Heaton, Trippier, Duff, Shackell, Ward, Arfield, Kightly (Sordell 84), Jones, Boyd (Chalobah 86), Ings, Jutkiewicz (Barnes 65)

Subs Not used – Gilks, Wallace, Keane, Mee

Everton Team

Howerd, Coleman, Alcaraz, Jagielka, Baines, McCarthy, Barry, Naismith, Eto'o, Lukaku (Barkley 65), Osman (Pienaar 82)

<u>Subs Not used</u> – Robles, Hibbert, Gibson, McGeady, Besic

Attendance – 19,927

Season Record – Played 9, Won 0, Drawn 4, Lost 5, Goals For 5, Goals Against 16, Points 4

League Position after Game 9 – 20th

I couldn't help but notice a lot of fans leaving in disappointment after the third Everton goal went in, and there seems to be a growing air of despondency. To a point this is understandable but we need to remain positive or we are sunk already. In his after match TV interview Sean Dyche seems still to be so whilst aware of the mountain we have to climb.

Personally I have no qualms about the result, we were beaten by a better team boasting a number of big name, top quality players. However, this is a scenario we are facing on a weekly basis. Are we as Merson suggests out of our depth? I fear the answer may well be yes.

The next game couldn't be any tougher, Arsenal away, and many fans fear the worst. We must get some confidence back into the team. Perhaps playing away to a major club will allow us to keep a better defensive shape as the onus will be off us to attack. We need to sort the centre midfield which is sorely missing Dean Marney. Maybe if Dean is still absent this is the time to try Chalobah, allowing Arfield to return to a wider position. Up front Jutkiewicz is a willing worker but is beginning to look like he will never score. Just a thought but with Mertesacker not the quickest central defender should we not go for pace in attack at Arsenal. Ings and Sordell should have plenty of that, but will they be able to make the ball stick when played up?

Incidentally for those of you who enjoyed the statistics, I made the return journey home in a walking distance of 1.29 miles, in 20.54 minutes, at an average walking speed of 3.69 mph. The return route was shorter not because I was walking on air, but because my wife came and picked me up anticipating my disappointment. As for the 'lucky wristbands' and the 'odd gloves', all I can say is anybody that believes in that codswallop needs certifying. That bloody Gnome is going out in the garden for the next game!

Interestingly at half time in the Everton game I heard a peculiar rumour that Dyche's position was in jeopardy if we failed to pick up points in the West Ham and Everton games. The story went that he would be replaced by David Moyes who was looking for a club near his home in the Clitheroe area. Moyes was spotted with Alistair Campbell at Turf Moor for the West Ham game. I can only assume that this is a classic case of putting two and two together! Surely we would not dump a manager who had just masterminded one of the greatest seasons in our history after nine games!

One topic of conversation during the half time break in the last game was the feeling of disappointment by many fans in regard to the summer transfer dealings. It seems generally that the fans felt more money could, and should, have been available to the manager for better quality deals. However without knowing the fees involved, and the wages required by players, the fans are unable to get a feel for the whole picture. Certainly many supporters are expecting some major transfer activity in the January window. We shall see.

As I anticipated Monday 27th October's televised evening game, QPR at home to the fast fading Aston Villa, results in a 2-0 home victory dumping us firmly back on the bottom of the pile. Ironically in a game between two poor sides, the points are won by two goals from ex Claret Charlie Austin. What we wouldn't give to have him now!

Even more worrying for my finances are the results of Preston North End who extend their winning run to eight games with a win at Leyton Orient on Tuesday 28th. This victory takes them second in League 1, two points behind Bristol City, with a game in hand. Jim (Skipper of the Yard) is already rubbing his hands!

It's the last day of October, Halloween, and the reason for our lack of success in the Premier League is suddenly clear. My wife reads an article in the Burnley Express under a headline entitled 'Dyche's Challenge', in which ace reporter Chris Boden states. *"Without a win in their opening nine league games, having spent in the region of £8 in the summer, the Clarets have come in for criticism for their perceived lack of investment."*

Well Chris, if that is the case then I have to totally agree with the critics, £8! I have just spent more than that in Lidl! What did we expect to sign for that sort of money? Surely we could have pushed the boat out to a tenner!

I think Chris and the proof reader may well have red faces after that one.

NOVEMBER

I have always had a bit of a soft spot for Arsenal, along with many football aficionados admiring their style of play. In our Championship days my daughter was a bit of a closet Gunners fan, and on a few occasions when they played at Blackburn we enjoyed some corporate hospitality provided by my friends and work associates at Blackburn Yarn Dyers. I can recall one memorable occasion when Thierry Henry ran box-to-box and finished exquisitely to sink the Rovers. Oh what joy!

Today however I will have no feelings of affection for our illustrious hosts and am hoping that we can get something against all the odds. In a break with tradition I have invited my nephew, James Spillett, a Gooner to write a review of the game from an Arsenal fans perspective. So here goes.

GAME 10 – Arsenal v Burnley, Saturday 1st November, 15.00 hrs

The first Saturday of November brought an unseasonably mild sunny day, and the visit of the mighty Burnley to the Emirates. Volunteered by my Clarets supporting Uncle who was keen for an Arsenal take on the game, this match not only provided me with my first ever match report, but also a great opportunity for us Gooners to show those Northerners how to play proper football!

Going into the game, the biggest concerns for us were: would Wenger have to play a ball boy at centre back? How many blind alleys would Jack Wilshere run down today? And how many goals could we get against bottom of the table Burnley?

In reality we expected a dogged Burnley display, buoyed on by the biggest away support of the season so far at the Emirates.

The first half saw our expectations realised, Arsenal were seeing plenty of the ball, but Burnley were getting plenty of men behind it and stifling most of Arsenal's play.

Midway through the half Burnley were lucky to escape conceding a penalty, with George Boyd performing his best volleyball impersonation. Flinging his hand in the air, and making contact with the ball from one of Arsenal's corners, but an action completely missed by the referee. He hardly redeemed himself when, with one of Burnley's brief forays into Arsenal's last third, his attempted shot embarrassingly dribbled out of touch for a throw in.

As the half wore on, we saw some equally woeful shooting from Santi Cazorla, and Alexis Sanchez. The 'on-fire' Chilean, the outstanding player of the half, going close on several occasions, but being denied by either great goalkeeping from Tom Heaton or poor finishing. At half-time Arsenal were clearly the better team having had 71% of the possession and 13 attempts on goal compared to Burnley's three. However, the longer the deadlock remained the more frustrated the crowd got, and whenever Burnley did win the ball they were tidy in possession. The combination of Marvin Sordell's pace, and Danny Ings forward play, looked like it could unsettle Arsenal's back line if given the opportunity.

Arsenal needed to start the second half strongly and put more pressure on Burnley, but typically they were lethargic after the restart. Burnley briefly grew in confidence and into the game, spurred on by the vociferous chants of "Burnley" from the increasingly audible away support. However, this was short lived, but Santi Cazorla was far too casual when presented with an almost open goal, seeing his effort thwarted by a fantastic lunging Michael Duff block.

Eventually the deadlock was broken by Arsenal's South American 'street footballer' on 70 minutes. A determined Alexis Sanchez tracked a Calum Chambers cross, ran and leapt between two Burnley defenders to nod home the first goal of the day. As Arsenal's confidence grew and Burnley tired, we were able to breach Burnley's goal on two more occasions, with Chambers prodding home from a corner and Sanchez having the last word when expertly working some space from a cross before driving the ball home from close range.

The game finished 3-0 to the Arsenal. The Gunners were clearly the stronger side but had the peerless Alexis Sanchez to thank for finally beating the outstanding Tom Heaton. The North Londoners walk away from the game with their third win on the trot, and will hopefully gain some momentum to make up for their slow start to the season.

As for Burnley however, I can't help feel if they continue to put in those types of performances, they have a real fighting chance of staying in the division. I was very impressed with Danny Ings and Tom Heaton today and the whole team put in a solid, disciplined performance. So we look forward to the re-match at Turf Moor in April, hopefully Arsenal top of the league and Burnley clear of the relegation zone!

Result – Arsenal 3 (Sanchez 70, 90+1, Chambers 72) – 0 Burnley

Burnley Team

Heaton, Trippier, Duff, Shackell, Ward, Arfield, Marney, (Chalobah 80), Jones, Boyd, Ings, Sordell (Jutkiewicz 68)

<u>Subs Not used</u> – Gilks, Wallace, Keane, Mee, Kightly

Arsenal Team

Szczesny, Chambers, Mertesacker, Monreal, Gibbs, Arteta (Ramsey 63), Flamini, Oxlade-Chamberlain (Walcott 80), Sanchez, Cazorla, Welbeck (Podolski 80)

<u>Subs Not used</u> – Martinez, Bellerin, Rosicky, Sanogo

Attendance – 60,012

Season Record – Played 10, Won 0, Drawn 4, Lost 6, Goals For 5, Goals Against 19, Points 4

League Position after Game 10 – 20th

Not a bad effort there from young James, well young compared to me. I think the 'mighty Burnley' may have been a bit tongue-in-cheek, but all in all I think a fair reflection of the day's events. I could also take exception to the 'show those Northerners how to play proper football' comment. As founder members of the Football league, with a history dating back to 1882, I think these particular Northerners know a thing or two about football. I will have to get his mother to have a word with James about that.

Half time during the Arsenal game signalled the quarter way point of the season. At this stage it's difficult to see anything but relegation as the eventual outcome. After ten fixtures in the first Premier League season 2009/10, we sat with twelve points, a whopping eight more than currently. This was as a result of our tremendous home form at the start of that season winning the first four games. Notable scalps in that sequence were Manchester United, and Everton, both dispatched 1-0, and both in the same week. Interestingly at this stage in 2009/10 we had won four, lost six, scored 10 goals, and conceded 22. That's five more scored, and three more conceded than this time. Goals were clearly easier to come by but we leaked like a sieve away from home.

Clearly we cannot afford another quarter season with a points return of only four. Coming up in November are three more, I hate to use the word, 'winnable' games. My personal feel is that the League is harder this time round and it's no coincidence that the bottom three in the table are Burnley, QPR, and Leicester City, that is all three promoted clubs. Hopefully we can get the elusive first victory on the coming Saturday at home to Hull City before yet another International break.

After the Arsenal game I got a text from one of the Preston Mob Dotcomers, the unfortunately named Chris McCann, who was holidaying in Olu Deniz, Turkey. Obviously keeping a keen eye on the Clarets fortunes he texted suggesting that PNE's three goal defeat at Rochdale was the equivalent of our loss at Arsenal. Now whilst this may be mathematically correct, come on, let's get real. I can't really think of a bigger contrast in the English game than a match at The Emirates in front of 60,000 and a local derby at Spotland! Anyway PNE's run of form that had me worrying about my fiver has temporarily come to an end with a second defeat in the week away at Swindon. That's better lads.

Next up is a game I have been awaiting for some weeks mainly as a result of a disproportionate amount of 'winding up' I have been receiving from my old mate Steve C. Steve and wife Noreen, with whom we have been friends for many years, took the decision to upsticks in their twilight years and move to Lincolnshire. I can only assume that this was a precautionary move to forsake the undulations of Lancashire for the flat midland plains, ahead of their failing mobility.

For some strange reason Steve seems to think he is now a Hull City fan, although I know for a fact he has only attended two league matches in the last 30 years, one at Doncaster, and one at the Turf, neither of which featured Hull City. He seems to have been badly affected by the Kelloggs Frosties advert and keeps telling me that the Tigers are 'grrrrrreat', how sad! *(But they are grrrrrreat! the author doesn't know I've added this……Steve C)* In retaliation I have taken to referring to them as Hole City, childish but necessary. Anyway the wind up has been ongoing and with increasing intensity as the early season form of the two clubs was at the opposite ends of the spectrum, the Tigers enjoying some early if unexpected successes. However, of late the toothless Tigers have started to slip back into their old ways. Steve has accordingly taken himself off for a two month break in Greece, but I am sure he is waiting to pounce should the worst happen in this fixture. I myself am similarly poised with both barrels loaded ready to blast him if today produces the long awaited first victory. Let battle commence.

GAME 11 – Burnley v Hull City, Saturday 8th November, 15.00 hrs

One of my walking buddies and member of the Burnley contingent, is a former GP, and one time Burnley FC club doctor. Mike M, his wife Lesley, and son Sam have a rather quaint match day tradition. They are kitted out with hip flasks filled with Malt Whisky for all home games. When the Clarets score it is the tradition to take a nip from the flask. I can imagine that last season this led to some pretty tipsy afternoons at the Turf. However this season goals have not been so forthcoming, to the point where Mike has been wondering if he will ever need to top up again. Ahead of the game I text him to say *"Get those hip flasks primed. Today is the day"*. His prompt reply is *"I've topped up"*.

I thought ahead of this game we may see a few changes in the starting line up. Ten games in and still without a win suggests it may be time to give one or two of the fringe guys a chance. Chalobah and Keane come instantly to mind, both on loan from top Premier League sides, Chelsea and Manchester United respectively. Both these youngsters have just been selected for the England U21 squad, along with Danny Ings, to play Portugal at Turf Moor on November 13th. Neither have had much game time since arriving on loan on transfer deadline day, although Chalobah has been edging nearer in recent weeks. It comes as something of a surprise then to find the only change from last weeks starting eleven is Ashley Barnes in for Marvin Sordell. Even more surprising as Barnes didn't even make the squad last time out. Sean Dyche obviously has a master plan.

The game starts brightly enough with Danny Ings latching on to a bouncing through ball in the box before firing wide in the first minute. Seemingly well in control of the game we manage to conjure one nasty moment as Michael Duff gifts a ball to the Hull striker Sone Aluko but Jason Shackell manages to avert the danger. As the half continues we look to have broken the deadlock. Following a right wing corner a powerful Ings shot is parried away excellently by Harper in the Hull goal. The ball then hits Hull central defender McShane and ricochets towards the goal only to be cleared off the line. The new goal line technology currently in operation in all Premier League games confirms the ball hadn't crossed. Despite lots of pressure the half ends goalless.

As I make my way for a half time comfort break Mike M, obviously aggrieved at the lack of goals texts:

"Sod it I'm having a nip for the booking"

Me – "Wise decision, can't see many other opportunities"

Prophetically, Me again – "Half time talk will do it"

The second half starts in similar vein with the Clarets making the running, but I am getting that uneasy feeling of a West Ham rerun. As I make this observation to my mate John W, he tells me not to even think it. And, at that point the MAGIC MOMENT arrives.

Interplay between Ings and Barnes results in a shot by the former being blocked. The ball is only cleared as far as Trippier in an advanced right wing position. Tripps promptly delivers a 'peach' of a cross, and rising between two defenders to power a header past the helpless Harper is good old Barnsey. Sean's master plan has come to fruition!

Mike – "Ah, the aroma of peat"

Me – "The half time talk!"

What a magnificent effort met with momentous acclaim from the delighted home fans. Immediately Hull Manager Steve Bruce, who by this time had seen enough, made two substitutions. These were followed by a third in the 59th minute. The visitors briefly try to step it up but we are in the driving seat now. Then disaster for Hull as centre back Curtis Davies goes down with what appears to be a back injury. After considerable attention from the physio he tries to continue but is clearly unable and goes off leaving 10 men to chase the game for the final minutes. Despite much huffing and puffing there are no real scares, and with one man down they are clearly vulnerable to a quick counter.

Referee Mark Clattenburg who had a highly erratic afternoon, enjoys a late spell of yellow card fever, finishing up with six for Burnley and four for Hull. Needless to say the worst foul of the lot receives no punishment at all. After five minutes added time it's all over and the victory is ours.

Success! At last! The first Premier League win of this campaign, and for the reasons aforementioned, how sweet! Messages were winging their way by text to Greece as soon as the final whistle blew, to be met with the expected reaction, *"Bugger off, jammy bastards"*.

Result – Burnley 1 (Barnes 51) – 0 Hull City

Burnley Team

Heaton, Trippier, Duff, Shackell, Ward, Arfield (Kightly 55), Marney, (Chalobah 80), Jones, Boyd, Ings, Barnes (Jutkiewicz 75)

Subs Not used – Gilks, Chalobah, Keane, Mee, Sordell

Hull City Team

Harper, Chester (Ben Arfa 59), McShane, Davies, Elmohamady, Huddlestone (Ramirez 51), Diame, Livermore, Brady, Aluko (Quinn 51), Hernandez

Subs Not used – Jakupovic, Rosenior, Robertson, Meyler

Attendance – 16,998

Season Record – Played 11, Won 1, Drawn 4, Lost 6, Goals For 6, Goals Against 19, Points 7

League Position after Game 11 – 20th

The immediate reaction to the win is mainly relief that we have finally 'got the monkey off our back'. The hope is that this victory will give both players and fans the confidence that survival is possible. We remain bottom due to Manchester City's failure to beat QPR at Loftus Road by three clear goals. In fact they fail to beat them at all, the game finishing 2-2. However the points gap is closed leaving us one point behind QPR, two behind Leicester and Crystal Palace, and four adrift of Aston Villa and Hull.

On Thursday 13th November I watch a very entertaining Under 21 International between England and Portugal at the Turf. Ings and Keane start for England and Chalobah is on the bench. Ings, playing in an unusual for him lone striker role, has a very impressive game notching two goals in a fine 3-1 victory. No mugs either these Portuguese who were unbeaten in their fifteen previous outings. Danny is clearly delighted at getting the opportunity to represent his country but I can't help feeling as I watch that he may have outgrown us. Still with no sign of him signing a new contract and his current one expiring in the summer, I fear we are seeing the last of Danny. If he is to go then the best chance of a reasonable fee would be to sell in the January transfer window, and those two goals won't have done his value any harm.

After what seems an eternity we once again return to Premier League action with an away fixture at Stoke City. The Potters were our first ever Premier League opponents when we opened the 2009/10 season with a 2-0 defeat at the Britannia Stadium. This set the tone for a dismal run of away results with only four points, one win and one draw, taken from a possible fifty seven in the season. Incredibly a win tomorrow in the sixth away game would take us beyond that points tally for the current season. However firstly there is the small matter of overcoming our opponents.

Stoke currently sit a very respectable ninth in the table, courtesy of four wins, three draws, and four defeats in the first eleven fixtures. It's fair to say their home form has been a bit mixed with two wins, one draw, and two defeats from the first five played. However the home form seems to be recovering with no defeats in the last three games. Here's hoping that timely win against Hull, and the rest period following, have set us up for a real go at this one.

GAME 12 – Stoke City v Burnley, Saturday 22nd November, 15.00 hrs

The team shows one enforced change from last time out with Scott Arfield, injured in training, missing out. Coming in is ex Potter Michael Kightly in a like-for-like change. Also missing from the bench is Nathaniel Chalobah injured in the England U21 International midweek.

Confidence is a wonderful thing and the amount gained from the win over Hull certainly manifested itself in the early exchanges at Stoke. A lively opening ten minutes from the Clarets should have alerted the hosts to the fact that they were in a game. If it didn't then minutes twelve and thirteen certainly did.

On twelve minutes Boyd won the ball and fed Marney, his pass found Barnes on the left of the box whose cross was only parried away by the Stoke keeper, under pressure from Kightly, straight into the path of Ings who couldn't miss. What a great start, and better was to come in less than two minutes as once again the Clarets wreaked havoc down the left flank. Ward's throw in being flicked on by Barnes to the menacing Kightly who left Bardsley for dead before crossing for another close range tap in for 'Ingsy'. Unbelievable, all of a sudden we have gone goal crazy.

Of course we all knew it wouldn't be so easy, and Stoke after taking a little time to recover their composure started to press. Game on after 32 minutes as Walters diving header from Bojan's cross had too much power for Heaton to keep out. Another nervy moment as Moses breaking into the box is suddenly sprawled on the deck. Television replays confirm that this serial offender has once again manufactured a momentous dive! This guy would surely never have been entrusted with leading the children of Israel back to the Promised Land. Perhaps he was momentarily practising carrying the 'tablets of stone' and finding them a bit on the heavy side. Referee Atkinson clearly spots this for what it is but mysteriously produces no card. Half time arrives with the lead intact but we are sure a second half battering is coming.

We are certainly given that, a match possession statistic of 73%/27% confirms Stoke's desire to rectify their calamitous start to the game. A shots total of 25/5 in favour of the hosts, plus a corner count of 14/0 are further evidence of their domination. However, perhaps the most telling statistic is the shots on target, 3/4. Yes, incredibly despite all their possession and pressure we emerge with more shots on target. Surely an indication of a magnificent rearguard action. For almost the entire second half Stoke threw countless balls into the box, bringing on the gangling Crouch to add his own particular menace. Through it all the defence, nay the whole team remained resolute and determined and protected the valuable lead without too many close calls. Finally after six minutes added time the victory was once again ours. Bloody heroes every man jack of 'em.

Back to back Premier League wins, who would have predicted that after none in the first ten? Danny Ings back from injury and back to his goal scoring best with three in his last two Burnley games, making it five from three counting his two goals in the England U21 fixture. But most of all once again a magnificent team effort, with everyone showing complete dedication to the task, and all prepared to go the extra mile to prove the doubters and detractors wrong. Hope is once again rising that this season will not be the disaster many predicted, and survival may yet be achieved. I don't think for one minute that the ever positive Sean Dyche ever thought anything else.

Result – Stoke City 1 (Walters 32) – 2 Burnley (Ings 12,13)

Burnley Team

Heaton, Trippier, Duff (Keane 76), Shackell, Ward, Kightly (Jutkiewicz 60) , Marney, Jones, Boyd, Ings (Reid 86), Barnes

Subs Not used – Gilks, Wallace, Mee, Sordell

Stoke City Team

Begovic, Bardsley, Shawcross, Cameron, Muniesa, Sidwell (Adam 68), N'Zonzi, Walters, Bojan KrKic, Moses (Amautovic 56), Diouf (Crouch 60)

<u>Subs Not used</u> – Sorensen, Whelan, Ireland, Assaidi

<u>Attendance</u> – 27,018

<u>Season Record</u> – Played 12, Won 2, Drawn 4, Lost 6, Goals For 8, Goals Against 20, Points 10

<u>League Position after Game 12</u> – 19th

The victory at Stoke takes the points tally into double figures and only one behind the record Premier League low held by Derby County. I'm not normally a betting man but I'll stick my neck out here and now and say that dubious honour will remain with the Rams. Saturday's results temporarily lift us to the dizzy heights of 18th but we drop back to 19th on Sunday as a result of Liverpool's capitulation at Crystal Palace.

Sean Dyche was clearly elated by the first away victory and spoke to the fans after the game saying:

"I said when I got here that they will always get a team who give everything for the shirt. Today they have given just that again in the Premier League, and I am proud of that make no mistake"

"There are things that people will know I hold dear. They are old fashioned values, but they have never been more relevant. Pride, passion, desire, and will, are all things that this team has in abundance. I have it, my staff have it, and the players too, and that was on show today".

He added: *"We said we wanted to make what has been deemed from the outside impossible, possible, but we don't think that. I believe in the players and the way we work".*

We had a tough start to the season and it will be tough again, but we didn't think we would just roll into this league and roll out victories. But the mentality of the group is good and if I were a Burnley fan, which I kind of am if you understand me, I'd be proud of that display today".

Clearly a very happy man, and well said! Now he just needs to get the same belief instilled in some of the less convinced fans and we will indeed be a force to be reckoned with.

Briefly returning to the subject of my walking colleagues, the Lancashire Dotcom Walkers (LDW). It is a tradition that every year around Christmas time we have our annual quiz which is usually held in our elected Pub of the Year (POTY). This year the quiz was held on Tuesday 18th November at the excellent Stork Inn, Conder Green, Nr Glasson Dock, Lancaster, which was actually our POTY in 2013.

Unfortunately, due to a malfunctioning central heating boiler, and the fitting of a new bathroom window, I was unable to attend. Obviously this seriously weakened an already depleted Burnley Contingent attempt to retain the crown won last year. Our chances were further hindered by once again I suspect some judicious team selection perpetrated by Quizmaster and North Ender, the highly corruptible Chris McCann. There was once again a whiff of the type of corruption employed at the summer Bowls Tournament. Needless to say the trophy this year went to the team from South Ribble!

However I was greatly honoured to learn that in the section of the quiz dedicated to the identification of famous authors, I had made the list! What a great achievement to find myself alongside the likes of, Shakespeare, Joyce, Du Maurier, and Solzhenitsyn. All this glory and so far based on my one and only published tome, 'A Season In The Sun'.

As usual my delight was quickly soured by the news that nobody had managed to identify me! The task had been to discover the authors by filling in randomly missing letters in their names.

At the next walk, Steve Glover another of the Nobbers, congratulated me on making the list and confirmed that he had indeed identified me. Marvellous, from zero to hero, until I was later informed that rather than identify me by my work, they had worked out the name by putting in letters and using a process of elimination! Oh well perhaps next year after publication of this blockbuster....

I suppose I was even more disappointed by the failure of my so called mates from the Burnley Contingent to pick up what should have been easy points on that question. However when I consider that the team could only manage a mediocre third out of five finish in the quiz, it should come as no surprise. A sad indictment of the teaching profession I'm afraid as the bulk of the team consisted of ex schoolteachers.

Thursday 27th November's Burnley Contingent walk to Musbury Tor provided another interesting and amusing incident. Shortly after lunch we were proceeding on our merry way along a bog sodden stretch of the Rossendale Way. At this point we came across a field containing a magnificent horse which could almost have been Red Rum Mk2. John W, not a great lover of horses, something to do with them having large teeth, decided he would conquer his fear and engage the horse in conversation.

It was then that we noticed that we had indeed to cross a wooden fence stile into the field where the horse was situated. All went over the stile without incident until just two were left, Geoff A (our previously mentioned ex Barden PE teacher) and John W. As John continued his one sided conversation with the totally disinterested horse, it turned its back on us, How ignorant I remarked! At this point Geoff was just astride the fence, when the horse let out a magnificent and tremulous fart! Geoff, shocked to the core, promptly lost his footing and almost something much more dear to him, his knackers! Oh what joy! It was impossible to go to his aid for the crippling effects of being doubled up with laughter. A memory I shall take to the grave with me! Fortunately the only thing hurt was his pride, but I could swear the horse was grinning malevolently.

That little bit of merriment set me in just the right mood for the upcoming challenge of two home games. First up are struggling Aston Villa who after a great start to the season have fallen away badly. A win over our fellow Clarets would chalk up a third consecutive success and take us above them in the table. Better not get ahead of ourselves though, the last team of Clarets to come here, West Ham, went home with the spoils. We shall see.

GAME 13 – Burnley v Aston Villa, Saturday 29th November, 15.00 hrs

Making my way to the Turf for this game I was confident but not over-confident of a positive result. Our two consecutive victories in the league had greatly lifted spirits among the fans and the feeling was that we were perhaps getting to grips with this league after a rocky start. Villa hadn't won in their last eight games losing six and drawing two, and this as I'm sure Sean Dyche would tell you, made them a very dangerous animal. Team news shows a first start in Clarets colours for loanee centre back Michael Keane, in place of the injured Michael Duff.

There's a lively start to the game with two early chances falling to the of late prolific Danny Ings, but both on this occasion untaken. The old adage that missed chances cost matches immediately pops into my mind but I try to quickly dispel it. It's certainly not one way traffic though and the Villains are looking quietly effective, with the pacy Gabby Agbonlahor deployed as a lone striker. He is getting good support from Joe Cole, and Andreas Weimann, and backed by a large following they are looking a real threat.

We have Dean Marney to thank for a couple of goal line clearances to keep us in the game. The midfielder is once again displaying what a vital player he is for us with his combative and skilful style making him a stand out player so far. The referee then decides its time he made his mark in the game and for a brief spell decides to arbitrarily deem some challenges bookable offences and similar ones not. It's from one of these decisions that Villa take a precious lead. The aforementioned Marney is involved in a full blooded 50/50 challenge for the ball with Villa's Clark. Harshly the referee decides this is a foul and a booking for Deano, and from the free kick the ball is fed down the right and slipped into the box for Cole to finish neatly from close range.

A jolt to the system but the game continues in fairly end to end fashion, both sides encouraged by very vociferous backing from the crowd. Half time sees us trailing to the solitary goal and with a difficult second half ahead.

The second period is largely one of Villa trying to kill the game with long periods of possession but no real goal threat. Kightly misses an early chance from close quarters hitting the keeper with the net beckoning but apart from that we are creating few clear cut chances. Off goes the highly effective but tiring Cole for Villa as they continue to try to stifle the game instead of pursuing a second, and no doubt match winning goal. We in turn introduce Arfield for Kightly, Jutkiewicz for Barnes, and finally Wallace for Jones, in a last throw of the dice.

As we opt for a more direct approach with time running out, on 87 minutes suddenly a lifeline! Jutkiewicz chasing a ball into the box is grappled to the floor by the burly Villa centre back and the referee has no hesitation in pointing to the spot. My mate John W fears a Crystal Palace repetition where Scott Arfield's late penalty was saved, but no such problem here as Danny Ings smashes the ball down the centre as Guzan dives to his right. GOAL and game on, as the fourth official signals five minutes added time.

There's only going to be one winner now as the rejuvenated Clarets go for the jugular. Ings gets clear in the box, pokes the ball goalwards, but with the keeper beaten it rebounds back off the post. This is a quickly followed by a close range Jutkiewicz header that lacking real power bounces agonisingly wide of the post. Just time for the Villa sub Grealish to fail to make the most of a final chance, and it's all over.

A game that looked lost ends with us ruing that we didn't take the maximum points! The three substitutes showed the importance of having fresh legs and options at the end of the game, and I am sure were instrumental in saving the point. Disappointed that we didn't get the three points, or relieved that we saved the one? It was hard to say in the immediate aftermath of the game, but on reflection I think a draw was probably about right.

Result – Burnley 1 (Ings 87 pen) – 1 Aston Villa (Cole 38)

Burnley Team

Heaton, Trippier, Keane, Shackell, Ward, Kightly (Arfield 65), Marney, Jones (Wallace 83), Boyd, Ings, Barnes (Jutkiewicz 65)

Subs Not used – Gilks, Long, Mee, Sordell

Aston Villa Team

Guzan, Hutton, Okore, Clark (Lowton 95), Cissokho, Cleverly, Westwood, Sanchez, Cole (Grealish 67), Agbonlahor, Weimann (Richardson 78)

Subs Not used – Given, Bacuna, N'Zogbia, Robinson

Attendance – 19,910

Season Record – Played 13, Won 2, Drawn 5, Lost 6, Goals For 9, Goals Against 21, Points 11

League Position after Game 13 – 19th

Ashley Barnes leads the celebrations as the triumphant Clarets celebrate the return to the 'Land of Milk and Honey'

Clarets team bus spotted on the streets of Lisbon

(For those of you looking in black and white the claret on the bus is next to the blue!)

Ouch! The author grimaces as he concedes the bet to PNE's Jim (Skipper of the Yard)

Sean the Gnome maintains a dignified stance as he hands over the 'dosh' to his rather surly and undernourished counterpart, Nobby the Gnome

Marker post spotted in the wilds of Calder Vale, Nr Garstang. Well done to the Calder Vale Claret!

Dotcom walkers dressed for all weathers, from L-R, Chris McCann, the author, Ed (Sherpa) Walton

Clarets dressing room ahead of the 2014 Championship fixture with Brighton, From L-R, John G, John W, Me, Some guy that just walked in, Daughter Stephanie, Judy W, Kath G

Claret's Hat making the long journey home after another successful Mediterranean cruise

DECEMBER

Coming hard on the heels of the Villa game is another home fixture, a rarity indeed, a Tuesday night Premier League game. The visitors this time are Newcastle United who after a rocky start, which almost cost Manager Alan Pardew his job, have recovered in impressive fashion, and currently sit in relative mid table comfort.

GAME 14 – Burnley v Newcastle United, Tuesday 2nd December, 19.45 hrs

The starting eleven shows one change from Saturday's game with Scott Arfield replacing Michael Kightly in a straight one-for-one swap. Young Michael Keane retains his place in central defence with Michael Duff still unavailable.

Starting the game in rather lacklustre fashion, I note after three minutes that I can't recall us having a touch of the ball. However slowly but surely we start to get a toehold in the game and I can settle a little further back in my seat. The best early effort comes as Arfield feeds Ings in the box to the left of goal. Turning to get the ball on his favoured right foot the in form striker shoots powerfully, only to be denied by a fine one handed save by the Newcastle keeper Elliott. Our visitors, boasting a veritable League of Nations line up, are similarly failing to impress.

On 34 minutes the deadlock is broken as a ball played up to Ings is headed back from the edge of the penalty area to Boyd lurking fairly centrally. Quick as a flash Georgie Boy unleashes a shot of great accuracy and no little power unerringly into the corner of the Magpies net.

Moving towards half time with little further goalmouth action, we see one of two match defining incidents. With just a couple of minutes to go to the interval clever interplay between Arfield and Ings on the left of the box sees Ings feed Jones through clear on goal. Preparing to launch myself to my feet in ecstatic goal celebration, I am rocked back as our midfielder fires over the top. A second goal at that point would I think have won the game. Still we go off at half time 1-0 ahead and in the driving seat.

Cue the second incident, within minutes of the restart, the usually ever so reliable Trippier inexplicably makes a hash of a clearance. Instead of pumping the ball to relative safety down the line, he fires it back in the direction of the penalty spot. Some last ditch defending appears to have saved the situation but the ball is recycled from the right wing to the waiting Cisse who guides it in from close range.

Buoyed by this early success Newcastle become more dominant and start to look dangerous with Sammy Ameobi posing a real threat down the left flank, until he is forced off with an injury. Mee joins the fray replacing Ward who appears to suffer a serious ankle injury. Finally the late introduction of Jutkiewicz in an effort to change the game wasn't really a success, and the game peters out to a second successive home draw.

Two draws from the last two fixtures and unbeaten in the last four mean we climb, for the moment at least, out of the relegation spots for the second time this season. Defeats for Leicester (home to Liverpool) and QPR (away to Swansea) leave them in 20th and 19th positions respectively. Hull City, without a game till Wednesday (away at Everton), come on you Toffees, currently occupy 18th place.

Result – Burnley 1 (Boyd 34) – 1 Newcastle United (Cisse 48)

Burnley Team

Heaton, Trippier, Keane, Shackell, Ward (Mee 66), Arfield, Marney, Jones, Boyd, Ings, Barnes (Jutkiewicz 85)

Subs Not used – Gilks, Long, Wallace, Sordell, Kightly

Newcastle United Team

Elliott, Janmaat, Williamson (Taylor 45), Dummett, Haidara, Abeid, Tiote, Gouffran, Perez (Cabella 45), Ameobi (Riviere 75), Cisse

Subs Not used – Alnwick, Anita, Armstrong, Streete

Attendance – 18,791

Season Record – Played 14, Won 2, Drawn 6, Lost 6, Goals For 10, Goals Against 22, Points 12

League Position after Game 14 – 18th

Unfortunately on Wednesday evening the Toffees are unable to tame the Tigers and a 1-1 draw puts us back into the drop zone but now only on goal difference.

The Burnley Express of Friday 5th December has a front page story regarding the club's annual accounts headlined, *'Clarets report loss of £7.6m!'* The report goes on to say that the deficit is a direct result of promotion to the Premier League. Before promotion the club were showing a profit of £300,000, but then promotion bonuses cost the club £7.9m. Turnover for the year had run at £19.6m but obviously promotion to the Premier League will reflect a quantum leap in this figure for the current year.

Co chairman Mike Garlick was proud of the figures and felt the club was in excellent health. *"None of the other two promoted sides (Leicester City and QPR) got close to breakeven – indeed, over the last five or six years not many will have, which gives us quite a unique record, of which we should be proud.*

"We've had to move towards the model of Financial Fair Play – we have no benefactor and can't run up losses of £20m-plus, so things have to be tighter.

"We have to cut our cloth accordingly.

"But we have cash in the bank now and have plans on other expenditure."

The plans include a full indoor training facility at the Gawthorpe training complex in order to help the club gain Category 2 status in the Elite Player Performance Plan – a youth development scheme initiated by the Premier League.

It's funny how the result of a football match can affect the mood. If I confess that it has taken me a good couple of days before I could write the report of the next match, I think you will guess that it is not good reading.

GAME 15 – Queens Park Rangers v Burnley, Saturday 6th December, 15.00 hrs

This game pits us against our former prolific goal scorer Charlie Austin, and coming face to face with ex Clarets always gives me an uneasy feeling. This is made none the less by Charlie's excellent form and strike rate while at QPR. I have to confess feeling that Mr Austin has been rather unstinting in his praise for what has been achieved at Turf Moor since his departure, and rightly or wrongly get the feel that he thinks he is 'bigger' than us. Perhaps it's just me getting a bit paranoid.

Unsurprisingly we show only one change from the team unbeaten in the last four Premier League games, Ben Mee replacing Stephen Ward, who it is revealed has a hairline fracture of the ankle sustained in the Newcastle match. Last year's corresponding fixture resulted in a pulsating 3-3 draw, and the early exchanges suggest a similar result may be on the cards. With the Clarets pushing hard they are denied in the first half by the usual combination of bad luck and heroic goalkeeping, none better than Robert Green's fingertip onto a post to keep out George Boyd's 25 yard thunderbolt. That's not to say that its one way traffic and we are kept on our toes defensively. Half time arrives goalless but with the Clarets way ahead on attempts at goal, and corners, but with nothing to show for it.

As so often seems to happen to us the half time interval interrupts our flow and we start the second half on the backfoot, QPR manager Redknapp clearly having instructed his players to seize the initiative. Within six minutes we trail to a Leroy Fer goal scored from a Charlie Austin assist. Perhaps some bad luck again in this one with Fer's shot hitting Mee's attempted block and the ball looping up over Heaton in goal. This goal seems to spur the Clarets back to life and once again we are playing some neat inventive attacking football but again being unable to find a finish.

Disaster then on 74 minutes as who else but Charlie Austin meets a ball cut back by Eduardo Vargas and buries a low strike. Incredibly then a clearly wound up Charlie, already on a yellow card for a nasty foul on Kieran Trippier, commits another one with an elbow in the face of Michael Keane, and on 76 minutes he sees red. QPR are down to ten men for the last 14 minutes but see the game out comfortably as the Clarets dismally fail to take any advantage.

Valuable points lost to a relegation rival and once again in a game that promised so much more than it delivered. The inability to take chances is once again proving a major contributory factor to our demise and the goals tally of only 10 from 15 games is clearly the main cause for concern.

Speaking after the game Sean Dyche admitted: *"Green's (QPR keeper) made a worldy save. We need to be more clinical. We have been earlier in the season and we weren't enough against QPR.*

The performance was good, there was organisation, energy, quality. We're putting in the right mixture but we need to win games. We have to turn that into wins."

Result – Queens Park Rangers 2 (Fer 51, Austin 74) – 0 Burnley

Burnley Team

Heaton, Trippier, Keane, Shackell, Mee, Arfield (Wallace 75), Marney, Jones (Jutiewicz 86), Boyd, Ings, Barnes (Sordell 89)

Subs Not used – Gilks, Long, Reid, Kightly

Queens Park Rangers Team

Green, Isla, Caulker, Dunne, Suk-Young, Vargas (Mutch 78), Barton, Henry, Fer (Phillips 91), Austin, Zamora (Kranjcar 66)

Subs Not used – McCarthy, Ferdinand, Onuoha, Hoilett

Attendance – 17,785

Season Record – Played 15, Won 2, Drawn 6, Lost 7, Goals For 10, Goals Against 24, Points 12

League Position after Game 15 – 19th

The evening of Monday 8th December is time for the draw for the third round of the FA Cup. In our elevated status which we have enjoyed for about the last fourteen years this is the entry point of the competition for us. Gone are the dark days of first round draws at places like Telford and Penrith, no…nowadays we only come in with the rest of the 'big boys'. I must confess that as I busy myself with other things I completely forget about the draw. It's only when I log in for a quick trawl of what's new on Claretsmad that I see the headline Clarets draw Spurs in the FA Cup.

So it's set for a replay of the 1962 FA Cup final, hopefully with a different end result. It might turn out to be a decent tie this with I think the Clarets fielding pretty much a full strength team. Our visitors on the other hand, who are still in the Europa Cup, may see the tie as less important, and be tempted to rest some of their regular starters. That could prove fatal as Rafa Benitez found to his cost as a weakened Liverpool side exited to the Clarets on a similar occasion in 2005.

Despite the defeat at QPR the previous four match unbeaten run had improved the league position significantly. In contrast, Leicester City and the unpleasant Nigel Pearson, had gone into a serious decline since failing to beat us, now lying bottom of the table and two points adrift of us. The eight points garnered from our little run had enabled us to close the gap on our other relegation rivals and we are once again back in the pack.

We now have a difficult run of fixtures coming up starting this coming Saturday at home to Southampton, the surprise form team of early season. Despite the Saints losing three consecutive games on the trot, this will again be a mighty ask for the Clarets. This game is then followed by no less difficult contests against Tottenham Hotspur (away), Liverpool (home), and Manchester City (away) before December is out. This will then see us at the half way point of the season. We must get some points from these games but it sure as hell won't be easy!

GAME 16 – Burnley v Southampton, Saturday 13th December, 15.00 hrs

The day starts out with a bitterly cold, clear December morning. Just the sort of weather we need to dispirit the 'southern softies' after their long trek north. From my seat in the James Hargreaves Upper stand I can see in the distance Burnley's iconic panopticon, The Singing Ringing Tree, atop snow covered Crown Point. Is there a better view in English football?

By kick off time the clouds are starting to roll in. That's ideal we'll give them a real mix of Burnley weather. Freeze them first, then soak them! Referee Mark Clattenburg gets the game underway promptly, so much so that I have barely had the chance to take my seat. Clattenburg's last game at the Turf saw his outburst of 'yellow card fever', where he managed to amass ten! Let's hope he has got that out of his system for today.

Southampton, after a brilliant start to the season are on the back of three straight defeats, albeit it to Arsenal, and both Manchester clubs. They will undoubtedly be fancying their chances to get back on track today. The Clarets are also looking forward to forgetting last week's blip at QPR which ended their four match unbeaten run.

It's quickly evident that we are going to see a game of contrasting styles. Southampton are silky smooth, with a neat passing game, and are enjoying lots of possession. We are more direct and combative. The first half is tight and with few chances at either end, but we have probably edged it. Our creative problems appear to stem from the slowness of our build up. On the few occasions we break quickly, the pace of Ings is causing the Saints defence problems. However, more often than not, the attacks are laboured and giving too much time for the visitors to get men behind the ball.

At half time as I go to relieve myself of two pre-match pints of 'Filly Close Blonde', an excellent tipple from the Reedley Hallows Brewery Company, I bump into an old mate of many years. Along with the son of his cousin, who has made the long trip from Melton Mowbray to support the Clarets, (there's dedication from someone who has never lived in the town), we discuss the first half action. They, like most fans, can see the endeavour being put in by the Clarets but bemoan the lack of a bit of quality to just make the difference. Whilst appreciating Ashley Barnes's unstinting efforts, we feel that we just can't see where a goal will come from. We all agree that we must not concede or we are sunk.

The second half starts in teeming rain, just what we ordered from the weather gods, but unfortunately it seems to be having the opposite effect. Southampton are out of the blocks in determined fashion and pushing us back relentlessly. We seem incapable of retaining any sort of possession and a goal against is looking inevitable.

On 60 minutes it looks like our worst fears are about to come true. The tireless George Boyd, is sold a dummy by the Saints full back Bertrand and sticks out a leg bringing him down just inside the penalty area. No arguments it's a penalty for sure. Up steps the Saints winger Tadic, who is apparently a penalty specialist. My mate John W somewhat ruefully informs me he has never seen Heaton save a penalty. To which my reply is "YOU HAVE NOW," as the magnificent Tom Heaton dives low to his left to push the ball wide of the post with both hands.

Quite often it's moments like this that change games and this is certainly the case here as the miss proves a pivotal point. Tom's save has given us fresh momentum and we start to gain a bit more self belief. From a Southampton throw in on their right, the full back Clyne's attempted pass down the line ricochets off Danny Ings as he closes him down. The ball falls invitingly into the path of none other than Ashley Barnes closing in on goal. In an instant Ashley shoots but the ball looks to be covered by the Saints keeper before taking the faintest of deflections off a defender and hitting the back of the net.

73 minutes gone, the Clarets ahead, and a moment to savour for the oft maligned Ashley Barnes. Still a long way to go in the game yet though and I sit back awaiting the onslaught. Surprisingly it doesn't seem to come, Southampton go close with a fierce shot just wide of the post from Nathaniel Clyne who is looking to make amends. A late chance falls to Wanyama who really should have done better but his header fails to test the keeper. After four minutes added time it's all over and the Clarets have their third win of the campaign.

Again the win moves us out of the bottom three taking our points tally to 15, 11 of which have been gathered from a possible last 18 available. QPR face a trip to Everton on the coming Monday evening and a defeat will see us remain out of the drop zone. Leicester's defeat at home to Manchester City leaves them trailing us by five points, whilst Hull's loss at Chelsea puts them second bottom.

Result – Burnley 1 (Barnes 73) – 0 Southampton

Burnley Team

Heaton, Trippier, Keane, Shackell, Mee (Lafferty 74), Arfield , Marney, Jones, Boyd, Ings, Barnes

Subs Not used – Gilks, Long, Jutkiewicz, Kightly, Wallace, Chalobah

Southampton Team

Forster, Clyne, Fonte, Alderweireld, Bertrand, Hesketh (Ward-Prowse 32), Davis, Wanyama, Tadic, Pelle, Mane (Long 78)

Subs Not used – Davis, Yoshida, Gardos, Mayuka, Reed

Attendance – 17,287

Season Record – Played 16, Won 3, Drawn 6, Lost 7, Goals For 11, Goals Against 24, Points 15

League Position after Game 16 – 17th

On the Monday night Everton duly oblige by doing the business on QPR. Their 3-1 victory at Goodison Park confirms our position outside the bottom three, and condemns 'Arry's men to their eighth consecutive Premier League away defeat. Millions spent, nothing gained!

Thursday 18th December marks the Burnley Contingent's 2nd Annual Christmas Lunch at our perennial

Pub of the Year, the Roggerham Gate, or Miss Haversham's house as I sometimes refer to it. The preceding day, as was the case with the 1st annual event, is one of continuous rain. This gives me some concerns over our proposed walk route to the 'Rogg'. The start will be from near my home in Harle Syke, via Thursden Valley then crossing Thursden Brook, and approaching the pub via Monk Hall/Shay Lane. The first part of this walk must rank as one of the wettest walks in England, and that's in summer! Last year's event had a particularly muddy conclusion following a route from Harle Syke via the Brun Valley Greenway, Houghton Hag Wood, the 'Rogg', Extwistle Hall, and Ogglity Gogglity. The sense of balance being not improved by the consumption of several pints of 'Rogger Ale'. I await the 18th with some trepidation.

True to form the rain didn't disappoint. This year our ranks are swelled by several new ramblers, and a bumper turnout of eighteen walkers were met at the pub by a further four, who were either unwell or wimped out due to the conditions. A mention here for a brave effort by another ex Barden teacher, Maureen Thornber, whose hip replacement operation was cancelled for the second time. This time Maureen made it as far as the gowning up stage but complications with the previous patient's operation meant the surgeon ran out of butchering hours. Geoff A attempted to cry off and just opt for the pub but was shamed into walking by his colleagues.

Heavy overnight and continuous morning rain made the outing seem a singularly unattractive proposition at the start. However suitably attired we managed to stay relatively dry, and provide some amusement for a local farmer at Cockden, who I think thought we had escaped from a nursing home for the slightly bewildered. (I can see where he was coming from.) This situation changed around Higher Halstead farm where the driving rain decided to do its worst. It would take more than wind and rain to dampen the spirits of this hardy bunch, especially as they now had the scent of the pub in their nostrils.

Arriving at the pub bang on cue at 13.00 hours, we were welcomed enthusiastically by our non walking colleagues and Jed behind the bar. I have to say the pub was a joy to behold, a proper pub selling proper beer, and not a whiff of plastic. Festooned in Christmas decorations and with a warming log burner, what a welcome for drenched walkers. Excellent food served in generous portions and a few pints of Rogger Ale soon had the party in full swing. A magnificent setting and a great day to end a glorious year's walking for the Burnley Contingent.

GAME 17 – Tottenham Hotspur v Burnley, Saturday 20th December, 15.00 hrs

Well this is a game that brings back memories for those of us old enough to recall the titanic struggles between these two major rivals of the late 1950s/early 1960s. When I was a lad these were the two teams that set the pace, Tottenham wealthy and flash, the Clarets homespun but equally their match.

Games in those days between the two always seemed to rain goals and even though the teams have met infrequently over recent years this is still usually the case. The corresponding fixture in our last Premier League adventure resulted in a resounding 5-0 victory to the Spurs, with our revenge coming in the final fixture of our campaign with a 4-2 victory at the Turf.

Going into the game Tottenham were on the back of two good victories away at Swansea in the league and at home to Newcastle in the Capital One Cup in midweek. Confidence was high and they sat just outside the Champions League qualifying places. Similarly our run of 11 points from the last 18, and last week's victory over Southampton had boosted the Clarets self belief.

The Clarets unsurprisingly went into the game unchanged and found themselves under some early pressure as the hosts looked to get off to a flier. After weathering the early storm we seemed to be getting on an even keel before being hit by an unfortunate opener on 21 minutes. A ball played down the Spurs left hit the in-form striker Harry Kane and flicked up striking Michael Keane on the arm. The quickly taken free kick, with some suspicion of a moving ball, was left by the clearly offside Eriksen but ran into the path of Chadli who crossed for Kane to head in from close range with the defence in disarray.

Didn't go down too well with Sean Dyche who in his after match comment stated.

"I can't actually be bothered to get into the whole debate about whether Eriksen was interfering with play. I'm more annoyed about the handball. It flicked off Kane and Keano (Michael Keane) could do nothing about it."

Undaunted by the setback we responded swiftly. Spurs winger Erik Lamela lost the ball in midfield to Dave Jones who fed George Boyd. Boyd's quick pass found Ashley Barnes in the inside left position about 25 metres from goal. Taking one touch with his left foot he advanced it on to his right then hit the most spectacular rising, curling effort inside the keeper's left hand post. Absolute belter! Really made up for Barnesy who now has three Premier League goals to his tally.

Lamela the Argentinian, a £30m signing from Roma in 2013, then decided it was time to torment us. One run into the box from the right flank had so many step-overs that poor Ben Mee was hypnotised. Fortunately his ball across the face of goal was missed by Kane and fired way over by Eriksen. Not so fortunate shortly after as on 35 minutes, Lamela again cutting in from the right, let fly with an unstoppable left foot curling effort that nestled just inside Heaton's right hand post.

So, at half time trailing 2-1 but still in the game. Obviously fired up by Sean's half time talk, Danny Ings went close on two occasions shortly after the restart, both saved by Spurs keeper Lloris. As the game started to drift away from us both wingers Arfield and Boyd, who had given their all, were replaced by Kightly and Wallace. In the final minute a foul on Ings outside the box gave Wallace an opportunity to repeat his heroic point saving effort at Leicester. Unfortunately this time his powerful free kick evaded the wall but was stopped by Lloris, who turned the ball away to safety.

So another brave effort, but no points on this occasion. Speaking later on Match of the Day on BBC TV, Phil Neville opined that he didn't think we would be relegated. Presenter Gary Lineker continued in his praise for the Clarets and there seems to be a growing feeling among the pundits that we are perhaps not as much out of our depth as they thought.

A Charlie Austin hat trick enabled QPR to overcome a 2-0 deficit at home to West Brom, and took them two points above us in the table. Defeats for Leicester (away at West Ham) and Hull (at home to Swansea), left them anchored below us. Crystal Palace's defeat at Manchester City kept them level on points with us but above on goal difference.

Result – Tottenham Hotspur 2 (Kane 21, Lamela 35) – 1 Burnley (Barnes 27)

Burnley Team

Heaton, Trippier, Keane, Shackell, Mee, Arfield (Wallace 78), Marney, Jones, Boyd (Kightly 78), Ings, Barnes (Jutkiewicz 89)

Subs Not used – Gilks, Long, Reid, Chalobah

Tottenham Hotspur Team

Lloris, Walker, Fazio, Vertonghen, Davies, Mason (Stambouli 44), Bentaleb, Lamela, Eriksen (Rose 90), Kane (Soldado 83), Chadli

Subs Not used – Vorm, Chiriches, Townsend, Dembele,

Attendance – 35,681

Season Record – Played 17, Won 3, Drawn 6, Lost 8, Goals For 12, Goals Against 26, Points 15

League Position after Game 17 – 18th

The only good thing I can say about Charlie Austin's hat trick for QPR last Saturday is that it didn't half boost my fantasy football league standing. Charlie's effort amassed 17 points, which as I had selected him as my skipper, boosted his tally to 34 helping me to a respectable 65 points for Gamesweek 17, and lifting me six places in the table to 11th. Well done Charlie but I won't be hoping for any more repeats, I am going to have to transfer him out.

On the subject of transfers January 1st will see the reopening of the transfer window, and the noises coming from Turf Moor are that we are more likely to be purchasers rather than sellers. The Danny Ings contract situation remains unresolved but statements from the Co-Chairmen and manager indicate he will not be sold in January and he will remain with us till the end of the season. That resolve may well be tested shortly, obviously come summer he will be out of contract and although because of his age we will be due some compensation should he move, it will be much less than we may be able to wheedle out of some desperate club in January. Indeed Tuesday 22nd December sees a reported bid by fellow strugglers Leicester City of £7.5m. I doubt that figure will be sufficient to prise him away but it might just alert other clubs and trigger an auction. Bids in the region of £10m may well be hard to resist. I am sure that behind the scenes at Turf Moor all the possible scenarios are being studied and hopefully a replacement strategy is in place if things turn for the worse.

Amongst the names so far linked as possible targets are an Italian International striker, I hope nobody briefs him what the weather is like during a Burnley winter. Then there is a rumoured interest in a midfielder currently playing with bottom of League 2 side Tranmere Rovers. Now this guy is interesting not so much for his pedigree but certainly for his name, MAX POWER. (How could you turn him down. Ouch!!!) What a great name to go through life with, you just know he is going to be special, turbocharged even. I am going to keep a keen eye out for this one. Another name being thrown into the ring is that of Serbian midfielder Nemanja Gudelj. This fellow is currently skipper at top flight Dutch outfit AZ Alkmaar, and has nine full caps for Serbia. The fee is reported to be in the region of £8m and this would smash the Burnley transfer record, which makes it seem unlikely.

However there seems definitely to be a move within the club to extend the scope of our transfer targets further afield than just the British market. Recently we have appointed former Manchester United and Everton scout Robbie Cooke to oversee the international operation, so these recent links may not be all that farfetched.

One very good piece of Christmas cheer comes with the news that Sam Vokes is ready to enter the battle for Premier League survival. Sam out since March after rupturing knee ligaments, played his second full 90 minutes in a friendly at Turf Moor on Monday 21st December, scoring twice in a victory over Blackpool. What a timely boost for the Clarets. Merry Christmas Sam, and Merry Christmas and hopefully a Happy New Year to all fellow Clarets!

GAME 18 – Burnley v Liverpool, Friday 26th December, 15.00 hrs

I think I may have mentioned in the first Premier League diary that I do love Boxing Day games. After the dietary excesses of Christmas Day it's great to get out for some fresh air, and at this time of year that's usually what the air is. There is always a good atmosphere in the pub as people take the opportunity for a bit of male bonding and show off their new Christmas jumpers. This year is no exception.

It's a full house at the Turf and a great atmosphere. Once again the Clarets are unchanged but the returning hero, Sam Vokes, gets a place on the bench. Immediately from the kick off the Clarets are into their stride and playing at a high tempo. The crowd, fuelled by alcohol and Christmas Pud, are extremely vociferous and the team are playing with great energy and intensity.

Our visitors playing in a ghastly all yellow kit with red trim, have surprisingly set up with a rather defensive formation, opting to play the pacy Raheem Sterling in a central striking role. It's soon apparent that the game plan is to catch the Clarets with swift counter attacks, but in the early stages this is meeting with little success as they are repeatedly pushed back. The dominant Clarets have the substantial away following of 'Scousers' extremely subdued. On 14 minutes we get the sort of ill luck that seems to be a regular feature for us of late. The dancing feet of Danny Ings create sufficient space for him to get a powerful shot away from the edge of the box. Keeper Brad Jones is well beaten but the ball rebounds from the foot of the post and Ashley Barnes can only blaze the rebound over the top. Statistics reveal that the woodwork at Turf Moor has been hit more times so far this season than at any other Premier League ground. Perhaps we should get the plane out and take a bit off the thickness.

Shortly after Brad Jones decides he has seen enough and decides his day is over being replaced by Simon Mignolet. Poor old Mignolet seems to be currently suffering a loss of confidence and this cauldron atmosphere is perhaps not the best place for him to refind it. An extremely nervy display from the keeper causes some interesting moments but unfortunately no goals as the Clarets continue to batter our famous visitors. The half ends goalless but nobody could have complained if we had gone off two goals up. Once again the lack of goals is a concern and we are aware that one mistake can be costly.

As so often happens the break proves seriously disruptive to our flow. Liverpool make changes to their personnel and shape and are much improved, whilst the Clarets are a bit off the pace. A breakaway on 62 minutes sees the jet heeled Sterling outpace the Burnley defence, go round keeper Heaton and roll the ball home. What a sickener! The magic of the first half has gone and we are unable to force an equaliser and once again it's a pointless return.

Once again a game we certainly deserved something from has yielded nothing. A Liverpool team fielding a midfield of England Internationals, Gerrard, Lallana, and Henderson, and the Brazilians Lucas and Coutinho, had for long stages of the game been dominated by the Clarets more humble names. The result coupled with Hull's victory at Sunderland drops us again to next bottom. Fortunately the other teams in the relegation battle also fail with defeats for, Leicester, Crystal Palace, QPR, and West Bromwich, and the situation at the bottom remains tight.

Result – Burnley 0 – 1 Liverpool (Sterling 62)

Burnley Team

Heaton, Trippier, Keane, Shackell, Mee (Jukiewicz 90), Arfield, Marney, Jones (Wallace 83), Boyd, Ings, Barnes (Vokes 80)

Subs Not used – Gilks, Long, Reid, Kightly

Liverpool Team

Jones (Mignolet 16), Toure (Can 46), Skrtel, Sakho, Henderson, Gerrard, Lallana, Lucas, Sterling, Coutinho (Lambert 73), Markovic

Subs Not used – Moreno, Manquillo, Ojo, Balotelli,

Attendance – 21,335

Season Record – Played 18, Won 3, Drawn 6, Lost 9, Goals For 12, Goals Against 27, Points 15

League Position after Game 18 – 19th

The next game takes us to the halfway point of the season, and it couldn't be harder, Champions Manchester City away at the Etihad stadium. This game is closely followed by the away fixture at Newcastle United on New Year's Day, another toughie. Please God give us something from these two!

The early games of the season saw us finding our feet. We now seem to have sussed it and established ourselves as genuine Premier League survival contenders; however the lack of goals is costing us dear. We are not, so far, with the exception of the West Brom game, being 'hammered' as was the case in our last Premier League adventure. We are close, but not yet close enough!

On Saturday 27th December the first managerial casualty of the Premier League season is announced, the highly unlikeable Neil Warnock getting the boot at Crystal Palace. One or two other guys must be sitting rather uneasily at the moment also, notably Nigel Pearson at Leicester, Alan Irvine at WBA, and Steve Bruce at Hull. Watch this space.

GAME 19 – Manchester City v Burnley, Sunday 28th December, 15.00 hrs

Last game in 2014, what a fantastic year for all Clarets fans, and they don't come any bigger. Twelve months ago many would have hoped, but not many really believed we would on this day, be facing the current Champions of

England in a Premier League game. Games are certainly coming thick and fast and how ironic to hear managers with huge squads stuffed full of International players complaining of player fatigue. No such noises coming from Sean Dyche though and for the fifth consecutive game, just 48 hours after the last competitive fixture, we go again with the same eleven.

I must confess going into this fixture I fear the worst. City are on a run of nine consecutive league victories, with a chance here to extend it to a record equalling ten. With Chelsea dropping two points in the lunchtime game, they have the opportunity to close the gap to a single point. Who would they choose to play in this fixture other than lowly Burnley, second lowest scorers in the division and the team with the worst goal difference. City second top, Burnley second bottom. We are tailor made for them, or are we?

The game starts in expected fashion with City enjoying lots of possession and everybody awaiting the flood gates to open. The Clarets for their part do not seem overawed and are playing some decent football and keeping the City defence on their toes. Then on 23 minutes the inevitable, Nasri plays in Navas on City's right, his cut back lands with Silva who has pulled off the defenders in the box. Given too much room Silva has the opportunity to spin and find the bottom corner by Heaton's left hand post.

Oh well it was what we were all expecting anyway! Worse to come on 33 minutes as from the edge of the box Fernandinho hits a cracking curling shot with his right foot that hits the underside of the bar and goes in. Who's betting if that had been a Burnley shot it would have hit the bar and bounced down and out? No further setbacks so it's in at half time two goals down, much as expected.

Now whether it was what City had expected and a classic case of counting your chickens before they hatch, or Sean Dyche's inspirational team talk galvanised the Clarets, it was soon to be **not** 'game over'.

On 47 minutes, a Clarets attack leads to a cross shot from left of goal by Danny Ings. Joe Hart in the City net appears to have it covered but at the very last minute George Boyd applies the faintest of touches taking it beyond his reach. Fantastic! A goal at City, albeit tinged with some good fortune as TV replays show Boyd in an offside position when the ball is played. So what! It's about time we got a bit of luck for a change.

That should have been the cue for our hosts to put their foot on the gas and blow us away, but no. The game then became a much more even affair with City's Nasri forcing Heaton to a save with a 25 yarder, whilst Ings replied in similar fashion for the Clarets. Arfield has an effort blocked by Demichelis and there is growing belief amongst Clarets fans and growing unease for City. That belief is rewarded on 81 minutes as a long free kick is played up into the City penalty area. The once again impressive Ashley Barnes wins the header which hits Michael Keane up joining the attack. The ball drops kindly to our Ashley who duly dispatches a thumping shot past the helpless Hart and into the net.

Words fail me at this point as it is impossible to express the sheer joy, relief, and pride that now overwhelm me and all of a Claret persuasion. Still nine minutes plus added time to play but there's no way the Clarets are now going to let their precious point slip. The final whistle blows and the unbelievable has happened, we come away with a most unexpected away point. How magnificent was that!

Almost immediately as the game ends my phone starts to go berserk with texts from well wishing fans, many who are not Burnley supporters. Scouse Brian texts, *"Bonus point in my plan. Did not think you would get anything today. Superb result for the dressing room and fans. Confidence will be high."*

PNE Ed is less verbose with, *"Great result"*. However, my ex colleague Alison with whom I worked closely for many years is less complimentary. Al is a City convert having previously been a Bolton Wanderers fan but given up on them after being driven to despair. Who wouldn't! She feels that we have only got the point as City have been forced to make changes. How churlish is that? A club with the resources of City can't beat lowly Burnley because they are without one or two players. I think Al has been drinking too much wine made with SOUR GRAPES.

Result – Manchester City 2 (Silva 23, Fernandinho 33) – 2 Burnley (Boyd 47, Barnes 81)

Burnley Team

Heaton, Trippier, Keane, Shackell, Mee, Arfield, Marney, Jones, Boyd, Ings, Barnes

Subs Not used – Gilks, Long, Chalobah, Kightly, Wallace, Sordell, Jutkiewicz

Manchester City Team

Hart, Zabaleta, Demichelis, Mangala, Kolarov, Fernando, Fernandinho (Sinclair 88), Navas, Silva, Nasri (Lampard 76), Milner (Jovetic 62)

Subs Not used – Caballero, Sagna, Clichy, Boyata,

Attendance – 45,608

Season Record – Played 19, Won 3, Drawn 7, Lost 9, Goals For 14, Goals Against 29, Points 16

League Position after Game 19 – 19th

The draw at City leaves us next bottom in the table but once again results have gone favourably for us. The only winners down the bottom end are Leicester who enjoy a rare victory away at fellow strugglers Hull. QPR and managerless Crystal Palace play out a 0-0 draw at Loftus road, whilst West Brom lose again at Stoke City. Leicester stay bottom on 13 points, then come Burnley, Crystal Palace and Hull all on 16. Above these are West Brom on 17points and QPR with 18. Still all to play for.

The toast of Turf Moor at the moment just has to be Ashley Barnes. Our unsung hero has three Premier League goals in his last four outings, and four in total. Not bad for a player with only eleven starts and six substitute appearances so far this season. Ashley I think it is fair to say, has not always been flavour of the month with some of the fans. I suppose it was difficult for him coming into a team where Sam Vokes and Danny Ings were so prolific and popular with the crowd. To be fair I have never heard one whinge from Barnesy about the situation, and whenever called upon he has never failed to give 100% effort. This effort is now being rewarded with goals, and some of the highest quality. I personally am delighted for the player and sincerely hope that with his growing confidence he goes on to make this season truly memorable.

By the 29th December my words of clairvoyance regarding the precarious position of certain managers is beginning to ring true. I suppose a minor surprise is Alan Pardew leaving a fairly comfortable position at Newcastle

United to take on struggling Crystal Palace following Warnock's dismissal. However I suppose in view of the abuse he received at the hands of the Geordies fans early in the season the move is not so strange as seems. Let's hope the disruption at Palace will take some time to settle and more points are lost in the process. Perhaps the timing of the move is ideal for us in that it leaves Newcastle, our next opponents, with a caretaker manager only in position for the New Year's Day game.

Much less surprising is the sacking of Alan Irvine at West Bromwich. The Scotsman always seemed to be a strange appointment and at a club not renowned for patience with its managers, was an accident waiting to happen. Leicester's win at Hull on the 28th December probably bought a little time for Nigel Pearson, whilst placing his counterpart Steve Bruce at Hull under increasing pressure. The merry go round may well yet see Bruce leaving Hull for the now vacant position at Newcastle. A strange old game isn't it? I only pray that following the Coyle fiasco at Burnley five years ago, which ripped the heart out of our last Premier League campaign, that we are not involved in any of the shenanigans this time.

JANUARY

What a way to end 2014, an away draw at City, but what a way to start 2015!

GAME 20 – Newcastle United v Burnley, Thursday 1st January, 15.00 hrs

Surprise, surprise, after the hectic schedule of Christmas games, the Clarets continue their policy of non squad rotation and go again with an unchanged side for the sixth consecutive time......well at least that is for a few first half minutes.

It's almost a spectacular start as in the first minute Ings feeds Barnes whose poked shot beats the keeper only to rebound off the post. Yes it's another woodwork incident for our trick shot experts. As usual our ill luck is further compounded by falling behind to a set piece goal from a corner on 15 minutes. However our discomfort is short lived as our hosts generously decide to even things up within four minutes. Newcastle central defender Dummett, under pressure from Ings, classically heads over his advancing goalkeeper to level the score. Good lad!

Sandwiched in between the goals is the loss of Jason Shackell to injury, a major blow, replaced by Kevin Long. The Magpies re-establish their lead on 26 minutes with an excellent 25 yard strike by Colback before further ill fortune hits the Clarets. Shackell's replacement Long lasts only 20 minutes before also succumbing to injury, and then Marney has to be replaced, victim of a viral illness. Newcastle continue to play some excellent football and hold the lead to go in 2-1 at the interval.

If the first half was eventful then the second half was phenomenal! It's almost one way traffic as Ings hits the crossbar and sees Barnes head the rebound against the post. Not to be outdone Ben Mee joins the fun seeing his header rebound off the crossbar. Would you believe it four woodwork interventions and still we trail! However there's no stopping the rampant Clarets now as Danny Ings levels the scores with a flicked header on 66 minutes.

Against the run of play the Magpies regain the lead on 78 minutes as Sissoko profits from a complete miscue in front of goal to fire home. After what had gone before, the loss of three players, and four timber mishaps, most teams would have decided it was not their day. Not these Clarets, no way will they be beaten as George Boyd levels on 86 minutes with a left foot shot across Newcastle keeper Jay Alnwick. The whistle blows for full time and we have an incredible 3-3 draw and another precious away point to take home.

I prayed after the Boxing Day fixture that God would give us something from the two difficult away fixtures coming up. My prayers have been answered and in what style! Who would have believed we would run in five goals in those two games? What odds would the bookies have given on that? The spirit in this team is unbelievable and the never say die attitude is winning admirers both near and far.

Result – Newcastle United 3 (Taylor 15, Colback 26, Sissoko 78) – 3 Burnley (Dummett o.g. 19, Ings 66, Boyd 86)

Burnley Team

Heaton, Trippier, Keane, Shackell (Long 17) (Reid 37), Mee, Arfield, Marney (Kightly 32), Jones, Boyd, Ings, Barnes

<u>Subs Not used</u> – Gilks, Wallace, Sordell, Jutkiewicz

Newcastle United Team

Alnwick, Janmaat, Taylor (Williamson 60), Colocinni, Dummett, Tiote, Colback, Perez, Sissoko, Gouffran (Haidara 71), Riviere (Armstrong 57)

<u>Subs Not used</u> – Woodman, Santon, Cabella, Anita,

Attendance – 51,761

Season Record – Played 20, Won 3, Drawn 8, Lost 9, Goals For 17, Goals Against 32, Points 17

League Position after Game 20 – 19th

Newcastle caretaker manager John Carver was unstinting in his praise of the Clarets after the game:

"I don't think I have been involved in such a game of, to quote the old cliché, two halves.

"We controlled the game and played really good football in the first half but the second half was pretty awful.

"I thought we had got out of jail (with Sissoko's goal) but they should have won the game. They were the better team over 90 minutes. They caused us more problems than we did them."

Claret's boss Sean Dyche was his usual level headed self:

"We had to make three changes and it was all going off in that first half.

We had to deal with it and after that I thought we were outstanding, right to the death when we were still looking to score.

The belief was still there and I thought some of the quality of our play was exceptional.

Going into Christmas people said we might not win a game but we have taken five points from five teams in the top 10 and two in the top four. We still need to get more points but we are going in the right direction and the performance levels are very high."

Monday 5th January is FA Cup Third round day for Burnley FC! Gone are the days of Saturday 3.00 pm kick offs for this ancient and noble competition. The competition is now seen by many Premier League clubs as almost an inconvenience. Once upon a time fans like myself would eagerly await FA cup draws, memorising the numbers of the balls that represented our own and the glamour clubs, and praying for a home tie. Now for many there is but a flicker of interest as the 'big boys' of the Premier League concentrate on more lucrative Champions League and Europa Cup competitions.

Our opponents this time are none other than our old adversaries, Tottenham Hotspur. Over the years some memorable cup ties have been played between these two clubs, principally the 1962 Cup Final won by Spurs 3-1 at Wembley. This despite a 50th minute equaliser scored by the Clarets Jimmy Robson, the 100th goal to be scored in a Wembley final, and what would have been a second equaliser by the same player given questionably offside. In recent years no Claret will forget the Carling Cup semi final in 2009. Trailing 4-1 from the first leg at White Hart Lane, the magnificent Clarets staged a remarkable comeback to lead 3-0 at Turf Moor going into extra time. The same score after the added 30 minutes would have seen the Clarets, then still a Championship side, on their way to Wembley again courtesy of their away goal. Cruelly on the night the gallant Clarets ran out of steam and two goals in the last couple of minutes by Tottenham ended the dream. Let's hope tonight is payback time.

Team selection for this tie should prove interesting with a good measure of how seriously the two teams are taking the competition. An in-form Spurs side, fresh from a 5-3 victory over title favourites Chelsea, have lofty ambitions of a Champions League place currently sitting fifth in the Premier League. They also have a continued interest in this season's Europa Cup and may therefore decide their priorities lie elsewhere. For ourselves we picked up injuries to Shackell, and his replacement Long, in the New Years Day fixture whilst Marney and Vokes were also affected by a viral illness. The situation regarding on loan central defender Michael Keane, very impressive in the recent run, is unclear. Will his parent club, Manchester United allow him to become Cup tied by playing ahead of a possible recall to Old Trafford? With a vital relegation battle looming at home to QPR on Saturday, dare I suggest that Sean Dyche may field a weakened team?

Saturday 2nd January saw the reopening of the transfer window, and within minutes the rumours are circulating of potential signings. By the 5th January, these include: Callum McManaman (Wigan), Henri Lansbury (Nottingham Forest), John Obita (Reading), Stuart Armstrong (Dundee United), Tom Lees (Sheffield Wednesday). Whether there is any substance in any of these rumours remains to be seen, however the first definite move in the window is a return of Nathaniel Chalobah to parent club Chelsea. Unfortunately for one reason or another the player has had very little game time during his loan spell and it has to be said that the move never really worked out.

FA CUP 3rd Round – Burnley v Tottenham Hotspur, Monday 5th January, 19.45 hrs

I mentioned in the preamble that these two sides had in the past produced some memorable cup ties. Can I just say now that this was not one of them!

Spurs make seven changes to the team that beat Chelsea but their replacements could still be billed as 'big names'. The Clarets make just the two changes, the injured Jason Shackell is replaced by Danny Lafferty with Ben Mee moving to the central defensive position. Dave Jones is out and his place goes to Michael Kightly with Scott Arfield moving to the central midfield berth. Manchester United grant on loan Michael Keane permission to play, a move which hopefully augurs well for an extension to the player's loan, or a permanent deal.

There is a strange atmosphere inside the ground with only three sides open, the Jimmy McIlroy stand being completely unsold due to a lack of interest. There is however a good following of Spurs fans, particularly for a Monday night in January, and they constitute approximately a quarter of the depleted crowd.

What can I say about the first half? Played in a sterile atmosphere, neither side could manage a shot at goal in the entire half. Dour was the only word for it, or maybe not, perhaps dire would be a more appropriate description. Spurs were neat and tidy in possession but with absolutely no cutting edge. We for our part were ponderous in the build up and completely one dimensional. A rating for first half entertainment value would be at best 3/10.

The second half starts with our visitors sensing a victory is theirs for the taking. Playing a more expansive game following the introduction of 'flavour of the month' Harry Kane, whose two goals against Chelsea have him brim full of confidence, the game is definitely moving in their favour. It's no surprise as they go ahead on 56 minutes as Chadli converts a left wing cut back by Davies.

Sensing the game slipping away Sean Dyche pulls his own master stroke, introducing Sam Vokes. The returning superhero now needs to inspire his colleagues for another mighty effort. Almost immediately the mood starts to lift and we are on the front foot and going forward. On 73 minutes Big Sam finds space in the box to convincingly put away a right wing cross from Michael Kightly. A fairytale return and how pleased are all Clarets for the lad.

It's a much more open game now and much improved on the first half. Half chances go begging at both ends, probably the best fluffed by current 'Golden Boy' Kane. However the game finishes 1-1, which is probably the last result either side wanted adding further congestion to a crowded fixture list. The winners of the replay will be at home to Leicester City in another all Premier League tie.

Result – Burnley 1 (Vokes 73) – 1 Tottenham Hotspur (Chadli 56)

Burnley Team

Heaton, Trippier, Keane, Mee , Lafferty, Kightly, Arfield, Marney, Boyd (Wallace 79), Ings (Sordell 79), Barnes (Vokes 60)

Subs Not used – Gilks, Reid, O'Neill, Jutkiewicz

Tottenham Hotspur Team

Vorm, Chiriches, Fazio, Vertonghen, Davies, Chadli, Dembele, Stambouli (Kane 45), Eriksen, Paulinho, Soldado (Townsend 67)

Subs Not used – Friedel, Dier, Naughton, Capoue, Onomah

Attendance – 9,348

On Monday 5th January we learn that the luckless Kevin Long, injured after 20 minutes of his Premier League debut, has suffered a cruciate ligament injury to his knee and his season is over. I say luckless but perhaps not, Kevin whose contract was up in the summer is revealed to have recently signed a new deal that will tie him to the club till the end of the 2016/17 season. This will ensure he continues to get the best possible treatment and rehabilitation for his injury. A sobering thought perhaps for Danny Ings! He seems intent on running his contract down to the summer when he will become a free agent, however a similar injury between now and then could seriously scupper his plans.

Great news announced on 8th January as it is revealed that on loan defender Michel Keane, has signed a permanent deal with the club. His three and a half year contract will now take him to the end of the 2017/18 season. Keane has impressed since establishing himself in the side following Michael Duff's injury and already looks the natural successor for 'Duffo'. The fee is rumoured around the £3m mark which should represent good value for an England U21 player just about to turn 22 this week. Already he is being mentioned as another Gary Cahill and if he lives up to his early promise he will become a key asset.

Two crucial home games in the league coming up next as we meet fellow strugglers QPR, and Crystal Palace. First up are QPR, who despite being two points to the good of the Clarets, have yet to collect an away point this season. An unusual game for us is this as we seem to start slight favourites! Let's hope the game continues our unbeaten run in 2015.

GAME 21 – Burnley v Queens Park Rangers, Saturday 10th January, 15.00 hrs

In many quarters this Game was billed as a 'must win' affair against our relegation rivals. QPR sat two points above us in the league but interestingly all their points had been won at home, with a truly dreadful away record of played nine, lost nine. Ahead of this game I saw a thread on the Claretsmad messageboard suggesting that some Clarets fan had insulted 'The God of Crossbars'. Caernarfon_Claret was referring to the number of times the woodwork had intervened to prevent us scoring. I couldn't help but hope that this particular God would today see fit to smile on us.

Team news revealed two changes; Jason Shackell fit again returning to central defence, with Ben Mee returning to left back and Danny Lafferty excluded. Dave Jones was recovered from his viral infection and returned in centre midfield, Scott Arfield reverting to a wide midfield role, and Michael Kightly back to the bench. Our old hero, now in the eyes of many fans turned villain, Charlie Austin returned as by far the visitor's main threat.

A pretty good turnout by the home support, clearly buoyed by recent results, but a pretty poor effort by the visitors. Conditions were far from ideal after a night of heavy rain and strong winds but I have to say that the pitch is now unrecognisable from the quagmires previous generations of Clarets had to play on. What would Ralph Coates have made of these lush green acres! Would Brian O'Neil have been able to perform his sliding tackles that carried him half the length of the pitch?

Backed by a noisy home crowd we are soon into our stride and George Boyd gets the first sight at goal but finishes tamely. Not long to wait for the opener though and what a beauty! Scott Arfield receiving a throw on the left flank spots an opportunity, bursting infield between two defenders and then circumnavigating the burly Richard Dunne, he curls a right foot beauty just inside Robert Green's left hand post. Twelve minutes gone and ahead, we couldn't have wished for a better start.

Clearly stung by this reverse QPR attempt to find a way back into the game and who else but Charlie Austin almost does it as he hits the post from a right wing cut back. 'The God of Crossbars (and goalposts)' has come to our rescue. Somebody or something has clearly appeased 'the Gods'. Unfortunately Charlie is not to be denied, on 33 minutes he controls a ball into the box, and steps away from Shackell. Before he can shoot Dean Marney sticks out a leg and Austin gleefully goes down over it. Made a meal of it but we couldn't really deny it. As expected Austin tucks the penalty away in the bottom corner with his usual aplomb, for his 14th goal of the season.

Our despondency however is short lived as Ashley Barnes lifts the ball forward in the direction of Ings. Danny's sharp brain and quick feet bring the bouncing ball down on the edge of the Ranger's box. Touching the ball away from Caulker and then turning past Dunne, he rolls it past keeper Green and into the net despite the efforts of Clint Hill to clear. It's edge of the seat stuff now and the Clarets lead at half time 2-1.

The second half sees QPR giving it a go but the Clarets mopping it up and looking to strike on the counter. Several chances come and go with the industrious Boyd outstanding. Ings and Barnes go close, but Danny is having a frustrating afternoon often making the opening but then either overdoing it, or not spotting a better placed colleague. Barnes has a 'goal' disallowed for a foul on the keeper, TV replays later show that in fact the initial foul is by Hill on Barnes and a penalty was probably the correct decision. The Clarets close the game out with just the one scare as Tom Heaton brilliantly touches over a Caulker header from a late corner.

A bit of late drama as QPR players applaud their fans as they leave the field. A few irate Londoners decide to vent their spleen against Richard Dunne in particular. Now Dunne is a man mountain and the last person I would choose to pick on. It all gets a bit heated with Clint Hill deciding to give as good back, and then what must be the strangest sight in football as serial troublemaker Joey Barton becomes the peacemaker! Clearly all is not well between fans and team at QPR but the opposite is certainly the case at Burnley as a jubilant crowd head for home and a study of the league table.

Result – Burnley 2 (Arfield 12, Ings 37) – 1 Queens Park Rangers (Austin 33 pen)

Burnley Team

Heaton, Trippier, Keane, Shackell, Mee, Arfield, Marney, Jones, Boyd, Ings, Barnes (Vokes 73)

<u>Subs Not used</u> – Gilks, Reid, Duff, Kightly, Wallace, Jutkiewicz

Queens Park Rangers Team

Green, Isla, Dunne, Caulker, Hill (Traore 75), Vargas (Zarate 76),Henry (Zamora 69), Barton, Fer, Austin, Taarabt

<u>Subs Not used</u> – McCarthy, Onuoha, Mutch, Phillips,

Attendance – 17,523

Season Record – Played 21, Won 4, Drawn 8, Lost 9, Goals For 19, Goals Against 33, Points 20

League Position after Game 21 – 17th

Saturday's round of fixtures leaves the league table with an intriguing look. No more than 5 points separate 12th placed Everton from bottom placed Leicester. The Clarets sit just above the relegation places, three points ahead of Leicester, and one ahead of QPR and Hull City. We are level on points with Sunderland and Crystal Palace, one behind West Bromwich Albion, and two away from Aston Villa and Everton. That's what they call tight!

The win against QPR means that we now equal the points tally of 20 gained from 21 matches achieved in the last Premier League campaign 2009/10. Quite an achievement considering only four points came from the first 10 games.

There is however a massive difference between the mood in the camp this January compared to that of 2010.

Following the defection of Coyle (can't bear to give him the dignity of a first name) to neighbours and relegation rivals Bolton, taking with him the entire backroom staff, the fans were distraught. The transfer window was open and all the targets lined up by Coyle followed him to Bolton. In addition the appointment of Brian Laws to replace him was universally unpopular.

Compare that to this time where the Clarets are on the back of a four match unbeaten run (three League, one FA Cup) including an away draw at the reigning Champions! Belief is what now fills the true Clarets breast. Whilst we are realistic enough to know there will be a real battle ahead, we stick with Dyche's mantra of 'one game at a time' and look to accrue sufficient points for survival. Interestingly in 2010 the next 12 games yielded a paltry further four points, surely we will better that this time round.

FA CUP 3rd Round Replay – Tottenham Hotspur v Burnley, Wednesday 14th January, 20.00 hrs

This was the game neither side really wanted. For Spurs yet another game in an overcrowded fixture programme as they chase honours on several fronts. For the Clarets an unnecessary distraction ahead of Saturday's relegation six pointer with Crystal Palace.

Sean Dyche's feelings about the game, whilst still maintaining that we go with our strongest side for all games, I think can be judged by the starting line up. No less than five regular starters are omitted from the starting eleven, Shackell, Marney, Boyd, Ings, and Barnes.

Waiting for the game to start I settle down on the sofa and establish my mission control. This consists of Tablet, opened at Claretsmad, and BBC Sport websites, Mobile Phone, and iPod to receive commentary from Radio Lancashire.

Before I have time to switch on the ipod my phone buzzes into action with a text message. This is from fellow Claret John W, who cryptically texts *"Bugger me"*. Frantically I search for the cause of this outburst. A quick look at the BBC Sport website reads zero shots at goal by either side, hmmm! Then as the page refreshes, GOAL! Marvin Sordell. Fantastic. As I fiddle with the iPod to get Radio Lancs, a second buzz on the mobile, *"Bugger, Bugger me"*. It can't be, but oh yes it can, the good old Beeb have it, GOAL! Ross Wallace. Unbelievable.

Now only a Burnley fan could feel uneasy about his side going 2-0 up inside eight minutes, but that's what I felt. Fears well founded as on 10 minutes, GOAL! Paulinho, and text from John W, *"could finish 27-28"*. Thankfully as we approach half time in a game going end to end there is no further goal action. As I contemplate going into half time with a one goal lead, wouldn't you just know it an equaliser with a shot from outside the box. A bad time to concede that; sending our hosts into the break having overcome our two goal lead and handing them the momentum.

Even worse early in the second period as we concede a soft goal from a corner on 49 minutes and three minutes later it's effectively game over as Spurs notch a fourth. Thankfully, though it's now practically one way traffic, there are no more goals and we emerge at least with our dignity intact if out of the Cup at the first attempt.

I think all Clarets fans would settle for an early exit in the Cup if it helps our chances of Premier League survival, so not too much disappointment on the night. On the plus side some valuable game time for some of the fringe squad members, and full 90 minute run outs for returning injured players Vokes, and Duff. Let's quickly put this one behind us and concentrate our energies on Saturday's battle to come.

Result – Tottenham Hotspur 4 (Paulinho 10, Capoue 45, Chiriches 49, Rose 52) – 2 Burnley (Sordell 3, Wallace 8)

Burnley Team

Heaton, Trippier (Reid 67), Keane, Duff, Mee, Kightly, Arfield, Jones (Marney 76), Wallace (Boyd 88), Sordell, Vokes

Subs Not used – Gilks, Lafferty, Ings, Barnes,

Tottenham Hotspur Team

Vorm, Chiriches (Dier 80), Vertonghen, Kaboul, Davies, Capoue, Stambouli, Townsend (Onomah 76), Paulinho, Rose (Chadli 59), Soldado

Subs Not used – Lloris, Kane, Naughton, Dembele

Attendance – 24,367

GAME 22 – Burnley v Crystal Palace, Saturday 17th January, 15.00 hrs

It's a cruel game! Just as you get your hopes up the football Gods contrive to smash them back down again.

Much of the pre match discussion over a couple of pints of Copper Dragon Brewery's, Golden Pippin, revolved around a comment made by a Clarets Player commentator during the cup replay with Spurs. During the game he came out with a gem, *"Rose turned like a tramp on a kipper"*. Now what exactly did he mean by that? Did Rose leave a bad smell? Or did he seize on the chance like a hungry man devouring a smoked fish? Whatever, it was a phrase worthy of Stan Ternent in his prime.

Enough of that let's cut to the game. The Clarets return to the usual line up after Wednesday's rush of blood by Sean, all the absentees are fit and back in the side. Once again it's a dream start in this relegation battle. On 12 minutes a Trippier corner from the left clears Palace keeper Speroni, and is headed home by a most unlikely scorer, Ben Mee. Just what we needed.

Even better on 16 minutes as Trippier belts a clearance in the general direction of our left wing. Clear favourite for the ball is Palace full back Ward, but in hot pursuit is Scotty Arfield who catches the dithering Ward on the left touchline. Now had I been Ward I would have simply rolled the ball out for a throw in, but not this lad Premier League players don't do that. Scotty promptly *"turns on him like a tramp on a kipper"*. As the ball stays in play on the line the two protagonists engage in a quick grapple off the pitch as Ward belatedly senses the danger. Scotty emerges triumphant from the tussle and plays in the onrushing Danny Ings, who gratefully fires low into the net. Sixteen minutes and two up in a 'must win' game, what could be better?

Unfortunately that's where it all starts to unravel. Palace decide they are not here to be smoked like kippers and embark on a series of attacks on our goal. Danger man Wilfried Zaha swaps flanks with Dwight Gayle and on 28 minutes the deficit is halved. From a cross by Zaha Palace midfielder McArthur has a shot brilliantly saved by Heaton but the rebound is straight to Gayle who fires home. Gone now is our early assuredness and we are struggling to create anything. Buoyed by the goal Palace are in the ascendancy and giving our defence a torrid time. Off at half time 2-1 up I can't help but remark that there is a long way to go in this one yet.

My half time unease is quickly justified as on 48 minutes the retreating defence allow Jason Puncheon to run deep at the heart and from 25 yards hit a low drive in the bottom corner for the equaliser. As we continue to struggle to get a foothold in the game, despite a Michael Keane header cleared off the line, there are ominous signs. Palace introduce Glenn Murray and the striker hits a post soon after his entrance. As the clock races towards full time it looks like we will have to settle for a point. Then tragedy, Puncheon swings a ball in from the right, Trippier is left woefully short of cover with two players lurking behind him. As the cross clears 'Tripps' it falls to the sure footed Gayle who buries his second of the day past Heaton.

That's it for the action and what started so joyfully ends tragically leaving us all muted and despondent as we trudge home to kick the cat. The only crumb of comfort is that most of our rivals have also lost. There are home defeats for Leicester, QPR, and Aston Villa, whilst Sunderland lose away. On the Sunday Hull City are 3-0 losers at West Ham and that result means they stay in the last relegation spot, one point behind the Clarets.

Result – Burnley 2 (Mee 12, Ings 16) – 3 Crystal Palace (Gayle 28, 87) (Puncheon 48)

Burnley Team

Heaton, Trippier, Keane, Shackell, Mee, Arfield, Marney, Jones (Wallace 90), Boyd (Sordell 90), Ings, Barnes (Vokes 73)

Subs Not used – Gilks, Reid, Duff, Kightly,

Crystal Palace Team

Speroni, Ward, Dann, Delaney, Kelly (Mariappa 83), Ledley,McArthur, Puncheon, Gayle, Sanogo (Murray 79), Zaha (Guedioura 70)

Subs Not used – Hennessey, Hangeland, Campbell, Thomas,

Attendance – 17,782

Season Record – Played 22, Won 4, Drawn 8, Lost 10, Goals For 21, Goals Against 36, Points 20

League Position after Game 22 – 17th

Dear Diary, it's now Saturday 24th January and it seems a while since I last made an entry. The simple reason for that is that there would appear to be precious little of note happening down Turf Moor way.

Every day I scan the papers and the Claretsmad website for rumours of imminent signings, but apart from a tenuous link to the West Bromwich midfielder Graham Dorrans, nothing! Even the stories of a queue of Premier League sides and some European teams pursuing Danny Ings seem to have dried up. The 'window' has been open now for the best part of three weeks but apart from the signing of former loanee Michael Keane, zilch!

I can only assume that behind the scenes there is frantic activity going on which will culminate in a last day spending spree that will rock us to the core. I suspect that deals are in the pipeline but that these are dependent on the selling clubs being able to satisfactorily conclude their own transfer business. A creative centre midfielder, would in my humble opinion, be the minimum requirement if we are to be successful in our goal of maintaining our hard won Premier League spot.

It's FA Cup 4th round day today so a blank Saturday for us on the playing front following our early demise at the hands of Tottenham Hotspur. It's probably not a bad thing as it will give our lads the chance of a much needed breather and the opportunity to heal some of the bumps and bruises we must be carrying. Another huge battle awaits, away to relegation rivals Sunderland, and we will need to be in peak physical condition for that one in a week's time.

On the walking front last Tuesday saw a very local walk for me as the Burnley Contingent hosted a Dotcom walk from on my own doorstep in Briercliffe. Led by the intrepid Sherpa Ed Walton, the walk took an eight mile circular route from St James Church in Harle Syke through snow covered fields via Catlow, to Walton's Spire, then back via Coldwell and Cockden. What a magnificent day for walking and the views from Walton's Spire were incredible.

Even the 'Flatlanders' of Preston and South Ribble were moved to grudgingly praise the outstanding scenery. Group leader Bob Clare (ex Barden School teacher) in his weekly address to the troops reported:

"It is going to take us all who were out on Tuesday sometime to come down from the 'Walker's high' we experienced. Those of us not of the Burnley Contingent are in a state of shock because we did not think it was possible for the words 'Burnley' and 'beautiful' to go into the same sentence. Yet that was the experience we had walking through the snow covered landscape of the South Pennines. So thank

you the Burnley Contingent and Edward for leading us on a superlative walk".

Well said Bob! I know it must have been hard for him to lavish such praise having the backdrop of Penwortham Power Station, and the murky waters of the River Ribble as the outstanding features on his own doorstep!

Tuesday 27th January is the Dotcom Walkers 7th Annual awards ceremony. It's a bit like the Oscar's, and the Bafta's, but without the glamour! After a short walk on Longridge fell (about 4.5 miles) we all reconvened at what is becoming the Dotcomers clubhouse, the Corporation Arms, Longridge. It's a bit unusual this year in that we are holding the ceremony in January instead of as is customary, December. The delay this year being down to an Antipodean adventure around Christmas time by Group Leader Bob Clare.

In his pre awards oration Bob did let slip that January may well become the favoured month, because in his own words; *"Some great offers in Poundland in January"*. I think readers that should give you an insight into how seriously the awards are valued! All the usual awards featured, Oldest Dotcomer of the Year, Youngest Dotcomer of the Year, Most walks completed, and the much coveted, Moll of the Year! Some pretty nasty catfighting goes on over that one. All this accompanied by as always, excellent fayre ensured another grand day out.

On Thursday 29th June it is reported that Burnley have had an offer of around £1.5m rejected by Dundee United for midfielder Stuart Armstrong. This is subsequently confirmed by Sean Dyche who goes on to say that the rejection now ends the interest in the player. Apparently he was seen as a 'development player', i.e. one for the future, not our Premier

League saviour. The identity of this guy is as yet to be revealed.

It's now Friday 30th January and as the transfer window closes on Monday 2nd February at 11.00 pm, activity is understandably hotting up. The big rumour of the day, fuelled by the national press and the BBC, is that Danny Ings is to be sold to Liverpool and loaned back to us for the rest of the season.

On first reflection it seems there may be some merit in this as he will 'walk' at the end of the season as a free agent. What's in it for Danny though? He can go at the end of the season and his new club will, it is anticipated, only have to shell out circa £3m in compensation. This will mean Danny is in a stronger position to negotiate his own terms.

What's in it for Liverpool? They will have to pay over the odds for a player that they won't have till next season, and who they could sign come summer for a fraction of the cost. It would however guarantee them the player and stop rival bidders.

The positive for Burnley would be that if as rumoured, other clubs are keenly interested (Spurs, Newcastle, Southampton all mentioned), it may now start a bidding war pushing up his price to our advantage.

As the 'Ings to Liverpool' thread surges past the 100 mark on Claretsmad, all conjecture is halted by the issue of a club statement:

Following growing media speculation Burnley Football Club would like to reiterate their stance regarding Danny Ings.

Ings has been heavily linked in the past 24 hours with a permanent move to Liverpool, with the suggestion that he would then be loaned back to the club for the remainder of the campaign

This kind of deal is prohibited by the Premier League under rule V7 which states that a player cannot be purchased and loaned back between Premier League clubs in the same transfer window.

Chief Executive Lee Hoos said: *"This type of move would violate Premier League rule V7 regarding transfers so simply cannot happen.*

"This is the last time we will be making any comments regarding the player's future.

"Over the course of the window, the player himself, Sean Dyche and the chairman have made it clear he won't be going anywhere and we consider that the end of the matter."

So back to action on the pitch tomorrow, and its Sunderland at the Stadium of Light, in another relegation 'six pointer'. After last week's lay off we will hopefully be primed and ready to go.

GAME 23 – Sunderland v Burnley, Saturday 31st January, 15.00 hrs

The day starts well with a convincing 3-0 away victory by Newcastle at relegation rivals Hull City. How much longer can Steve Bruce hang on there? This consigns Hull to a spot in the drop zone whatever happens in the other games today. A win for us would take us four points clear of the 'toothless tigers'.

Sunderland has not been a great place for us in recent years and it is 43 years since we last managed a victory there. You can probably make that 44 now after today's faltering effort.

Two first half goals, one from Connor Wickham, his first for almost two months, and one from the recently signed Jermain Defoe, his first for the club, were sufficient to defeat the Clarets.

A better second half performance but with no real threat saw us come away empty handed again. Interestingly in the second period Dyche chose to substitute the two players who have probably been our most influential attackers this season, Ings and Boyd.

Dyche referring to the growing transfer interest in Ings went on to say:

"I think all the speculation has affected him. It was almost too much and I wasn't going to play him at one point. I took him off because it has affected him. Hopefully the rumours will die down and he can crack on and be a Burnley football player."

For the 9th consecutive Premier League game Burnley named the same starting eleven, highly unusual for this league. Whether this is a reflection of the boss's confidence in his team, or down to the lack of quality depth in the squad, is one that only he can answer. However with the last day of the transfer window almost upon us, many fans are once again disappointed by the lack of incoming players. It has long been apparent that the squad is woefully short of central midfielders, with only Marney, and Jones recognised options. Failure to bring in at least cover for these two would be seen by many as a major mistake with survival in a very congested bottom half of the table still a distinct possibility.

We are becoming far too predictable and the injection of a bit more creativity is a necessity as we approach a very difficult series of matches. In the last two games we have lost to two teams very much involved in the relegation battle and this is a worryingly similar situation to that which occurred in our last Premier League season. Let's hope Monday 2nd February sees us not only hang on to Danny Ings but also bring in one or two new faces to freshen up the squad.

Result – Sunderland 2 (Wickham 20, Defoe 34) – 0 Burnley

Burnley Team

Heaton, Trippier, Keane, Shackell, Mee, Arfield, Marney, Jones, Boyd (Wallace 61), Ings (Jutkiewicz 61), Barnes (Vokes 76)

Subs Not used – Gilks, Reid, Duff, Kightly,

Sunderland Team

Pantilimon, Reveillere, Vergini, O'Shea, Van Aanholt, Bridcutt, Gomez, Larsson, Wickham (Graham 75), Defoe (Fletcher 75), Johnson (Alvarez 86)

Subs Not used – Mannone, Jones, Coates, Giaccherini,

Attendance – 44,022

Season Record – Played 23, Won 4, Drawn 8, Lost 11, Goals For 21, Goals Against 38, Points 20

League Position after Game 23 – 17th

On the brighter side results generally went well for us on the day leaving us still precariously just outside the dead men. Defeats for QPR (away at Stoke), and Leicester (away at Manchester United), coupled with the Hull result kept the bottom three as it was. West Bromwich, our next opponents were thumped 3-0 at home by Spurs leaving them just two points ahead of us. On Sunday, Aston Villa were thrashed 5-0 at Arsenal keeping them also just two points ahead. Sunderland's win lifted them three points in front of us, level with Crystal Palace who also lost for the first time under Alan Pardew, 1-0 at home to Everton.

FEBRUARY

Well it's the big day, Transfer Deadline day, and Clarets fans all around the world wait with baited breath to see what will transpire.

The early morning speculation has Graham Dorrans of West Brom the prime target. There are also still suggestions that the deal for Stuart Armstrong at Dundee United may not be dead.

On the negative side Radio 5 Live are reporting a rumour from a 'good source' that Danny Ings has signed a pre contract agreement with Real Sociedad. The Spaniards are now managed by ex Everton and Manchester United boss, David Moyes, who has certainly been a visitor at Turf Moor recently. This deal if true would be a bitter blow in terms of financial compensation when the player leaves. The common feeling is that should he leave for another English club, compensation of around £2-3m could be expected. However if Europe is his destination this figure could be as low as £300K.

The next player linked is Bradley Johnson at Norwich City, and the general concencus is that he would be just our type, being a midfielder who 'likes to get stuck in'.

By late morning Burnley FC are denying knowledge of any agreement between Ings and Real Sociedad and reaffirming that the player will be here till his contract expires. Reports in the media are adamant that Liverpool are still trying to get a deal done today for the player to avoid a tribunal in the summer.

At 12 o'clock our old friend, journalist Alan Nixon, friend of disgraced ex manager Owen Coyle is tweeting that our search for new players is bordering on frantic. Dorrans is too dear, Armstrong's price is too high, and now there is a new bid in for Henri Lansbury of Nottingham Forest a previous target during the summer.

As we move into early afternoon Sky Sports News reveal that Dorrans is on his way to Norwich City for £4m. There's no way the Clarets value the player at that price so it looks like another one biting the dust!

19.00 hours, only four hours to go and still no incoming. Panic is mounting on the Claretsmad messageboard and blame for the failure to land targets is being liberally dished about. God knows what will happen if we reach 23.00 hours and the situation remains as is. The latest rumour is that we have offered £2m for Lansbury, will that be tempting enough?

Exciting stuff is this! Now being reported that Dorrans to Norwich includes a player going in the other direction and the deal is now valued at £5m. I wonder if that player might be Bradley Johnson just to rub salt in the wounds!

At 22.00 hours I have had enough of the suspense and decide to call it a day. I go to bed hoping but not really expecting that someone/anyone, now I am getting frantic, will sign. My expectations are fully justified next morning when a quick check of the internet reveals no incoming activity. A late bid is reported for Matt Jarvis at West Ham United but it amounts to nothing.

How disappointing was that! My immediate reaction is that this failure to add to the squad may well have scuppered our season. Driving through town I notice a headline board for the Lancashire Evening Telegraph which is boldly proclaiming, all the Clarets deadline day action. I can't see that generating many sales, the article won't even run to a paragraph!

The whole transfer window saga has left the supporters feeling decidedly 'flat' and the mood is almost one of dejection. It feels almost akin to the period where Owen Coyle deserted us in our hour of need in 2010/11. Disappointed would be an understatement. What are the recruitment staff at Turf Moor doing to justify their salaries? Surely following the failures in the summer window lessons would have been learnt, but apparently not.

One would have assumed that in the period between the 'windows' realistic targets would have been identified. Why all the last minute brinksmanship? The window has been open for a month! It seems incredible that of all the professional footballers out there, we could not find one or two affordable one's that would strengthen our position and give us more options.

If the fans are despondent I sincerely hope that the feeling is not shared by the management and playing staff. I'm sure that Sean Dyche, whatever his personal feelings are, will continue to project a positive approach and attempt to lift the players ahead of a crucial game against West Bromwich Albion.

In typical Dyche fashion and in true Churchillian spirit the boss rouses the troops ahead of the game:

"I've come to value the people here and there has been so much positivity recently that I've got a feeling Burnley people get

over their disappointment quickly and realise what we are and get right behind it. I'll be amazed if that doesn't happen.

"I will say that I think myself and the club are always honest with the fans. We always are, and it's not an easy situation for us, even more so at this level.

"Signing players often comes down to the numbers and it's hard for the club and the board to write off large chunks of money when the club going forward might not be able to deal with that. It has to be measured, but I can assure the fans that we have been out there looking, despite the story of this email to agents. We all know the movers and shakers in the market and that was to prompt any last minute moves.

"We are giving honesty, not hiding behind the market. We said its tough and we have tried and tried, but there has to be a level within reason because otherwise the club will fall into big trouble in a very, very short future. That's the challenge and it's a tough one.

Referring to the transfer deals where the plug was pulled on us at the last minute Sean added:

"That can happen, but I will remind everyone that we have a fantastic group of people here and we are 17th in the highest level of world football.

"Let's not forget where we are, what we are doing and what got us here. Let's remember what this club is built on and the pride we've all jointly taken in how we go about our business. So before anyone gets this weird mindset of negativity, let's remember the positive journey and the people who have been key in that, not just the players, but the fans too.

"After ten games we hadn't won a game, but our fans were amazing. We're now 17th so how are there suddenly these question marks? They are key markers and there is a bigger picture. We want to operate in the market, we made that clear. We couldn't but we will look to do it again.

"Let's not forget what has got us here and that's a group of players giving everything for this football club. Let's also not forget what we are, a fantastic, deep, rich football club full of history, so let's protect that, safeguard it and keep working hard at that one club mentality because that is vital.

"It's one of our unique selling points, an aligned club all pulling in the right direction. That's a powerful thing and it needs to be protected."

That makes me feel a little ashamed of my earlier negativity and I shall consider myself well and truly rebuked. Now I have my head up again and looking forward to the WBA game.

This week we are once again a Sky TV featured match so we move to a Sunday 12.00 kick off time. I ask you, is that any sort of time to play a football game?

Anyway this gives us a chance to see how our relegation rivals fare in the Saturday fixtures. Generally speaking it's good news as Leicester are beaten at home by resurgent Crystal Palace, QPR also go down at home to a very late goal from Southampton. Hull City surprisingly hold a one goal lead at champions Manchester City from the 35th minute only to be thwarted of a vital three points by again a very late equaliser. It's tragic how bad luck conspires against teams at the bottom. The point for Hull temporarily lifts them above us on goal difference and pushes us back into the bottom three. Aston Villa are also beaten at home but put up a much improved performance against league leaders Chelsea. So it's all to play for once again at Sunday lunchtime.

GAME 24 – Burnley v West Bromwich Albion, Sunday 8th February, 12.00 hrs

A cold morning and as kick off approaches so does the freezing fog. Thankfully not sufficient to put the game in jeopardy, but enough to worry the Sky TV camera crews. Unsurprisingly we name an unchanged starting eleven whilst WBA include new signings Darren Fletcher and Callum McManaman. WBA manager Tony Pulis drops young England prospect Saido Berahino to the bench, presumably in retaliation for comments made to the media about wanting to move on to 'better things'.

A lively opening by the Clarets has a fingertip save onto the crossbar by Foster in the WBA goal denying us an early lead. But not for long as on 11 minutes Ashley Barnes nods us ahead. Our visitors who had clearly come with a plan for containment are quickly forced into a change of plan. They enjoy a brief spell on attack but pretty quickly normal service is resumed as the Clarets continue to dominate. On 32 minutes the lead is increased as an Ings header finishes a brilliant move involving Trippier and Boyd with the latter providing the cross. 2-0 up for the third time in four games surely nothing can go wrong now!

WBA are forced into a change up front as the 'bullying' Victor Anichebe is forced off by injury to be replaced by the aforementioned 'bad boy' Berahino. No real dangers for the Clarets until in first half injury time we concede a corner. In typical Burnley fashion we contrive to spoil an excellent first half by allowing Chris Brunt to head home unmarked from the cross. Still I suppose better to go off 2-1 up than 2-1 down.

An uneasy feeling of déjà-vu at half time, not helped by a passing fan's advice to, *"hold on tight for a bumpy ride."* A change in formation for the Baggies at the start of the second half, as defender Chris Baird, yellow carded in the first period, is sacrificed for another attacker, Brown Ideye. Just a change of player for us as Dean Marney injured in the first half fails to reappear. He is replaced by Michael Kightly who goes to the right wing with Scott Arfield moving to centre midfield.

The start of the second period sees WBA in the ascendancy as we struggle for any fluidity. The switch of Boyd to the left flank to accommodate Kightly is not helping, his link play with Trippier being a feature of the first half. On 67 minutes disaster as the recently introduced, and extremely niggly, and 'gobby', Ideye levels the score heading in at close range from a corner. Our two goal lead blown away yet again, and with two soft goals down to our inability to deal with set pieces.

It's really a game that can go either way now, a close thing with a Shackell header cleared off the line by Lescott. Then a 'nailed on' penalty denied by referee Mike Dean as McAuley sticks out an arm to deflect a Mee cross. TV replays clearly show the players deliberate intent. At the other end a good save by Heaton and a scrambled clearance by Mee from a Berahino effort. The switch of Kightly and Boyd on the flanks allowing Boyd to link again with Trippier, gives us fresh impetus but it's too little too late. We have to settle for a point in a game where we really needed all three particularly in view of a decidedly difficult run of games coming up.

The draw is enough to lift us out of the drop zone again taking us one point above Hull, two ahead of QPR, and now four in front of Leicester. We close to within one point of Aston Villa, whilst remaining two behind WBA., and three adrift of Sunderland.

Result – Burnley 2 (Barnes 11, Ings 32) – 2 West Bromwich Albion (Brunt 45, Ideye 67)

Burnley Team

Heaton, Trippier, Keane, Shackell, Mee, Arfield, Marney (Kightly 45), Jones, Boyd, Ings (Jutkiewicz 61), Barnes

Subs Not used – Gilks, Reid, Duff, Vokes, Wallace, Jutkiewicz

West Bromwich Albion Team

Foster, Dawson, McAuley, Lescott, Baird (Ideye 45), Fletcher, Yacob, Brunt, McManaman (Morrison 82), Anichebe (Berahino 18), Sessegnon

Subs Not used – Pocognoli, Wisdom, Rose, Gardner,

Attendance – 16,904

Season Record – Played 24, Won 4, Drawn 9, Lost 11, Goals For 23, Goals Against 40, Points 21

League Position after Game 24 – 17th

Tuesday 10th February and it's time for another Dotcom walk this time from Spring Wood car park at Whalley. The route is planned down through Whalley and out to Mitton returning via Wiswell. Once again we are to enjoy a rare pub lunch of Soup and Sandwiches washed down with a pint of ale. I have to say that I think last week's similar offering at The Strawberry Duck at Entwistle will take some beating in terms of both quality and price.

On learning the destination of our lunch stop, suffice it to say a hostelry not noted for pensioner friendly prices, I had my reservations. I must say on that score the pub did not disappoint. I feared the worst, but it was worse than I feared! A soup and sandwich (singular) ran out at a handsome £10 with a pint of Reedley Hallows beer at £3.80! As I suspected a poor effort compared to The Strawberry Duck. However undaunted and still suffering hunger pains we completed a very enjoyable circuit back to Whalley. Our leader Nigel Hext (another ex Barden teacher) estimated the walk at 7.5 miles but in true Dotcom walking fashion the actual distance was 8.68 miles measured by GPS. Our leaders are becoming notoriously economic with the truth in relation to distance and elevation, slightly undulating often being the description of a mountain climb!

On returning home a quick check of Clarets news reveals another disaster, as it transpires Saturday's injury to Dean Marney is much worse than anticipated. Once again the curse of the cruciate Knee ligament has struck and Deano is out for the rest of the season. What a tragedy, and how this highlights the folly of not securing centre midfield cover in both transfer windows. This is potentially extremely damaging to our survival hopes and must surely prompt a serious tactical rethink. For the second time in a day I find myself fearing the worst, but praying that it won't be worse than I fear!

The loss of Marney, who I consider one of our most underrated players, could well have dealt us a critical blow. Who can step up to the plate? Will it be Arfield moving permanently to the centre, and a chance for Kightly or Wallace. Will the little used Steven Reid come in? How far is Matty Taylor, recovering from Achilles problems, from a return? Will Sean throw in one of the untried youngsters such as Hewitt or Howieson. This time he is really going to have to pluck the rabbit out of the hat!

As the Tuesday evening kick off scores start to flash up, Claretsmad messageboard poster Rowls dubs the day 'Black Tuesday'. Marney is out for the season, and the latest scores put us second bottom. He asks has anybody killed a sacred cow? I have to say it certainly feels that way. QPR get their first away points with a 2-0 win at Sunderland, Hull beat Villa 2-0 at home, the only losers below us are Leicester and that in a close game at Arsenal 2-1.

GAME 25 – Manchester United v Burnley, Wednesday 11th February, 19.45 hrs

Wednesday night and all set for the mismatch of the fithy rich against the plucky rag, tag, and bobtail challengers from East Lancashire. In front of a 75,356 crowd at Old Trafford you expect the game to be pretty much dominated by one team, what you don't expect is that team to be Burnley!

In the wake of the Marney injury the vacant starting place went, as I think most of us expected, to Michael Kightly. Scott Arfield moved to a central midfield role and Kightly took his position on the left flank.

Within five minutes of the kick off United are forced into a substitution as Phil Jones leaves the field with an ankle injury to be replaced by Chris Smalling. What a sensational start for Smalling as he heads United in front with his first touch of the ball, yes you guessed it, from a corner! In view of recent events that could have been enough to knock the stuffing out of the Clarets but not on this occasion. It only served to ignite the blue touch paper as our heroes roared back. On 12 minutes we are level with a brilliant Danny Ings diving header from a superb Kieran Trippier cross.

The Clarets then proceed to humble United in front of their massive home support. The attempts on goal tally for the first half running out at ten for Burnley against three for the Red Devils. Former United player Phil Neville commented on BBC Match Of The Day:

"Make no bones about it United were really poor in the first half. Burnley were magnificent and could have been a few goals up."

With Kightly tormenting the United defence and Ings the outstanding striker on a pitch graced by Rooney, Van Persie, and Falcao, it was a heart warming 45 minutes. Until on 45+3 minutes United stole the lead with another Smalling header, and yes you guessed, from a corner!

How heartbraking, but also how predictable! Why is it that all the goals that we score are beautifully crafted and most that we concede are straightforward close range headers from set pieces? This regular concession is hurting us badly. It is becoming reminiscent of displays under Eddie Howe's management when no matter how many goals we scored, the opposition would equal or better it.

At the start of the second half a golden chance for Danny Ings to level matters again, but alas not taken. After this the game somewhat petered out with the Clarets unable to reach the heights of the first half and United looking uninspired. As the game reached the last ten minutes, Kightly saw his volley deflected over and from the resulting corner the game was over. Scott Arfield failed to get the ball back into the penalty area and United broke through Di Maria. In his anxiety to atone for his mistake, Scotty chased Di Maria and brought him down in our penalty area. Van Persie duly converted the spot kick and what could have been a magnificent night once again ended in disappointment.

Result – Manchester United 3 (Smalling 6,45, Van Persie 82 pen) – 1 Burnley (Ings 12)

Burnley Team

Heaton, Trippier, Keane, Shackell, Mee, Arfield, Kightly (Vokes 86), Jones, Boyd, Ings, Barnes (Jutkiewicz 92)

Subs Not used – Gilks, Reid, Duff, Lafferty, Wallace,

Manchester United Team

De Gea, Rojo, Evans, Jones (Smalling 5), McNair, Di Maria, Blind (Herrera 39), Rooney, Januzaj, Falcao (Wilson 74), Van Persie

Subs Not used – Valdes, Valencia, Mata, Fellaini

Attendance – 75,356

Season Record – Played 25, Won 4, Drawn 9, Lost 12, Goals For 24, Goals Against 43, Points 21

League Position after Game 25 – 19th

Once again a mention of the away support is called for. This hardy bunch of travellers created a superb atmosphere despite being heavily outnumbered and for much of the game were by far the loudest. Their positivity does them great credit and one day soon this will surely be rewarded. Notable amongst the mocking chants on the evening was 'we only spent £3', belittling the vast sums of money spent by United on a team who were for large parts of the evening given the run-around.

On the same evening, Aston Villa beaten at Hull City on Tuesday finally lost patience with boss Paul Lambert and decided to dispense with his services. No surprise there, I just wonder why it took so long to come to that conclusion.

Thursday 13th saw a small party of Burnley Contingent walkers enjoy a lovely ramble from Nuttall Park, Ramsbottom to Peel Tower via Stubbins, and Holcombe Moor. Despite flirting with the DANGER AREA, which is a military firing range, all walkers returned safely. Pub choice for the day was the excellent GRIFFIN at Haslingden and at £1.90 a pint it certainly did not disappoint. Contrast that with Tuesday's effort in the Ribble Valley at £3.80, bloody robbery! A great day out was topped off with a Cissy Green's Meat Pie, truly a Prince among pies. I'm sure the hostelry and pie shop will figure much more frequently on subsequent outings.

After 25 games we are roughly two thirds of the way through the season. A simple bit of mathematics means we would realise 32 points for the season if that points per game ratio were maintained. This would almost surely be not enough to retain our Premier League place. Common feeling is that a minimum of 36 points would perhaps be sufficient. However life is rarely so simple.

Starting with the recent defeat against Manchester United the fixture list has been, on paper, exceedingly unkind to us. The next seven games are Chelsea(a), Swansea(h), Liverpool(a), Manchester City(h), Southampton(a), Tottenham Hotspur(h), Arsenal(h)! All but Swansea of those teams currently sit in the top seven of the league, and Swansea are ninth!

What sort of points return can we expect from that batch of fixtures? The pundits would probably predict zero. Assuming this worst case scenario came true then that would leave us requiring 15 points from the last six games to make a total of 36. Clearly that would be too much to ask. We must once again somehow conjure some points from unlikely sources. We must shake off the habit of playing well but still getting beaten. The defence needs to revert to its miserly habits of early season, particularly with regard to set pieces. What better place to start than this coming weekend at Chelsea.

I was just thinking to myself how quiet things were on the Clarets front when a Friday evening peek at the Claretsmad website ahead of the Chelsea game made my eyes do a double take. The headline to an article by Claretsmad editor Tony Scholes was, *"Have we found a midfielder in Norway"*. The article went on to reveal that the Norwegian media were suggesting a deal for 22 year old midfielder Fredrik Ulvestad may be imminent, and suggesting that the player was currently training with us. The youngster who is currently a free agent, has been capped by Norway at Under 21, and Under 23 levels, and also has one substitute appearance for the full Norwegian side. He has previously made 106 appearances for his home town club Aalesunds FK, scoring 14 goals. It would appear nothing is signed yet but at least, and at last, we are taking a look at our limited options.

GAME 26 – Chelsea v Burnley, Saturday 21st February, 15.00 hrs

Well certainly a game here to get the tongues wagging and plenty of controversial incidents to wind up the serial moaner/hypocrite, Chelsea manager Jose Mourinho. On top of that a great result, almost unbelievably, against a team that had they won would have led the table briefly by 10 points.

For this game I am unfortunately at the Trafford Centre! After a nightmare journey, stuck in heavy traffic between junctions 16-12 on the M60, and a light lunch at John Lewis, my mind turns to the game. My first thought is to follow the game via the BBC website but I am having difficulties with the Wi-Fi on my mobile phone. As the next best option I decide to contact my old mate PNE Ed, who seems to have some sort of mission control going on match days and has reliable info on all games.

The texts soon start coming thick and fast and it's no surprise when on 14 minutes he informs me Chelsea lead 1-0 with a goal from Ivanovich. I have the Chelsea full back in my Fantasy Football team but I would gladly have done without the points that goal gained. At this point my Wi-Fi is sorted and I start checking the BBC and note that results on the other games are not going well for us. However we seem to be making a decent fist of things, and equal Chelsea for shots on goal, but unfortunately and more importantly, not for shots on target.

The game gets to half time with no more distressing texts, although Ed does keep me updated with other scores. Notable in his half time sequence is, *"Direshites 1-1 Sewerpool."* This thanks to my excellent powers of deduction I realise means Blackburn are level with Blackpool, clearly two of Ed's favourite local teams.

As the second half gets underway I am on way home, and thankful that I can follow the game on Radio Lancashire. But can I? Can I hell. The radio has developed the knack of flicking between Radio Lancashire frequencies thereby covering two games at the same time. Today at Trafford this tops the lot by alternating on almost every other word. It can be quite disconcerting to hear that we are on the attack, and in the next breath that Gestede has the ball. Almost impossible to follow the game but I have to persevere and hope things improve as I get nearer home.

Eventually this does seem to be the case and as the radio settles I can make out that Chelsea midfielder Matic has been red carded! This is a great boost for us and with still some twenty plus minutes to go we are in with a shout. Typically, the bloody radio then decides to switch back to the Rovers game! After a few minutes we are back at the Bridge and I can detect by the commentator's excitement that we are unbelievably LEVEL. Ben Mee has headed in direct from a corner, how ironic is that!

As I frantically try to will the remaining minutes away, my palms start to sweat and my nerves jangle. Referee Atkinson adds four minutes additional time but it's the Clarets who go closest as Ings fires over following a quick break. Game over and an extremely valuable and unexpected point is ours. Can't help feeling our friend Mr Mourinho, the 'Special One', is going to be not too pleased about that.

Sure enough I am home in time to catch his after match interview on TV. Jose, then in his most impressive sulking and hard done by demeanour, goes on to define the game cryptically in four minutes. These are minutes, 30, 33, 43, and 69. Later TV reviews of the game highlight these defining moments as

Minute 30 – Ashley Barnes aerial challenge with Branoslav Ivanovic leaves the Chelsea defender rolling around on the deck after receiving what looks like a knee in the back. He can't be too seriously hurt as on realising the referee is taking no action he bounces up to deliver an angry rant.

Minute 33 – An Ivanovic shot at goal hits Michael Kightly's outstretched arm in the Burnley penalty area as the Claret's player turns his back on the ball. Referee's decision no penalty!

Minute 43 – Diego Costa theatrically hits the deck in the Burnley penalty area following an apparent push by Jason Shackell. Again the referee awards no penalty.

Minute 69 – Ashley Barnes plays a ball in the direction of Dave Jones, his foot's follow through catching the onrushing Nemanja Matic badly on the shin. Slow motion replays look horrific but Matic is trying to tackle Barnes, not vice versa, and has come on his blind side. The referee sees no problem and waves play on but Matic reacts badly pushing Barnes to the ground and leaving the official no alternative but to send him off.

How bloody hypocritical of Mourinho, it's only a matter of days since Ivanovich escaped punishment after having an Everton midfielder in a headlock. In Diego Costa they have the most bullying attacker in the Premier League and his disciplinary record clearly reflects this. But still he tries to blacken our good name over one incident which none of the officials at the game deemed notable.

What a fantastic result for the Clarets but straightaway you just know that all the controversy whipped up by Mourinho and the media are going to take the shine off the achievement. But I'm not going to let that spoil my Saturday night, and I'm going to kick it off with a bottle of 'London Pride', how very apt.

Result – Chelsea 1 (Ivanovic 14) – 1 Burnley (Mee 81)

Burnley Team

Heaton, Trippier, Keane, Shackell, Mee, Arfield, Kightly (Vokes 79), Jones, Boyd, Ings, Barnes

<u>Subs Not used</u> – Gilks, Reid, Duff, Ward, Wallace, Jutkiewicz

Chelsea Team

Courtois, Ivanovic, Terry, Zouma, Luis (Drogba 85), Fabregas, Matic, Cuadrado (Willan 63), Oscar (Ramires 72), Hazard, Costa

<u>Subs Not used</u> – Cech, Azpilicueta, Cahill, Remy

Attendance – 41,629

Season Record – Played 26, Won 4, Drawn 10, Lost 12, Goals For 25, Goals Against 44, Points 22

League Position after Game 26 – 18th

As expected following the airing of the game on BBC's Match of the Day (MOTD) programme the media went to town on the Barnes/Matic incident. The MOTD pundits, Alan Shearer and Robbie Savage, both ex Blackburn Rovers players, unsurprisingly sided completely with Mourinho's views.

What everybody seems to have completely missed in their various descriptions of the horrific tackle/challenge by Barnes is that it was evidently no such thing! Video evidence clearly shows that the tackle/challenge is by Matic on Barnes who has clearly played the ball before connecting with Matic on his follow through. Furthermore there is no coverage in the programme of the later blatant kick on Shackell by Costa in an attempt to provoke some retaliation. Neither is the unsporting incident where Heaton throws the ball out of play to allow treatment to Mee, is followed by Chelsea's failure to return the ball to Burnley from the resulting throw. The only person from the programme to emerge with any credit is Gary Lineker, who at least makes the experts pass comment on Burnley's claims for a penalty as the ball rolls down the arm of Chelsea defender Luis. Needless to say they didn't feel this a valid claim.

By Sunday morning the attacks on Barnes's character are reaching fever pitch as the Sunday papers throw their weight of support behind the vitriolic Mourinho, who is now claiming the Barnes tackle is 'criminal'. He even goes to the point of appearing on 'Goals on Sunday' to continue his tirade against referee's in general, and Ashley Barnes in particular. The London based media, clearly knowing which side their bread is buttered on, decline to challenge the 'Special One'.

Speculation is mounting on Monday that Barnes could be facing retrospective action by the FA, which would certainly result in a ban. This is given more credence as Chelsea announce they are to appeal against the Matic sending off. On what grounds for God's sake? The guy has clearly assaulted Barnes and what's more in a cowardly fashion from behind his back.

Thankfully by Monday afternoon some semblance of common sense has prevailed as the FA reveal that Ashley Barnes will face no disciplinary action as a result of the Matic incident. The ruling being that retrospective action is only taken against off the ball incidents which are unseen by the match officials. As this was clearly a 'live' incident in the game and the officials are presumed to have seen it without deeming anything amiss, there is no case to answer. Praise the Lord!

The weekend results which at various stages seemed to be going horribly against us finally end up quite favourably. Our miraculous and merited draw lifts us one place in the table going above Aston Villa who go down to a late goal at home to Stoke. QPR lose at fellow strugglers Hull and now occupy fourth bottom position but only by virtue of a one goal better goal difference than the Clarets. Leicester surrender a late lead at Everton, courtesy of an own goal, to leave them still four points adrift of the next three. The draw between Sunderland and West Bromwich does neither any favours. Crystal Palace are beaten at home by Arsenal, so all in all not too bad a weekend. After all the media exposure, almost all of which attempted to cast us in a bad light, I am now looking forward to a quieter few days.

On Tuesday the media and their hatchet men are still having a go, and still incorrectly referring to the Barnes incident as a tackle by our man, which once again I will reiterate was no such thing. Matic's appeal is overturned by the FA but they reduce the three match ban to two. Didn't we just know that would happen! The pressure applied by Mourinho and the press almost guaranteed that the gutless administrators would make concessions. Chelsea however are still unhappy with the outcome, and await the written explanation before further comment. I think they have already said enough on this one. It is high time that the FA grew some balls and stood up to the rich and powerful clubs.

Text conversations with PNE Ed, and discussions with pals of other northern clubs during Tuesday's Dotcom walk at Wigan, are generally in agreement with Burnley's dignified reaction to this provocation. Chris McCann, another North Ender, and also a referee's assessor in local league football, finds no argument with referee Martin Atkinson's handling of the affair. If it's good enough for Chris then it'll do me.

PNE Ed has some scathing comments to make on Mourinho, feeling that he tries to trample on the Burnley's of this world. I am also of the opinion that we, and our town club Lancashire neighbours, are easy prey for this sort of attack. We are relatively small backwater clubs who without the media machine behind us are easily ignored, so it does no harm to kick us.

Quick recommendations here for the pub that we used for our lunch on the Tuesday walk. The Crook Hall Inn, Wigan catered a full menu for 26 hearty eaters at an extremely acceptable price. Mine hosts were very welcoming and the food plentiful and delicious. To cap it all there was a good selection of real ales, also reasonably priced, and we would readily recommend this pub to anybody who finds themselves in the area.

Also a mention of the Burnley Contingent walk on Thursday 26th, a smaller than normal gathering set off from the Bay Horse pub in Baxenden for a scheduled 8.5 miler. Some time limitations here as Dave and Theresa Preedy (ex St Theodore's) needed to be back before 3.00 pm to pick up grandchildren. Suffice it to say this was the worst walk for some time in relation to unclear pathways, defective stiles, acres of mud, and gallons of running water. After two hours continuous slogging uphill we break for lunch, having achieved a distance somewhat under three miles. No way is this planned route going to get us back to Baxenden by three o'clock. A necessary decision to revise the route results in a satisfactory finish time and a distance of 5.94 miles in a time of 3.26.30, slow progress indeed. The day ends in the Bay Horse a pleasant enough hostelry but with a very disappointing pint of Thwaites, Light Touch ale. Not a beer I fear to be looked for again.

GAME 27 – Burnley v Swansea, Saturday 28th February, 15.00 hrs

Following a week of mauling of the club in the media we are back in action again at the Turf in a fixture that it goes without saying, we need to win. After the customary couple of pre match pints at the Talbot, not aided by some rather slower than usual beer dispensing, we make our way to the hallowed turf.

On arrival shortly before kick off time it feels as though the previous week's events have united the fans and once again engendered a powerful siege mentality. Swansea despite a lofty league position are fairly poorly represented in terms of travelling support. So we are hopeful that we can claim the spoils albeit in rather difficult playing conditions.

What follows is a pretty tepid first half with few goalmouth incidents, probably the closest to a goal being a Barnes close range effort blocked by Swans keeper Fabianski. Our visitors are proving difficult to breakdown but offering little of an attacking threat.

At half time I meet up with some old mates in the Gents toilet. Now I don't think they are habitual frequenters of these premises but it does give us the chance of a quick catch up. We all agree that we are anxiously awaiting the deluge of second half goals, but realistically concurring that on the evidence of the first half, this is unlikely to happen.

The start of the second half sees the Clarets at least operating at a higher tempo and pushing Swansea back on the defensive. The best opportunity comes as Michael Kightly cuts in along the bye line but his shot/cross is again foiled by a good save from Fabianski. But on 64 minutes its disaster time again as we once again concede from a corner calamity. From Shelvey's flag kick an almighty scramble ensues with Heaton tipping the ball onto the crossbar. As it is recycled in the general direction of our goal Trippier appears to have the opportunity to clear, but somehow pokes the ball back in the direction of the now grounded Heaton. The keeper for a moment seems to have saved the day but the next moment I see him rolling in the back of the net along with the ball. Bloody corners!

There's plenty of huff and puff from the Clarets as we go in search of a leveller, but precious little guile and no cutting edge. A good shout for a penalty as Swans full back Taylor hauls down substitute Sam Vokes but it goes unheeded. Perhaps we should get Mr Mourinho to comment on the unjustness of that! After a paltry three minutes of added time the referee blows up and we trudge off home, once again pointless.

Later that evening I am out at a friend's birthday celebration at the Sparrow Hawk, Fence. Among the other guests is a former Clarets central defender, who suggests we may have seen the 'first nail in the coffin'. I tell him I sincerely hope not but in my own mind I believe I have thought for some time that our Premier League status is gradually slipping away. Fortified by a hearty meal, good company, and several pints of Reedley Hallows, No Nay Never, I end the evening feeling much brighter.

Result – Burnley 0 – 1 Swansea (Trippier og, 64)

Burnley Team

Heaton, Trippier, Keane, Shackell, Mee, Arfield, Kightly (Vokes 75), Jones, Boyd, Ings, Barnes (Jutkiewicz 90)

Subs Not used – Gilks, Reid, Duff, Ward, Wallace

Swansea Team

Fabianski, Naughton, Fernandez, Williams, Taylor, Ki, Cork, Shelvey, Carroll (Montero 61), Gomis (Oliveira 90), Routledge (Amat 90)

Subs Not used – Temmell, Rangel, Britton, Emnes

Attendance – 17,388

Season Record – Played 27, Won 4, Drawn 10, Lost 13, Goals For 25, Goals Against 45, Points 22

League Position after Game 27 – 18th

MARCH

No game at the weekend for Leicester it being Capital One Cup Final day, and a narrow defeat for Aston Villa at Newcastle mean our position in the relegation dogfight remains unchanged. But considering the upcoming run of fixtures Swansea at home would certainly have been a game from which we would have hoped for some points return. Eleven games to play now and still only 22 points on the board. Our current points per game ratio is only 0.81 and if that is maintained we will amass approximately nine more points, way short of what will be required. We have clearly somehow to manage a much greater points haul in the final run in than we have so far all season, and at the moment this doesn't look likely.

Undeterred, and with hope springing eternal, on Monday 2nd March I renew my season ticket for 2015/16. Will it be Premier League or Championship football? Que sera, sera!

It's still Monday and after a day of snow, hail, sleet and biting wind, I eagerly await Tuesday's Dotcom walk, which this time is on home turf. The walk is described by Group Leader Bob Clare as 7.5 miles with one climb. Now I did say earlier that Bob was getting a little economical with the truth regarding distance and elevation. A bit of inside info gleaned from walk leader, Dave Preedy, leads me to believe the route is from Towneley Riverside Car Park to Burnley's Panopticon, The Singing Ringing Tree, high up on Crown Point. Well he may be right in that there is one climb, but that looks to me, and any of you that know Burnley, like one continuous climb of about half the total distance. With snow, sleet and rain showers again forecast I can't wait to see what the 'Flatlanders' of Preston and South Ribble make of that!

On the subject of Preston, disturbing events of late, as our winless run continues, North End are on a charge and now lie joint second in League 1 with a game in hand. It's not looking good for my bet with Jim (Skipper of the Yard) that both teams will be still be in different leagues next season, and I am starting to say my prayers.

The Singing Ringing Tree did not disappoint every facet of winter weather and a distance of 9.2 miles, mostly uphill. Mud in abundance and in parts a veritable paddy field, that's what I call East Lancashire hospitality.

GAME 28 – Liverpool v Burnley, Wednesday 4th March, 20.00 hrs

Our season unfortunately seems to be becoming very predictable. Same team, same formation, same result. I could almost have written the script for this one before a ball was kicked. Plucky underdogs battling bravely but ultimately no match for better quality hosts. Non stop running is no match for skill allied to work rate.

Injured Liverpool captain Steven Gerrard remarked in his programme notes, *"nobody has it easy against Burnley."* The Reds obviously heeded the message and burst out of the blocks requiring a Heaton save from Sturridge within the first minute. More chances came in quick succession and a long hard night was on the cards. In typical Burnley fashion though we hung in and occasionally looked like we might make a game of it.

That was until the inevitable happened and our hosts took the lead on 29 minutes as Henderson dispatched a swerving 20 yarder into the net. Sturridge had the chance to wrap the game up on 42 minutes but failed, and Barnes let them know we were still alive with a header saved by Mignolet.

The start of the second half saw us come out fighting but quickly our hopes were snuffed out as Liverpool took complete control Sturridge heading home a Henderson cross. Two down on 52 minutes and once again, game over.

Perhaps tiredness is beginning to take its toll, and loss of confidence after a poor series of results. We expected a difficult sequence of games with Manchester United, Chelsea, Swansea, Liverpool, Manchester City, Southampton, Tottenham, and Arsenal. We are now half way through that lot and anticipated a poor points return, currently one from a possible twelve. What can we glean from the next half? On current form not many, and my optimism is rapidly fading to pessimism. Fortunately on the same night Leicester and QPR also lose to limit the damage but we are now three points adrift of Aston Villa in the safe spot.

Result – Liverpool 2 (Henderson 29, Sturridge 52) – 0 Burnley

Burnley Team

Heaton, Trippier, Keane, Shackell, Mee, Arfield, Kightly (Wallace 54), Jones, Boyd, Ings (Jutkiewicz 90), Barnes (Vokes 66)

Subs Not used – Gilks, Reid, Duff, Ward,

Liverpool Team

Mignolet, Can, Skrtel, Lovren, Lallana, Henderson, Allen, Moreno (Toure 73), Sterling (Lambert 90), Sturridge (Johnson 83), Coutinho

<u>Subs Not used</u> – Ward, Balotelli, Williams, Markovic

<u>**Attendance**</u> – 44,717

<u>**Season Record**</u> – Played 28, Won 4, Drawn 10, Lost 14, Goals For 25, Goals Against 47, Points 22

<u>**League Position after Game 28**</u> – 19th

There's no game on the weekend of 7th March due to FA Cup games. My wife and I along with a couple of friends take the opportunity of a long weekend in Paris via Eurostar. Excellent trip enhanced by lovely weather, but boy is Paris expensive! I return wiser but poorer! During a brief bar break in the hotel I notice on the TV that QPR are losing at home to Spurs in the only Premier league fixture, but the game is quickly displaced by the Paris St Germain v Lens game on the screen. Fortunately I later learn that QPR have lost again so that keeps them firmly in the mire.

I was wondering what had happened to our young Norwegian trialist Fredrik Ulvestad. Then out of the blue on Tuesday 10th March came the news that we had signed him on a three year deal taking him to the end of the 2017/18 season. No rushed panic signing this as he has been training with us for a couple of weeks and Sean Dyche presumably sees something in the guy. It is reported that he has a good 'engine' and that is something that is certainly a necessity for anyone coming to us. I don't think we will see much of him in first team action this season, the step up from the Norwegian League to the Premier being a huge leap. It looks like he is one for the future and the remainder of this season should give him a chance to acclimatise to his new surroundings before he gets a full pre season and is ready to go next time. Perhaps if we are relegated with games still to play we may pitch him in to see how he fares, but he is too big a gamble whilst it is still all to play for.

Ahead of the Manchester City game this coming Saturday I am becoming apprehensive. Our recent home record against them is not pleasant reading and we have been on the receiving end of some serious hammerings. Two that stick in the memory are a 0-5 defeat in Stan Ternent's reign, and the 1-6 reverse in our last Premier League campaign. In that particular game we were blown away with three goals in the first seven minutes, and five down by half time. Please, please not another of those games!

Another thing I don't fancy about the City game is the lousy kick off time, 17.30 on the Saturday! What sort of a time is that for football? It completely louses up Saturday evening for the paying spectator forcing him to eat either mid afternoon, or later in the evening, seriously curtailing 'boozing time'. I suppose I should get used to this as the next two home games after this are also moved to accommodate the TV viewers. But that's life in the Premier League where paying supporters present at the stadium's needs are insignificant as the club's pander to the global TV millions.

GAME 29 – Burnley v Manchester City, Saturday 14th March, 17.30 hrs

After a day that seemed to last forever, and heartened by the news that QPR have lost again I set off on my way to the Turf. The three o'clock kick off games are just coming to an end and the big shock in the relegation battle is Aston Villa's 4-0 away win at Sunderland. Bad news is that this victory puts the Villains six points clear of us but the flip side is that it leaves Sunderland temporarily only four ahead. Leicester have failed to beat ten man Hull City leaving them still three points adrift of the Clarets.

It's a cold but clear early evening and the ground is full to the rafters despite the game being televised live by Sky TV. We surprisingly make two changes to the starting line up with the experience of Michael Duff being preferred to young Michael Keane in central defence. Michael Kightly returns to the bench and it's a first Premier League start for the now fully fit Sam Vokes, who leads the line with Ashley Barnes moving to wide left.

In almost the first action of the game Barnesy in his own inimitable style makes his presence felt in a crunching challenge with City fullback Zabaleta leaving him crumpled on the deck. I am half expecting a yellow card for Barnes but he gets away with it, although the referee Andre Marriner soon afterwards leaves Ashley in no uncertainty that an early bath will be the consequence of any recurrence. The game quickly settles into a pattern of determined pressing by the Clarets and a lot of possession for our illustrious visitors. Both sides are quickly into their stride and we are giving a good account of ourselves. For City Aguero is looking sharp and ready to exploit any slip ups whilst Silva and Toure attempt to craft the openings.

A half hearted early appeal for a penalty as Demichelis catches Ings in the face is summarily dismissed, and a more 'giveable' one following a handball by Clichy on a Trippier cross suffers the same fate. Ben Mee next puts a header over whilst City enjoy lots of ball but not much penetration. Not until 25 minutes do the reigning Champions manage a shot on goal but Dzeko's shot goes harmlessly wide. Inspired by this they manage a couple more attempts but Heaton and the rearguard are equal to them. At the other end Hart is called into action to save from Scott Arfield who is enjoying a good game in exalted company in centre midfield. Boyd is his usual busy self and Trippier is getting forward down the right flank frequently. One more chance for City as half time approaches but we reach the break deservedly level.

In the interval a little drama is played out for the TV viewers. A young couple are invited on to the pitch and it transpires the young lady is a Burnley fan (cue much cheering) whilst her boyfriend is a City fan (cue much booing). The young fellow explains that he has bought the tickets for the game as a surprise for his girlfriend. He then goes on to say that he has another surprise for her (cue one or two smutty jokes) and promptly proposes marriage. This is met instantly by the crowd chanting *"You don't know what you're doing"*. The young lady promptly accepts the proposal and as they contemplate a life of wedded bliss, the real action resumes.

I must admit that despite our excellent first half showing I am still extremely nervous and apprehensive. The Clarets though have once again come out fighting and are taking the game to the visitors. George Boyd tries a 'range finder' with a fierce volley but just wide on this occasion, then it's City's turn as a quick break by Aguero is wasted as Silva's first touch takes him too wide and we are able to recover. Referee Marriner is having a dire time giving the Clarets precious little whilst allowing our opponents, Demichelis in particular to get away with some barely concealed thuggery.

How ironic as from one of the rare free kicks that we are given we take the lead. On 61 minutes Trippier's free kick is firmly headed clear by Kompany to the edge of the box. Unfortunately it is straight to the left boot of George Boyd who returns it unerringly with pace and direction to nestle in the corner of Hart's net. What a sweet strike, and how the stadium erupted. Such scenes of unbridled joy, mixed with a little disbelief.

Still 29 minutes to play, can we hold out for a highly improbable win? If I had been nervous before it was nothing to what I was feeling now. City ring the changes with Bony replacing the ineffective Dzeko, to be followed by Jovetic on for Silva. The final throw of the dice sees Yaya Toure replaced by Frank Lampard but it's all to no avail. The Clarets now with their tales up are not going to give this one up easily. A superbly marshalled defence is equal to everything thrown at it and the shape and energy of the team is perfect. Defending from the front as the strikers continue to harry and the midfield are quick to close down we gradually edge our way towards full time. The officials somehow manage to find four minutes added time. Zabaleta sprawls in the box following a Mee challenge in a vain attempt to win a penalty, but not this time.

The whistle blows and all three points are ours, what a MAGNIFICENT effort and thoroughly deserved result. As I arrive home congratulatory texts are coming thick and fast, my mate Scouse Brian texts, *"life's good sometimes."* He goes on to say that, *"I hear a door opening and it isn't a trapdoor. Great result."* Even the North Enders, clearly buoyed by their teams thumping 5-1 win against Crewe are complimentary, I suppose they are not all bad. Home before 8 o'clock and time for a celebratory G&T to be washed down with copious amounts of beer!

I wonder if the relationship between the newly engaged couple can survive this result. I sincerely hope the young lady is giving her 'beau' hell!

Result – Burnley 1 (Boyd 61) – 0 Manchester City

Burnley Team

Heaton, Trippier, Duff, Shackell, Mee, Arfield, Jones, Boyd, Barnes, Ings (Reid 90), Vokes (Ward 87)

Subs Not used – Gilks, Keane, Wallace, Kightly, Jutkiewicz

Manchester City Team

Hart, Zabaleta, Kompany, Demichelis, Clichy, Navas, Fernandinho, Toure (Lampard 81), Silva (Jovetic 74), Aguero, Dzeko (Bony 63)

Subs Not used – Caballero, Sagna, Mangala, Nasri

Attendance – 21,216

Season Record – Played 29, Won 5, Drawn 10, Lost 14, Goals For 26, Goals Against 47, Points 25

League Position after Game 29 – 18th

Oh me of little faith, not for the first time this season had I doubted the team's ability to compete, following the defeat at Liverpool. How wrong have I been proved yet again. In Sean Dyche's own words on some occasions we have been dented but never broken. The spirit in this bunch of players is indomitable, and the belief and unity is incredible.

This is surely down to the positivity of Dyche and his coaching staff who have been unwavering in their belief that the impossible may indeed be possible. Once again I am ashamed of my doubting nature and resolved to maintain a positive approach for the remaining nine games.

The City result has kept the dream alive as we leapfrog QPR, and close to within one point of the freefalling Sunderland. Unsurprisingly on Monday 16th March the Mackems dispense with the services of their manager Gus Poyet in response to their embarrassing home defeat to Villa. Leicester remain bottom six points adrift of the Clarets with a game in hand, however this being a difficult one against Chelsea. QPR are now three behind, whilst we once again have Villa, and Hull City in our sights.

An interesting little observation from a non football orientated but highly intelligent co Burnley contingent walker whilst out on a Thursday ramble. On the previous evening Manchester City had exited the Champions League by virtue of a 1-0 defeat away to Barcelona. With impeccable reasoning the good lady Dr Walton opined that if we had beaten City 1-0, and in the same week Barcelona had beaten them 1-0, surely if we were to play Barcelona the score would be 1-1! How could I argue with that? We are clearly destined for bigger things.

GAME 30 – Southampton v Burnley, Saturday 21st March, 15.00 hrs

I think it's fair to say that prior to the win over City; our biggest scalp of the campaign had been the victory over the Saints at Turf Moor. Buoyed by last week's fantastic feat could we repeat the success and record our first double of the season?

A quick glance at the stats on Saturday morning shows we have a pretty good record away against Southampton in recent meetings, although these have not been all that frequent. A decent day for weather with a distinctly Spring like feel, coupled with my new found resolve to be positive has me feeling quietly confident about this one.

A race against time as I try to erect a new washing line in the back garden to replace the winter weather ravaged old one, but I make it just in time for Radio Lancashire's commentary. A few minutes into the game and I leave the room for a few moments, to hear on my return that the Saints keeper, Fraser Forster, has been substituted following an innocuous collision with Sam Vokes. This could be good news for us if not for Fraser as he boasts the most clean sheets in the Premier League this season. His replacement, the veteran Kelvin Davis, seems to have been around long enough to be my Dad. Let's hope those arthritic old joints aren't up for the job.

The Clarets are quickly into their stride and fielding the same side that started the magnificent win over City are soon giving their hosts major concerns. Unfortunately Kelvin is not as arthritic as hoped and is keeping them level with good saves from Ings and Vokes. Also a close call for a penalty as Fonte upends Boyd in the box. But on 37 minutes, and probably against the run of play, we find ourselves behind. A deflected ball into the box finds Shane Long lurking near the 'back stick' with Mickey Duff playing him onside. From close range he needs no second invitation to poke Southampton ahead and we are in a familiar position of trailing away from home. A good response by the Clarets and a further good effort from Vokes amount to nothing and we go in at half time one down.

After the first half performance I am not unduly worried and as we seem to be creating plenty of opportunities, I am confident we can turn this one round. It's at this point that I realise just what is missing from our performance. It's the 'lucky wristbands'. Without further ado I hurdle the stairs to retrieve them from the bedroom drawer. Now fully kitted out I text my mate John W at St Mary's to assure him that all will now be well. I decide to ditch the Radio Lancs coverage at this point as they are well known to be a bloody jinx, and decide to follow the BBC website text updates.

On minute 57.08 up comes the unbelievable, *"Own goal by Jason Shackell, Burnley. Southampton 2, Burnley 0."* Immediate text to John W, *"These bloody wristbands are shite."* What is it with own goals recently? Tripps against Swansea now Shacks! Bloody Hell lads it's hard enough trying to keep the other buggers out without doing the job for them. But how can I be critical of our 'Captain Fantastic' who has once again had a magnificent season and been a model of consistency. Unfortunately this incident seems to end the game as a contest and the Saints start to coast to another victory to keep them in touch with the Champions League places. The game ends 2-0 and once again whilst not disgraced we come away empty handed.

Fortunately Leicester lose a close encounter at White Hart Lane going down 4-3 to Spurs and remain 6 points adrift of us. Villa also lose, at home to Swansea, and in the evening kick off Sunderland are beaten by a late goal at West Ham.

Text arrives from John W, *"What can I tell u boys. MOTD tonite see 1st half only! Shambles second half Saints really turned it on. Now in pub drinking Ruddles County."* A long way to go for no points and a few pints, but c'est la vie!

Result – Southampton 2 (Long 37, Shackell o.g 58) – 0 Burnley

Burnley Team

Heaton, Trippier, Duff, Shackell, Mee, Arfield, Jones, Boyd, Barnes (Wallace 82), Ings (Sordell 88), Vokes (Jutkiewicz 74)

Subs Not used – Gilks, Keane, Reid, Kightly,

Southampton Team

Forster (Davis 14), Clyne, Fonte, Aldeweireld, Bertrand, Davis, Schneiderlin, Long, Mane, Tadic (Wanyama 45), Pelle

Subs Not used – Yoshida, Gardos, Djuricic, Ward-Prowse, Elia

Attendance – 30,864

Season Record – Played 30, Won 5, Drawn 10, Lost 15, Goals For 26, Goals Against 49, Points 25

League Position after Game 30 – 18th

Sunday 22nd March sees two more relegation strugglers in action. QPR go down at home 1-2 to Everton, whilst Hull lose 2-3 at home to Chelsea despite coming back from two goals down in the first nine minutes. Incredibly all the bottom six teams lose in game week 30 and it's exactly as you were, albeit for minor changes in goal difference. No real damage done but no advantage gained, and now down to eight to play. Increasingly it is looking like three teams now from the bottom six to drop, but we still have a fighting chance!

Tuesday March 24th is the date for a Dotcom walk at White Coppice. Needless to say the North Enders are in high spirits following an impressive run of results. They are now sitting in the second automatic promotion spot in League 1 with points and a game in hand. My counterpart in the Clarets/PNE end of season wager, Jim (Skipper of the Yard) whilst conceding that the bet could go right to the wire, is already making plans for the handover ceremony of the cash!

There are wild suggestions of venues with photoshoots at Deepdale or Turf Moor already being mooted! Perhaps we should get the opposing team captains, or better still managers, to present the prize. Honestly, all this fuss over a £5 bet.

Our walk from White Coppice takes us over and around Great Hill, which to the Burnley Contingent brought up with the towering peaks of East Lancashire, strikes us as not so great. On reaching the summit of the said mound, our friends from the lower echelons of the football pyramid seem excited to point out some hideous white structure in the distance. This of course turned out to be Deepdale, but to a man (and woman) the Burnley Contingent stoically refused to acknowledge its existence and cast our eyes further afield to Blackpool Tower. I can only assume the 'giddiness' exhibited by our flatland friends was attributable to some form of altitude sickness associated with lower oxygen levels up the hill.

Some great ammunition to fire at my PNE adversaries arrives courtesy of two Daily Mail articles on 26th March. The first is a bit of nonsense dreamt up by the Mail entitled 'How Big Is Your Club?' Now I don't want anyone to get the wrong idea here, this is not about the size of male organs of procreation. Instead the article attempts to rank the top 50 teams from the 59 who have played in England's top division,

Premier League or previously Football League, for at least one season, ever. These top 50 were ranked in six categories to assess how 'big' they are in each of them. The categories being: crowds, global fanbase, trophies, league finish, player quality and income. An absolute load of tosh but useful for a slow news day! The Clarets end up in mid table in the rankings, occupying 26th position. The top three are Manchester United, Arsenal, and Liverpool respectively. Unfortunately some way above us in the chart are Blackburn Rovers in 17th spot, but skulking in the lower regions are Preston North End at 39th. I shall have to point this one out to them at our next meeting when they start to get uppity.

The second article is non football related and goes under the banner, 'Unhealthiest High Streets in Britain'. The Mail seems to like tables and this one lists the top ten towns which are perceived as the unhealthiest in terms of proportion of bookies, pay day loan shops, fast food shops, and tanning salons in the main shopping areas. Such businesses being viewed as having a negative effect on health. Surprise, surprise, who should top the charts on this one, none other than 'Proud Preston'. Now I have to say this didn't surprise me at all. I have always suspected the citizens of that proud city to be Tango'd, kebab guzzling, ne'er do well gamblers. Neither does it surprise John Swindells, deputy leader of Preston Council who said: *"There are no surprises here. These results mirror our own concerns. It's not all bad news. We are seeing a greater variety of shops, restaurants and bars opening here."*

Perhaps the leaders of Preston council should make the short journey over to Burnley and visit our cornucopia of juice bars, libraries, gymnasiums, and health spas. Unsurprisingly our town does not feature in the top ten, all of which are in the North or Midlands with the exception of Eastbourne! What's going on there? The Pensioner's Paradise a hot bed of gambling, carbohydrate overloading, and vanity, surely not!

The last Saturday in March is a football free zone as far as far as Premier League action is concerned. England continue their relentless pursuit of a Euro 2016 finals place with an easy 4-0 home victory over Lithuania on Friday 27th March. Among the goal scorers is Harry Kane who marks his England debut with a goal within 60 seconds of his entry as a second half substitute. Harry has certainly got the Midas touch at the moment but I am praying this deserts him before our upcoming home game with Spurs on Sunday 5th April.

APRIL

Game 31 is once again moved for television, our home clash with Tottenham now scheduled for a 13.30 Sunday kick off. This gives us the chance to see how most of our rivals fare on the preceding Saturday.

The two sides currently viewed as the bookmakers favourites to drop, Leicester and Queens Park Rangers, infuriatingly win. QPR with an impressive 4-1 win at West Bromwich, with only their second away points of the season, go temporarily above us on goal difference. Whilst a late goal for Leicester gives them an invaluable 2-1 home victory over West Ham, closing the gap on us to three points with a game in hand. This was definitely not what we wanted.

However two of the 'catchable' teams above us, Aston Villa and Hull City both lose 3-1 away at Manchester United and Swansea respectively. The gap between bottom and sixth from bottom once again 'concertinas' up and emphasises the fact that nobody should be written off at this stage. It's up to us now to go and get a result against Spurs and hope that Newcastle can take points from Sunderland in Sunday's Tyne-Wear derby.

Before the game against Spurs there is some real praise from Ex Liverpool centre back Jamie Carragher in an article entitled 'This Week I'm Looking Forward To...' Jamie then elaborates, *"Seeing if Burnley can make Turf Moor bounce again. Back in August many people would have expected Burnley to be adrift at the foot of the table at this stage of the season but they are still in there fighting. Sean Dyche has done an excellent job and the recent win against Manchester City has given them a decent chance of defying the odds and staying in the Barclays Premier League. They face Tottenham tomorrow and it's the type of match in which they have excelled. They have taken points from games many thought would be comfortable defeats and they need to keep doing that. Dyche said after losing at Anfield last month that his side would be 'relentless' in the run-in and it will be interesting to see how they return from the international break. Turf Moor is a tremendous old stadium and the atmosphere is always good. If they beat Spurs, they will put intense pressure on Sunderland 30 minutes before the Tyne-Wear derby."*

GAME 31 – Burnley v Tottenham Hotspur, Sunday 5th April, 13.30 hrs

After early morning heavy mist Easter Sunday turns into a glorious sunny day, perhaps not the kind of weather we would have wanted for a visit by the 'southern softies'. What we would have preferred is some proper Burnley weather, driving rain and hailstones. I miss out on a trip up Pendle Hill with friends and family owing to the switch to a Sunday game so it better be worth it.

No surprises in the Clarets line up, Ashley Barnes again plays wide left with Sam Vokes and Danny Ings up front. Michael Duff retains his place in central defence, and the only minor eyebrow raiser is the inclusion of new signing Fredrik Ulvestad on the bench. I doubt he will get any action but it is a further step in his acclimatisation to English football.

'Golden Boy' Harry Kane is rewarded for his glorious season's efforts for Spurs and now England by being named as Captain. Once again we face a very strong line up with an equally impressive bench which includes the likes of Andros Townsend, scorer of England's equaliser in the friendly international in Italy last week.

What we need now is a performance of the quality we delivered against Manchester City and at a lovely sunny Turf Moor the crowd are certainly up for it. Starting brightly it looks like the team are also and on five minutes we should be ahead. Danny Ings goes clear in the penalty area in front of goal but his shot lacks any conviction and is easy meat for Spurs stand-in keeper Vorm. A costly chance gone begging? I can't help feeling that had that chance fell to Kane in his current form he would have gobbled it up.

Still it's no good bemoaning the miss we have to get our heads up and keep plugging away. This is indeed what we do and in a half of few chances we are probably edging it in terms of performance. Once again our high pressing game is limiting Spurs threat and forcing them backwards. Danny almost redeems himself nearing half time as he moves infield to launch an 'exocet' destined for the top corner before Vorm's outstretched hand saves the day. So it's in at half time all square.

Bizarrely, Spurs full back Kyle Walker injured in an incident just before half time re emerges for the second half, clearly limping badly. Obviously in considerable discomfort he hobbles around for a few minutes as Burnley launch all their attacks down his flank. Not surprisingly he then sits down on the floor and waits to be substituted. What were the Spurs medical staff thinking? If he couldn't walk at half time how the hell was he going to play a half of Premier League football!

Buoyed by an increasingly vociferous crowd clearly enjoying their day in the sun, the Clarets continue to press relentlessly but lacking a 'cutting edge'. The Spurs goal survives some close shaves with Vorm equal to all that we throw at him. As the game rolls on our attempts become more direct with a lot of direct ball into the box but to no avail. The nearest being a header from George Boyd from a headed pass by Lukas Jutkiewicz on as a substitute for Sam Vokes, which drifts agonisingly wide of the post. A special mention here for Ashley Barnes who in this game combines his usual unstinting muscular effort with great ability to hold the ball up and give the Spurs defenders a real contest.

Our visitors are looking to catch us on the break as we push ever forward in search of the precious goal that would mean so much to our survival hopes. Lamela, scorer of a wonder goal against us at White Hart Lane, is introduced in a straight swop, winger for winger with Chadli. Finally Townsend enters the fray late in the game, presumably to exploit tiring legs in our defence. I am anticipating a final few minutes of blistering pace from the speedy winger, but thankfully it doesn't transpire.

Still lots of 'huff and puff' from the Clarets but no final reward, and after three minutes of added time the referee blows his whistle and the game ends goalless. Three points would have been invaluable but one is better than nothing, and it takes us back to 18th spot once again above QPR. Unfortunately the fast fading Newcastle are unable to take anything from Sunderland who pick up 3 invaluable points with a 1-0 win at the Stadium of Light.

The weekend's fixtures it could be argued leave us in a weaker position than before. QPR and Leicester have closed the gap behind us, and Sunderland have extended their lead over us to three points. On the other hand we now sit only two points behind Aston Villa and Hull City, just one win adrift of two teams that we still have to play.

Result – Burnley 0 – 0 Tottenham Hotspur

Burnley Team

Heaton, Trippier, Duff, Shackell, Mee, Arfield, Jones, Boyd, Barnes, Ings, Vokes (Jutkiewicz 76)

Subs Not used – Gilks, Keane, Ward, Ulvestad, Kightly, Sordell

Tottenham Hotspur Team

Vorm, Walker (Davies 47), Dier, Chiriches, Rose, Mason (Townsend 83), Bentaleb, Eriksen, Paulinho, Chadli (Lamela 64) Kane

Subs Not used – Friedel, Stambouli, Dembele, Soldado

Attendance – 18,829

Season Record – Played 31, Won 5, Drawn 11, Lost 15, Goals For 26, Goals Against 49, Points 26

League Position after Game 31 – 18th

Continuing bad news on the wager front as Preston continue to pile on the points. Consecutive victories in the Easter period, 1-0 at home to Rochdale, then 3-0 away at Bradford, open up an eight point gap over third placed MK Dons who have a game in hand. With only six left to play this is a substantial lead. Not wanting to appear churlish I text my congratulations to some of my PNE walking buddies, and at the same time remind them of my concern for my fiver.

What a fine chap Scouse Brian turns out to be! Despite him being a Liverpool fan who has leanings towards North End, he immediately replies that should, God forbid, the Clarets fail in their quest he will pay the fiver. His agile mind then gets into overdrive and starts to suggest ways of wriggling out of the payment, such as looking at alternative understandings of the word five...r. Then he even offers to rifle his grandson's piggy bank and make the £5 payment in pennies. I like his thinking on this, it is not only lateral but also devious. Hopefully it will not come to this but I am retaining his text offers just in case!

On Tuesday evening 7th April MK Dons reduce the deficit with a 2-0 victory over Scunthorpe in their game in hand. That makes the gap now only five points and PNE have a tough game coming up next at home to league leaders Bristol City.

On the same night an important clash affecting the Clarets chances is played out. Aston Villa meet QPR at Villa Park and Clarets fans debate what will be the best outcome. Personally I feel that for both teams to lose would be ideal, but as this is impossible a draw would best suit. A Villa win would take them five points clear of us and difficult to catch, a QPR win would take them two points to the good, and give them some real momentum with consecutive away victories in a week.

Following the game intermittently via the BBC website I see QPR have taken an early lead, but this is short lived and by half time they trail 2-1 to two Christian Benteke goals. Early in the second period QPR equalise and entering the final stages again go ahead with a goal from, yes you guessed, Charlie Austin. I'm not over enamoured with this potential outcome, despite Charlie racking up more good points for my Fantasy Football team. However Benteke steps up to fire home an immaculate free kick to pocket the match ball and level the scores again whilst sending all Clarets happily to bed. The potential damage is limited as we drop a place below QPR but only on goal difference, and Villa extend their lead to a manageable three points. PHEW! This relegation battle is a nerve wracking business.

Saturday 11th April is not only the date for our home game with Arsenal but also its Grand National day. This fact reminds me that our biggest ever Premier League victory came on National day in 2010, a thumping 4-1 away win at Hull City. What a fantastic day that was. Will this be the same?

As usual wife, daughter and myself make our considered selections for the race, based not on form, weight and jockey, but on more important factors like the horse's name, and what colours the jockey wears. It can't be a bad method, my wife Julie won last year with Pineau De Re. I settle down to watch the race whilst hastily cramming my early tea down ahead of the 5.30 kick off at the Turf. Unfortunately last year's success was not to be equalled and the best we manage is Julie's horse in sixth, daughter Stephanie's 10th, and both of mine failing to finish. I hope this is not a bad omen!

GAME 32 – Burnley v Arsenal, Saturday 11th April, 17.30 hrs

Another live TV date for the Clarets and I'm at the ground in surprisingly good time having managed to park with less difficulty than anticipated. It's a bright day but blustery and quite cool out of the sun. As expected there are no changes for the Clarets although a welcome return to the substitutes bench for Matty Taylor following a long spell out with an ankle injury. Arsenal, also as expected, field a glittering array of talent assembled at a cost that we can only dream of.

We start the game as usual attacking the cricket field end playing in to a stiff breeze. We seem to be having difficulty clearing our lines but whether this is down to the wind or the strength of the opposition is not immediately obvious. Nevertheless the best early sight of goal falls to the Clarets as Sam Vokes, not noted for his lightening pace, outstrips Mertesacker and gets into the box but is thwarted by Arsenal keeper Ospina. An encouraging sign though that this lack of pace may be an opportunity to exploit.

Our visitors then proceed to assert some dominance as they move the ball precisely and intelligently and the signs are becoming ominous. It's no surprise as we fall behind on 12 minutes. A poor clearance is picked up in the midfield and quickly shuttled forward. Ozil's shot from the left is well blocked by Heaton with the ball falling to Sanchez, whose effort is then blocked by Duff. Unfortunately the rebound falls to Ramsey who powerfully shoots into the top of the net. A bit typical of the goals we concede, a lot of ricocheting about but the ball always seeming to fall for our opponents, bad luck or bad play?

I must confess at this point I am fearing the worst and dreading the sort of purple patch that Chelsea hit us with in the season's opener. Indeed there are many similarities between this Arsenal side and their London cousins. However the onslaught doesn't materialise and after a few minutes we start to get a foothold and the game becomes more even. We are being handicapped though by Arsenal's willingness to go down at the slightest hint of physical contact, and referee Mike Dean's gullibility to fall for it. Sanchez is a prime example of this tactic and bends the referee's ear at every possible opportunity.

Dean is clearly not a lover of Claret, but on a couple of occasions manages to award us free kicks in dangerous areas, greeted by loud ironic cheers from the crowd. Nothing comes from the first but from the second Trippier's fine effort brings a good save from the Gunner's keeper. It's a shocking first half performance by the referee but we go in at half time just the one goal down.

It's a better opening to the second half as the Clarets showing some belief, and with the wind at their backs, signal their attacking intent. Unfortunately we are now starting to play much more directly and hitting rather too many long hopeful balls into the opposition box. The best chance however comes from a great run by Ben Mee, he skilfully evades a defender and gets into the area on the left side, his cross eludes a crowd of players and lands at the feet of George Boyd, who promptly completely misses his kick!

Having weathered the storm, with about 20 minutes to go, the Gunners start to show a bit more attacking interest as they go in search of the second killer goal. The Clarets maintain their excellent defensive shape and limit their opponents to mainly long range efforts. Despite the introduction of Welbeck for Giroud they are unable to add to their tally and settle for a hard fought, if somewhat scrappy one goal win.

Once again a game of few chances ends in a narrow defeat. Once again the fans remain till the end to applaud the team and manager for another tremendous battling performance. Once again we can't fault the team for effort, organisation and fight, but we wish fervently that we had that little bit of quality that we lack in key areas. Our opponents are clearly well blessed in that respect and with players of the calibre of Cazorla, Ozil, Ramsey, Sanchez, and Giroud are rightfully mounting a late if albeit hopeful title challenge. Their strength in depth means that players such as Welbeck, Walcott, Rosicky, and Flamini can only make the bench, how can we compete with that?

Result – Burnley 0 – 1 Arsenal (Ramsey 12)

Burnley Team

Heaton, Trippier, Duff, Shackell, Mee, Arfield, Jones (Taylor 90), Boyd, Barnes, Ings, Vokes

Subs Not used – Gilks, Keane, Ward, Ulvestad, Kightly, Jutkiewicz

Arsenal Team

Ospina, Bellerin, Mertesacker, Koscielny, Monreal, Ramsay, Cazorla, Coquelin, Ozil, Giroud (Welbeck 82), Sanchez (Chambers 90)

Subs Not used – Szczesny, Gibbs, Rosicky, Walcott, Flamini

Attendance – 20,615

Season Record – Played 32, Won 5, Drawn 11, Lost 16, Goals For 26, Goals Against 50, Points 26

League Position after Game 32 – 19th

Yet another defeat and earlier in the days wins for Leicester at West Bromwich, and Aston Villa at Tottenham, do nothing to improve our survival chances. The only good news from Saturday's fixtures are defeats for Hull City who go down 2-0 at Southampton, and Sunderland thrashed heavily 1-4 at home by the resurgent Crystal Palace. Queens Park Rangers have no game till Sunday when they meet Premier League leaders Chelsea at Loftus Road. Come on you Blues!

In his after match summation Arsene Wenger is unusually complimentary to the Clarets. *"I am pleased with the performance because it was more of a fighting performance than a fluent performance. Many people question us on that side but I would first say that I'm surprised by the quality of Burnley. It would be a shame if they go down as they are fantastically well organised, they press very well, they have a great solidarity, they are very fit and I understand now why they took points from the big teams here.*

"We had to fight, we had to be combative until the end and we couldn't score the second goal, our defenders played well today and won us the three points.

"It was a different test. At some stages at the start of the second half I thought we were under pressure to concede a goal because we didn't start very well. In the last 20 minutes it looked like they got a little bit tired and we could have scored a second goal, but there were periods in the game where we need to be tight, well organised and calm at the back and I think our defenders and goalkeeper deserve credit,"

Good old Arsene I think he is a Clarets convert. Compare that to the odious ramblings of Leicester boss Nigel Pearson after we took a point from them. I know which manager commands my respect.

Anyway a bit more good news on the Sunday as another notorious whinger's team, Chelsea do the decent thing and take all three points at Loftus Road. A brave battle by QPR limiting Chelsea to one shot on target, but vitally that was the goal scored by Cesc Fabregas on 88 minutes. The defeat leaves the Rangers level on points with us but above on goal difference, vitally though they have played one game more.

Tuesday 14th April should have been my first Dotcom walkers outing following the fortnight Easter break, and an opportunity to hit them with my 'dry powder' should they start 'lording it' about promotion. However my powder will have to stay in store as instead I enrol on a Cardiopulmonary resuscitation course (CPR) run by the British Heart Foundation and promoted by Radio Lancashire at Burnley Library. The radio station has swung its support behind the scheme since the collapse and near fatal cardiac incident suffered by comedian and presenter Ted Robins on stage in Manchester recently. Ted came along and also Graham Liver (Boo! Hiss! Blackburn Rovers fan), presenter of Radio Lancashire's breakfast programme. A very informative session which hopefully gave me the knowledge and confidence to attempt to save a life if God forbid I am ever called upon. A fine walking day sacrificed but in a noble cause.

Apparently and quite unexpectedly it appears I have become a TV celebrity. Unknown to myself the resuscitation course I had just taken part in was filmed and shown on BBC's Look North West teatime programme on Tuesday 14th April. I was of course blissfully unaware of this. On Thursday 16th we assembled for the regular Burnley Contingent walk, or as I like to think of it, another episode of 'Walking with Dinosaurs'.

On getting out of the car I was heckled in an unseemly manner, across a busy main road, by several of my fellow perambulators. The gist being that now I was famous I was too good to speak to them. I of course ignored the fatuous comments whilst mentally making a note to see if I could catch the programme on the BBC iPlayer. Who knows this could be the start of a career in television, maybe a part in Casualty next! Fortunately after a while they got tired of the ribbing and by the next outing it will be completely forgotten about, that's what dementia does to you. What's more so probably will all the training just undertaken.

GAME 33 – Everton v Burnley, Saturday 18th April, 15.00 hrs

I must say that I don't have many recollections of Goodison Park being a happy hunting ground for the Clarets. However I do have a bit of a soft spot for the Toffees as my daughter was able to do some voluntary work with Everton in the Community back in her University days. Unfortunately they made her wear an Everton tracksuit and this has mentally scarred her to this day. No room for sentiment in this game though, three points vitally needed by the Clarets to kickstart the survival push

This game turns out to be for me a rather difficult one to summarise. Firstly on account of the fact that I have only scant knowledge of what transpired. The game coincides with a visit to the North Lakes for my family to meet the parents of my daughter Stephanie's boyfriend Tom. Stu and Sue are residents of Bampton Grange in the North Lakes and we have booked an overnight stay at the excellent village inn, the Crown and Mitre.

Leaving Burnley around kick off time for the journey north I decide to leave off the Radio Lancs commentary, one to ease conversation, and secondly to relieve stress levels. By Preston this has been abandoned as the girls instruct me to switch it on. Now, I have had problems with this station in the past whilst mobile. It has an innate ability to switch to a commentary on any other game than ours. Today is no exception. Instead of Everton v Burnley in the Premier League I am treated to full match commentary of the League One fixture Doncaster v Fleetwood. This is further enhanced by summaries from Blackpool v Fulham, and Morecambe v Burton. The Doncaster game seems to be a rather dour affair, whilst the Morecambe one is even worse. Already relegated Blackpool are probably best not mentioned.

Sporadically little snippets filter through from Goodison Park. The first one informs me that Tom Heaton has saved a penalty from Ross Barkley. What the Hell is going on with penalty taking there? Leighton Baines is a recognised spot kick expert but recently Mirallas, and now Barkley have taken the responsibility and both missed!

Is this a good omen? Are the footballing Gods going to be in our favour today? Apparently not as the next reference to our game informs that the aforementioned Mirallas has put the Toffees one nil up. No more news until right on half time then more bad news as the commentator lets us know Ashley Barnes has been sent off for a second bookable offence. That's enough for me, I can't take anymore of this Doncaster stuff and switch off, hoping that on arrival I will find that we have made a miraculous second half come back and taken the spoils. Whilst however, realistically fearing that our ten men will have been overwhelmed, and our already inferior goal difference further damaged.

Well it certainly wasn't the first scenario, nor the second. A brave second half performance results in no further goals for either side and we are beaten again for the 17th time this season. Furthermore Leicester who are now on a charge have beaten Swansea 2-0 and leapfrog us in the table, dumping us bottom in the process.

A bad start to what is meant to be a very enjoyable weekend, but I am determined not to let the result spoil it. A good night out at the pub with our new friends Stu and Sue, and their two sons Tom and James ends with us being reportedly 'last men standing' at the bar. Stu, a Sunderland fan by birth, does his best to seem concerned about our plight whilst not exhibiting any confidence in the Mackem's survival chances.

A quick glance at the Internet tells me all I need to know about the game. Once again an inept refereeing performance has cost us dearly. A penalty to Everton that should not have been, two better shouts for us not given. A sending off for Barnes, but no similar punishment for Mirallas for a much worse challenge on Boyd.

It's not looking good now as we enter the last five games, the next being an absolutely 'must win' at home to Leicester City. Changes will be inevitable as Barnes sits this one out suspended, however with only one goal in our last seven matches perhaps this is not a bad thing. The tide has got to turn now but with most of the games to come against sides also fighting for their lives, will we be good enough?

Result –Everton 1 (Mirallas 29) – 0 Burnley

Burnley Team

Heaton, Trippier, Duff, Shackell, Mee, Arfield, Jones (Taylor 84), Boyd (Wallace 84), Barnes, Ings, Vokes (Jukiewicz 59)

Subs Not used – Gilks, Keane, Ward, Kightly,

Everton Team

Howard, Coleman, Stones, Jagielka, Baines, McCarthy (Besic 88), Barry, Barkley, Lennon, Kone (Naismith 80), Mirallas (Lukaku 61)

Subs Not used – Joel, McGeady, Garbutt, Alcaraz

Attendance – 39,496

Season Record – Played 33, Won 5, Drawn 11, Lost 17, Goals For 26, Goals Against 51, Points 26

League Position after Game 33 – 20th

I was right about the Doncaster v Fleetwood game. On Thursday 23rd April the Radio Lancashire Sports bulletin ran with a story about last Saturday's match. Apparently Doncaster had posted on their club website a video of the match highlights. This consisted of the two teams running out, followed by a guy kicking the ball as the referee blows for full time. Total running time 27 seconds.

The Fleetwood manager, ex Claret Graham Alexander, was not amused and called it 'disrespectful'. Oh come on Graham, lighten up a bit!

Ahead of Saturday's now absolutely vital must win game at home to now third bottom Leicester city, Sean Dyche is as ever staying positive to the end, but trying to play down the importance.

"It's the same for any game, but particularly against teams in and around you, you want to win. It's an important game, as they all have been, and obviously we want the points.

"Performances generally have been good, we just have to keep creating chances and take more of them."

Agreed Sean, now let's get out there and ram the disrespectful drivel that Leicester boss Nigel Pearson came out with about our club right back down his throat. It's sure to be a feisty atmosphere with so much at stake and Pearson not having endeared himself to Clarets fans. With home support based for the last two home games in all four stands, the return of home fans to the Cricket Field stand should ensure a loud and hostile reception for the Foxes. Let battle commence.

GAME 34 – Burnley v Leicester City, Saturday 25th April, 15.00 hrs

The penultimate home game of a hard and often difficult season sees us bottom of the pack, but with probably now just five teams contesting three relegation places, still in contention. Nobody in their right mind thought it was going to be easy and to be still in with a shout at this stage is probably as much as we had a right to ask for.

A week of lovely weather in East Lancashire has given way by Saturday to the more familiar cold and cloudy climate that we all know and love. Suntan cream and shorts are replaced by woolly hats and gloves as I make my way to the pub for pre match pints. Undaunted by the cold we sit outside with our beer and discuss everything from personal ailments to boyhood in Burnley Wood with not a mention of football.

I must say that in view of the fast approaching vital fixture I am remarkably relaxed and suffering no pre match tension. Little do I know what is about to unfold.

With one enforced team change due to the suspension of Ashley Barnes following his dismissal last week at Everton, Sean decides to go with a more cautious replacement in Matty Taylor rather than the unpredictable Michael Kightly. The formation remains pretty much the same with Taylor taking a wide left midfield role but perhaps a little deeper and narrower than we have seen from Barnes. A late shock is the unavailability of Sam Vokes through injury, and he is replaced like-for-like by Lukas Jutkiewicz. One notable absentee from our visitor's team is our nemesis David Nugent, and for that I am truly thankful.

An early sight of goal for the Clarets as a poor clearance by Leicester allows Taylor to play in Ings but his shot is straight at an oncoming defender. After that the game settles into a nervy affair with few attempts at goal despite much huffing and puffing. Leicester produce one half chance with the pacy Vardy's spin in the box, but his shot is comfortably saved by Heaton. Our best chance of the half comes on 31 minutes as Trippier's corner is headed on by Duff to Taylor whose close range effort is brilliantly saved by Schmeichel in the Foxes goal. Not much then of note till half time and the teams troop off level, 0-0.

Reflecting on the first half, I am of the opinion that for a game we need to win our performance is way short of the mark. We lack any real creativity with no penetration whatsoever. There is nobody getting to the by-line and cutting crosses back into the danger area, perhaps Kightly would have been the better option.

On to the second half and once again a determined push on the restart but no real sign of the excruciating drama that is shortly to be played out. Then in the 59th minute the deciding point not only of this match but probably our season. Danny Ings wriggles free in the box and fires a shot which is parried by the excellent Schmeichel. The ball however falls into the path of Taylor who is promptly upended by Leicester full back Konchesky. A penalty, for a team with only one goal in seven games, manna from heaven.

The crowd, as a man, rise to their feet to see Danny Ings surely complete the formality and fire the Clarets into an invaluable lead. But no, striding to the spot with the ball in his hands is Matt Taylor. Why? Our highly rated top scorer is out there on the pitch, why is a guy who has missed most games through injury entrusted with one of the most important kicks of the season? Still he has scored from the spot at Turf Moor, albeit against us in the colours of West Ham, so surely he won't miss. But oh yes he will! His left foot shot sends Schmeichel the wrong way but hits the base of the post and goes out.

Disbelief in the space of a minute turns to abject despair as Leicester break down the right. Albrighton's cross is scuffed towards his own goal by Duff, Heaton has to desperately amend his body shape to keep it out and the onrushing Vardy completes a scruffy poke over the line. How cruel is that! What have we done to so offend the footballing Gods? The sheer look of horror and despair on the faces of the Burnley crowd and the delight on our counterpart's visages says it all. I think that this is the moment that has doomed us! As The Mail on Sunday's reporter put it *"GONE IN 60 SECONDS."*

Substitutions aplenty and another reflex save by Schmeichel but it's all too little, too late. The game fizzles out in a third consecutive 1-0 defeat for us and a fourth consecutive victory for our fast escaping visitors.

Leaving the ground I am lost for words. Others in the crowd claim, and possibly quite rightly that our season has floundered on two missed penalties, today's and Scott Arfield's saved effort early in the season at Crystal Palace. If those two had gone in we would probably have been 5 points better off, exactly the distance we are now off safety. But I am sure every team in the dogfight can point to ifs and buts. I can't help feeling our demise is down to something more basic, i.e. a lack of quality in most positions, a lack of depth in the squad, and on occasions a lack of adventure.

Result –Burnley 0 – 1 Leicester City (Vardy 60)

Burnley Team

Heaton, Trippier, Duff, Shackell, Mee, Arfield, Jones, Boyd (Wallace 71), Taylor (Kightly 86), Ings, Jukiewicz (Sordell 71)

Subs Not used – Gilks, Keane, Ward, Ulvestad,

Leicester City Team

Schmeichel, Wasilewski, Huth, Morgan, Konchesky, Albrighton (De Laet 72), Cambiasso, King, Drinkwater (James 77), Vardy. Ulloa (Kramaric 65)

Subs Not used – Schwarzer, Upson, Mahrez, Wood

Attendance – 19,582

Season Record – Played 34, Won 5, Drawn 11, Lost 18, Goals For 26, Goals Against 52, Points 26

League Position after Game 34 – 20th

Saturday night is spent mentally trying to come to terms with the impact of what I have just witnessed. The Beer Helps! Hull City's 2-0 away victory at Crystal Palace further compounds a dreadful day for the Clarets. QPR pick up a point in a home draw with West Ham, but at this stage of the season that is probably not enough. Ironically Mr Dependable himself, Charlie Austin, also misses a penalty in that game. We remain anchored at the bottom now one point behind QPR, four behind Sunderland, and five adrift of Hull and Leicester. Aston Villa lose the evening game at Manchester City to stay six points ahead.

To me survival now looks a lost cause, we need a minimum of two wins to overhaul three sides and that without them collecting any more points. Furthermore the three sides nearest to us all have a game in hand. Realistically we need at least three wins from the remaining four fixtures to stand any chance, but considering we have only managed five from thirty four, this seems a tad over optimistic. I am already mentally preparing myself for regular Saturday afternoon football at a sensible kick off time, and an extra four home games for my money.

Sean Dyche, who inwardly must have felt worse than me, summed it up perfectly in his after match interview.

"The game is cruel sometimes and that was the game at its cruellest today. We miss a penalty and they score from a knock into the area."

Maintaining his permanent positive stance, he went on to say.

"Our performance had been good enough to win, especially in the second half. It's a blow for us to lose but we've been written off all season so we're not in new territory."

Asked if his team could stay up, Dyche said: *"Never say never…it's do-able."*

On this Black Saturday for the Clarets further irony is heaped on us as close season target Troy Deeney, scores the opener for Watford in a 2-0 victory at Brighton that sees them promoted to the Premier League.

Saturday's tragic events again focus my mind on my increasingly foolhardy wager with Jim (Skipper of the Yard). The defeat plunges my money into further jeopardy as the survival gap widens. One half of the equation could have been settled on Saturday 25th with PNE winning 3-0 at home to Swindon. Fortunately the gallant MK Dons came to my rescue with a 3-2 away victory at Rochdale, taking the race for the second automatic promotion place in League One to the final game.

A defeat would have seen Preston promoted so it's now down to this coming Sunday as MK Dons host already relegated Yeovil, and North End travel to second bottom Colchester. A win for MK Dons means that anything but victory for PNE will dump them into the play-offs. With their past history of play-off failures this will be the last thing they want.

Still feeling a bit down about the Leicester game, I text Scouse Brian to see if he can lift my spirits. His ever optimistic reply is that all is not lost. He then goes on to predict the results of the remaining fixtures for the bottom six. Now I have to say there are some flaws in Brian's predictions. He feels that QPR and Leicester will go down, but has the Foxes finishing on 38 points! He then forecasts two wins and two draws for the Clarets, the last draw coming at Villa Park. However he also predicts Villa will beat Burnley. Hmmm... I suggest he takes more water with it!

On Monday 27th April Bournemouth, managed by our old friend Eddie Howe, ensure automatic promotion to the Premier League, with a 3-0 home win over Bolton. What a magnificent achievement for a club even smaller than ourselves and with a ground capacity of only 12,000. Surely a lesson there to some of the more profligate Championship big spenders.

Tuesday 28th and following a lovely walk in the Silverdale area with some very nervy North Enders, our survival chances become even more remote. Hull City defeat Liverpool 1-0 at the KC stadium to record their second victory in four days. This stretches the gap to eight points and puts them virtually out of our reach. Thanks Liverpool! It's amazing how at the business end of the season the struggling sides suddenly find some form. Leicester with four wins on the bounce and now Hull with two, unfortunately the same can't be said for the Clarets.

Wednesday 29th sees Leicester take on Chelsea at the King Power Stadium and a victory for them in this one will put them similarly almost mathematically uncatchable. Fortunately Chelsea after a lacklustre first half, and trailing 1-0 at the break, find the same scintillating rhythm that they had at Turf Moor. By the end of the game they have blown Leicester away by the same 3-1 scoreline, and the points gap between the Foxes and us stays at five.

The last day in April sees a seriously depleted Burnley Contingent head out for the customary ramble. The absence of 'Sherpa' Walton, currently enjoying(?) backpacking the West Highland Way with wife Gwen, provides an opportunity for husband and wife team Dave & Theresa Preedy to nominate the walk and take the lead.

Suffice it to say that these two are currently building a reputation for walks with long steep ascents and in Theresa's case, an abundance of water. This occasion does not disappoint on both scores. This walk has strong analogies with the Clarets current plight in that it proves too have, 'Many Rivers To Cross', and 'Ain't No Mountain High Enough'.

A supposed 10 miles walk (changed initially from a 7.5 mile walk) turns out to be in effect 11.5 miles. The walk concludes with at least three 'walking wounded' from a party of seven, five out of seven rescued by car, a total walk time of six hours twenty minutes, and a late tea with a return home at 19.00 hours! I think the next time a 'Preedy walk' is announced the sick absence figures will make interesting reading.

MAY

GAME 35 – West Ham United v Burnley, Saturday 2nd May, 15.00 hrs

To be strictly honest my own feelings ahead of this fixture were that the game was well and truly up for us. Although mathematically still possible the reality of the situation was that we were not likely to pick up anywhere near enough points to survive.

This game just confirmed my thoughts and in a manner that has become customary in the last few weeks. Yet again a 1-0 defeat, yet again a man sent off, yet again a penalty against (scored not missed), yet again a referee doing us no favours.

The early exchanges seemed to bode reasonably well as we registered some shots at goal, which in itself is becoming a rarity. The best chance fell to Danny Ings on 18 minutes but his free header from 12 yards missed the target completely.

However any optimism was quickly dispelled on 23 minutes as Kouyate weaved his way in the box and Duff's lunge brought him down. No arguments about the penalty decision, but then referee Jonathan Moss flourished an extremely harsh red card to effectively end the game as a contest. Noble despatched the penalty with no problem, if only Matty Taylor had done the same last week, and we are once again facing Everest. Down to 10 men and almost an hour to play was too much to ask even for this bunch of wholehearted triers.

As usual the Clarets refused to be rolled over and Barnes was unlucky to see his goalbound header saved by the foot of West Ham custodian, Adrian. But once again we showed whilst we have an admirable ability to contain the opposition our creative skills are sadly lacking.

Sean Dyche expressed amazement at the sending off. *"There was a stadium full of people surprised it was a sending off. I can only imagine their manager was surprised it was a sending off. The staff were surprised it was a sending off. The subs were surprised it was a sending off. The groundsman was surprised it was a sending off. Other than that..."*

But Sean did concede that the decision was not the reason that we find ourselves now almost certainly doomed. The reality is that we now have to overturn an eight point deficit and a weak goal difference in our final three games. At a time when fellow strugglers with the exception of QPR have found some form and results, we have lost four on the trot, the conclusion is inevitable.

Result –West Ham United 1 (Noble 24 pen) – 0 Burnley

Burnley Team

Heaton, Trippier, Duff, Shackell, Mee, Arfield, Jones, Boyd (Keane 46), Taylor (Wallace 81), Ings, Barnes (Sordell 79)

Subs Not used – Gilks, Reid, Jutkiewicz, Kightly,

West Ham United Team

Adrian, Jenkinson, Collins, Burke, Cresswell, Downing, Noble, Kouyate, Amalfitano, Nolan (Nene 79), Valencia (Cole 82)

Subs Not used – Jaaskelainen, O'Brien, Oxford, Song, Jarvis

Attendance – 34,946

Season Record – Played 35, Won 5, Drawn 11, Lost 19, Goals For 26, Goals Against 53, Points 26

League Position after Game 35 – 20th

After Game 35 it looks like QPR and ourselves are almost crashing through the trap door, but two points then separate the next five clubs and a real battle to come for them in the remaining three fixtures. In free fall are Newcastle United having lost eight on the bounce and now involved heavily in the dogfight.

Sunday 3rd May brings a little consolation regarding the Burnley/Preston wager. With the Clarets now almost certainly destined for the Championship, half my bet is lost, however Preston must match MK Dons result to clinch the cash for Jim (Skipper of the Yard). In typical PNE fashion they bottle it! MK Dons romp home 5-1 whilst PNE go down 1-0 at relegation battlers Colchester. My cash is for the moment safe pending the results of the play-offs.

On Tuesday 5th May the Clarets appeal the controversial red card handed out to Mickey Duff at West Ham. By Wednesday the red card appeal has been successful and the suspension rescinded, making Duffer available for the remaining three games. Whilst being happy that justice has been done, I am still vexed that due to a wrong refereeing decision we have been obliged to play more than two thirds of a 'must win' game with a major handicap. Doesn't seem right somehow.

Once again the outcome of my financial speculation causes concern as Preston take a big advantage in their semi final play-off away leg with a 1-0 victory at Chesterfield. This lead sets them up nicely for the home leg to be played on

Sunday 10th May. A draw now will be enough to take them to a Wembley final, and one step nearer the return to the Championship.

Friday's Burnley Express Sports section leads with a story 'Dyche defends Clarets' ambition'. This followed claims in the national press that Burnley had 'failed to be competitive' and claiming that we should have splashed the cash.

However Dyche felt the club had acted prudently with regards to future stability.

"There has to be a story, and ours is of truth, reality and positivity. Someone will always go against that with their story – that's life, it is what it is. The main values the club have instilled, certainly in my time here, have been of positive realities, and a club which wants to build and move forward.

The club has had years of trying to punch above it's weight, but is now trying to sustain a level and build for the future. It's not just about today, it's about tomorrow – the club has come out of a situation where they HAD to sell one player, Charlie Austin, and now has a platform to allow real growth for many seasons. There is a counter balance to the argument."

He went on to highlight the inflation in the transfer market caused by the ridiculous fee paid by Fulham for Ross McCormack on his pre-season move from Leeds.

"The truth is shown in the transfer market. It ignited from a Championship player moving to a Championship club for a deal that, somewhere down the line, will cost £11m. It's no one's fault, but if you look at the numbers after that...

You were looking at £2/3/4m in a market where you had to look at £7/8/9/10m. Where does that live at a club like Burnley? Do you want to put the club in trouble again? There has to be a reality, and for us, we want to build for the future, which costs a lot of money, and if you want to put that on the pitch immediately, it costs a lot more."

Well I for one, and I am sure many more realistic supporters believe that Sean is right in this respect. We could have thrown all the Premier League cash at it and still failed, as others will. Then where? Oblivion?

The next game up is Hull City away and you may remember from an earlier chapter that the game has some significance for me. This relates to an antagonistic old mate of mine who since his move to Lincolnshire, for some reason believes he is a 'Tiger'. Now although I know for a fact he is only doing it to wind me up, he has been succeeding! To be fair since our recent run of cataclysmic form he has gone easy with his jibes about our impending demise. This may be due to the fact that Hull City are also in a precarious position! I am therefore praying for a Clarets victory not only to keep alive our slim hopes, but also to scupper theirs.

GAME 36 – Hull City v Burnley, Saturday 9th May, 15.00 hrs

Hull has in the recent past been a happy hunting ground for the Clarets with four wins from our last four visits. How we would love that run to continue! In our previous Premier League season we completed a fine double over the Tigers, and with a home win already under our belt against them, could this be a repeat? However with only one win in the last 14 matches, and no goals in 569 minutes, and only one in 819 minutes, that is going to be easier said than done.

With Mickey Duff available after his red card from last week was rescinded, we go again with the standard line-up.

Bad news ahead of the game is that the fellow strugglers have somehow managed to come away with a 2-0 away victory from Everton, putting them now beyond our reach.

A nervy occasion for both teams, probably more so for Hull than us given our respective positions, made for a less than enthralling first half. The nearest to a goal for Hull being a Brady free kick which hit the bar. Our best effort coming from Barnes which brought a save from the keeper. Half time arrived with no score, and once again a competent defensive performance with little goal threat.

The second period started more promisingly with a Barnes overhead kick going close and a shout for a penalty as Ings working his way across the penalty area went down under a challenge. Then on 62 minutes the unbelievable, a Burnley goal! Hull down to 10 men as centre back Dawson received attention on the touchline for a nose injury, conceded a corner.

In truth it was the type of goal that we usually concede. From the corner there was a bit of a scramble in the box the ball finding its way to Boyd to the right of goal near the touchline. The ball was fed to Mee whose cross was headed by a Hull defender hitting another before falling kindly for Ings. Now for Danny who of late had come in for some stick this was an opportunity he was not going to miss. A deft turn and a well struck left foot shot from the centre of goal and the ball nestled in the net.

A clearly delighted Ings, along with his equally also delighted teammates set off to milk the rapturous acclaim of the travelling Clarets. At this point presumably unaware of the disastrous results going against us in other fixtures, believing a lifeline had been grabbed.

Hull clearly stung by the goal and its implications attempted to rally, but with little threat. Another Brady free kick rattled the bar but the defence bolstered by the introduction of Keane and Ward stood firm. Four minutes of added time came and went and how happy we were to taste victory again.

How Burnley was that? We score after 10 hours of goalless football, and win our second away victory in the Premier League, but as a consequence of other results are RELEGATED. I can't feel too down, for me we had lost the fight some weeks back, and were awaiting the inevitable. Once again though we had given everything and this time got not only a good performance but also a positive result. This team may be going down, but they are going down with HEADS HELD HIGH, and all associated with the club, manager, staff, players and fans, should feel PROUD.

Result –Hull City 0 – 1 Burnley (Ings 62)

Burnley Team

Heaton, Trippier, Duff, Shackell, Mee, Arfield, Jones, Boyd, Taylor (Ward 76), Ings (Keane 88), Barnes

Subs Not used – Gilks, Ulvestad, Vokes, Jutkiewicz, Kightly,

Hull City Team

Harper, Chester, Dawson, McShane (Jelavic 57), Elmohamady, Livermore (Meyler 57), Huddlestone, Quinn, Brady, Aluko (Hernandez 66), N'Doye

Subs Not used – McGregor, Rosenior, Bruce, Robertson

Attendance – 24,877

Season Record – Played 36, Won 6, Drawn 11, Lost 19, Goals For 27, Goals Against 53, Points 29

League Position after Game 36 – 19th

Needless to say at the final whistle I am texting my erstwhile mate in the Lincolnshire heartland;

Me – "We are down but we are taking you with us"

Steve C – "Bollox" (sic)

Me – "And it's a double over Hull City. Can we play you every week"

Steve C – "Well by the look of it, twice next year. Think I'll support someone else"

Game, set and match I do believe!

Shortly after the game there are stories speculating that Sean Dyche will not necessarily commit himself to the Clarets for next season. These are largely based on comments made by the manager in his darkest hour, straight after relegation has been confirmed. Probably not the best time to interview the guy, and he basically said he wanted to get back to his family and assimilate the impact of what had happened.

Hopefully after coming to terms with our plight Sean will 'gird his loins' for another attempt at promotion, our own version of climbing Everest. To lose the boss would be a bigger tragedy than losing players. It would throw the whole of the progress made in the last two and a half years up in the air. But it would be understandable if Sean in his disappointment were to feel that he had taken the Clarets as far as he could. Should tempting offers come his way it would only be natural for an ambitious man to give them due consideration.

On Sunday 10th May Preston duly complete the semi final victory over Chesterfield with a 3-0 home win in the second leg, and an impressive 4-0 aggregate. It's off to Wembley now, and my wallet trembles slightly in my pocket. Worse still I will have to face the jubilant North End Dotcomers on Tuesday's walk. Should I call in sick? Fortunately the walk is scheduled on home territory from Haggate with some 'undulations' promised, that may take the wind from the Flatlanders sails.

On the same day, Queens Park Rangers become the second team to be relegated from the Premier League. Needing an unlikely scenario of winning their remaining three games whilst others lost their final two, they might just have escaped on goal difference. Not so now, they go down 6-0 at Manchester City and drop out the top flight ignominiously.

On Saturday's Match of the Day whilst discussing the relegation issue Gary Lineker puts up an interesting table showing the sums spent this season by the relegation strugglers. Not surprisingly Burnley weigh in with a measly £8.2m, whilst QPR have frittered £33m and even more astonishingly, Hull City who look almost certain to join us in the Championship an eye watering £46m!

What do the advocates of spending to survive have to say about that? Furthermore the repercussions of relegation back to the Football League may well be catastrophic for QPR who face, as a result of their previous profligacy, a Financial Fair Play penalty of almost £60m. I await the outcome of the QPR case with great anticipation, but fear the punishment will be averted or reduced significantly.

Needless to say within one day of being relegated it is reported that QPR are raising a legal objection to their Financial Fair Play penalty. What a surprise!

Some better news comes ahead of the final Premier League game at Turf Moor as Sean Dyche in his pre match press conference appears to dispel doubts about his future commitment. Speaking about comments made following the Hull game that raised concerns he said.

"I think the media has a job to do – people are looking for a different story, but the story was we had just been relegated.

"I just thought it was irrelevant in that moment – I was irked by the fact I was asked about my future 10 minutes after coming out of the Premier League.

"I am not bigger than the club – I am a custodian, whose job it is to look after the club and take it forward.

"It was a bad day for the club.

"I must make it clear for anyone trying to read into my words. I did a piece with Alistair Campbell recently and said the same thing as regards my future – I am focused on the club.

"After the season, we will have a chat about the way forward and take it from there, that's how this business works.

"I feel I understand the media more after this season, but it was an inappropriate time to speak about my future."

Hopefully that will go some way towards reassuring the fans that Sean is not on the verge of quitting and we can relax and enjoy the summer break.

Further good news comes with the announcement by the club of a new one year contract for the injured Dean

Marney, with the option of a further year to follow. 'Deano' will be unavailable for the early part of the season whilst he recovers from his cruciate ligament injury, but I am looking forward to his return asap.

GAME 37 – Burnley v Stoke City, Saturday 16th May, 15.00 hrs

It's my wife's birthday and unfortunately it coincides with the final home game of our season in the big time. Normally we would try and take in a weekend away on her big day, but with commendable understanding she has settled for a lunch out with her friends and dinner out with family after the game. Come on lads make it worth it, win it for Julie!

Also a notable occasion for one Danny Ings as it marks probably his last game at the Turf in Burnley colours. I hope the crowd give him a real good send off, he has been a credit to the club in his four seasons with us and the last two have seen some truly memorable and glorious days. Go out on a high Danny, a hat-trick will be fine!

Reasonable if not beachwear weather provides the opportunity for a couple of alfresco pints of Moorhouse's Premier Bitter at our clubhouse, the Talbot hotel. I wonder what the brewer will do next season, will it be Champion Bitter? Two pints but not much discussion about the upcoming game, I think the whole atmosphere has turned a little flat as we play out the 'dead rubbers'. More talk of rambling the moors and summer holidays now.

At the Turf and a supportive but somewhat subdued crowd are ready to see the Clarets end the season on a high note. The early exchanges certainly seem to give some promise that this is indeed what will happen. An unchanged Clarets XI are making the early running and carving out some chances. Ings cutting in from the left evades defenders in a mazy run but on arriving around the penalty spot can only find a weak finish more akin to a backpass. Undaunted our heroes continue to apply the pressure but find Stoke keeper Butland in immaculate form.

Not a lot of threat in the first 20 minutes from the visitors but as the half wears on they begin to come more into it. Their best chance falls to Diouf whose attempted diving header goes well wide. Half time arrives and a game that started promisingly for us now seems to be following a familiar pattern as we show plenty of aggressive intent but no cutting edge.

Half time is brightened by a piece of pork pie provided by a Gentleman occupying a seat on our row in the stand. A splendid gesture to end the home season and a shining example of the Pie Maker's art!

The second half continues the downward trend of the latter part of the first. We latterly seem to have developed a habit of becoming less creative and more direct. It might just be me but it seems the longer the match goes, the longer our game goes. This may be all well and good in the Championship, but against Premier League defenders is largely ineffective. It may also be more beneficial if you have a giant 'beanpole' striker like Peter Crouch, but unfortunately he is just about to enter the fray for Stoke.

I can't honestly recall many chances for us second half and not a lot from the Potters either. Michael Kightly gets a late run on as a substitute, ironically it was he who was largely responsible for a 2-1 away victory at Stoke which seems eons ago and which gave us great hope. Unfortunately he is unable to reproduce the magic today. Also a few minutes pitch time for our Norwegian recruit Fredrik Ulvestad who gets a taste of Premier League football for the first time. Fredrik is obviously a signing with next season in mind and we all hope that we have unearthed a hidden gem. We shall see.

So the game ends 0-0 and the crowd give the team a good hand as they depart the field. There's no booing and I think that everybody whilst recognising the squad's shortcomings, are appreciative of a magnificent effort in a very difficult league. There is no shame in our relegation, we have given everything and if that was not enough, so be it.

Last to leave are Danny Ings and Kieran Trippier who themselves are giving the crowd a good round of applause. For Danny as we have all been aware for some time this is probably the last time he will grace the Turf in a Burnley shirt. He has been in his time here an exemplary character. His first two seasons have been blighted with injury but the last two have been a pleasure to watch and his prodigious efforts in the Championship runners up season have been invaluable. Now he has the opportunity to go on to possibly even greater things, and I for one wish him well for the future.

I'm a bit concerned that 'Tripps' prolonged departure from the pitch may also be a last farewell. Unlike Danny he is still under contract but there are rumours of a £3.5m buy-out clause which may well be triggered by Premier League predators. Already rumours are circulating that Stoke, and Bournemouth may be interested. Southampton may also be in the market should they lose Nathaniel Clyne in the summer. Kieran will be dare I say a harder act to replace than Danny, he is our most creative outlet and his skill and desire make him I believe one of the best full back's seen this season. Fingers crossed that we can hold onto him.

Result – Burnley 0 – 0 Stoke City

Burnley Team

Heaton, Trippier, Duff, Shackell, Mee, Arfield, Jones (Ulvestad 88), Boyd, Taylor (Taylor65), Ings, Barnes (Vokes 83)

<u>Subs Not used</u> – Gilks, Ward, Keane, Jutkiewicz,

Stoke City Team

Butland, Cameron, Muniesa, Shawcross, Pieters, Whelan, Adam (Sidwell 83), Nzonzi, Walters (Odemwingie 59), Diouf, Arnautovic (Crouch 69)

<u>Subs Not used</u> – Begovic, Ireland, Wilson, Wollscheid

Attendance – 18,636

Season Record – Played 37, Won 6, Drawn 12, Lost 19, Goals For 27, Goals Against 53, Points 30

League Position after Game 37 – 19th

The season is not even ended with the final game still to come at Aston Villa on Sunday but by Monday 18th May comings and goings, or should I say goings are already happening at the club.

Monday sees the announcement that Steven Reid, signed on a one year contract, will be retiring from the game. No real shock this as he has been sorely plagued with injuries in his latter playing years and these have finally taken their toll on him. His Burnley career will not linger long in the memory having made only one start, and five substitute appearances.

Second one out on Tuesday is Ross Wallace who it is announced will be leaving the club having not been offered a new contract. Again not really a big surprise, although the player had been with us for five seasons his appearances have been few and far between in the last two. He has been a good servant to the club and scored some memorable goals, none more so than the brilliant equaliser at Leicester City in the Premier League which so irked Mr Pearson. Thanks for that Ross!

Tuesday's Dotcom walk at Calder Vale, Nr. Garstang was expected to be a day of fending off excited ribbing from the expectant PNE fans ahead of their play off final this coming Sunday. Fortunately our 'friends' are still in somewhat subdued frame of mind, probably down to the failures in all of their nine previous play-off encounters. How refreshing therefore it was to see, in an area not noted as a Clarets hotbed, a marker post emblazoned with a Burnley FC emblem proclaiming 'Keep the Faith'. It brought a tear to my eye! Whoever you are, Claret in Calder Vale, well done your work has not gone unnoticed.

More surprisingly is the news on Wednesday that chief executive Lee Hoos will be leaving the club and taking up a similar role at Queen Parks Rangers. Mr Hoos seems to have come in for a fair amount of stick from some sections of the fans, primarily down to the perceived failings in the transfer market, and the season ticket retainer row which upset many at the start of the last campaign. He will certainly need his wits about him to sort out the finances at QPR who are serial overspenders. A bigger contrast between clubs would be hard to imagine! He will be replaced as chief executive by David Baldwin who joined the club as chief operating officer in November 2014 and seems to be highly regarded by those in the know.

Great news for goalkeeper Tom Heaton on Thursday 21st May as he is called up to the full England squad for the upcoming games against the Republic of Ireland and Slovenia. I must confess I didn't see that one coming, I wonder if Tom did. That is tremendous reward for another excellent season with the Clarets in which, up to press, he has not missed a single minute of League action. There are also honours for both Danny Ings and Michael Keane who are called up for Gareth Southgate's England U21 squad.

GAME 38 – Aston Villa v Burnley, Sunday 24th May, 15.00 hrs

Sunday May 24th brings an end to a long and exhausting season for the Clarets. The trip to Villa Park whilst meaningless in terms of preserving our Premier League status, still has two achievable objectives.

A point today will mean that we have bettered the points tally achieved in the 2009/10 campaign. We must also attempt to better Queens Park Rangers result (away at Leicester) in order that we stay above them in the table. With a reputed £1m available for finishing each place higher, it's a not inconsiderable sum.

Well a Clarets side showing two changes to the starting line up, a debut for Fredrik Ulvestad who replaced Matty Taylor, and the return of Michael Keane for Mickey Duff, went out in style. Not content to settle for one point they came home with all three courtesy of a Danny Ings sixth minute header. A fine end of season flourish, the last three games resulting in two away wins and a home draw, sees us finish 19th in the table comfortably ahead of QPR beaten 5-1 at Leicester. No goals conceded in the final three matches and two goals for Danny Ings to send him on his way in good spirits.

Perhaps Villa's minds were preoccupied with next week's FA Cup Final against Arsenal, and already safe in their league position they were perhaps ideal final day opponents for the Clarets. Ings scoring early following Barnes's header back across the box from Ulvestad's assist set up the third away victory of the season. Tom Heaton chipped in with some terrific saves to celebrate his England call up, so all in all a highly satisfactory end to the campaign.

A good first half for the Clarets with further chances not taken, a stronger second half by Villa with the same outcome. At the end a good hand by the fans for the players and manager which was enthusiastically reciprocated.

Interestingly on the last day, Stoke City who drew 0-0 at the Turf last week, hammered Liverpool 6-1! Hull City as expected took the final relegation place after drawing at home to Manchester United, whilst Newcastle ensured their safety with a home win over West Ham.

Result – Aston Villa 0 – 1 Burnley (Ings 6)

Burnley Team

Heaton, Trippier, Keane, Shackell, Mee, Arfield, Jones, Boyd, Ulvestad (Taylor65), Ings (Reid 87), Barnes (Vokes 34)

Subs Not used – Gilks, Duff, Kightly, Jutkiewicz,

Aston Villa Team

Steer, Bacuna (Hutton 80), Vlaar, Baker, N'Zogbia, Cleverley (Sinclair 72), Westwood, Delph, Agbonlahor, Benteke, Grealish

<u>Subs Not used</u> – Guzan, Weimann, Sanchez, Green Robinson

<u>**Attendance**</u> – 40,792

<u>**Season Record**</u> – Played 38, Won 7, Drawn 12, Lost 19, Goals For 28, Goals Against 53, Points 33

<u>**League Position after Game 38**</u> – 19th

Compared to 2009/10, we gained three more points, but had one less win. This time we were beaten in 50% of the games, 2009/10 in 63%. Goals scored this time 28, last time 42. Goals against this time 53, last time 82. The statistics tell the story, a much better defensive show this time but at the cost of goals scored. On reflection though a much more harmonious and enjoyable affair than first time round. Bring on Round 3!

And finally, the BET. On Sunday the 24th May the unthinkable happened! Preston North End claimed their rightful place back in the Championship with a convincing 4-0 victory over Swindon in the Play off final at Wembley. That means that both PNE and ourselves will next season play in the same division and Jim (Skipper of the Yard) takes the spoils of the wager. I can see some real ribbing ahead in the next few weeks but I shall smile (through gritted teeth) and take it all in the spirit intended. Well done North End!

REVIEW

So that was it, a second season in the Premier League ended in the same way as the first. Or did it? My overwhelming memory of the first was one of a season ripped apart by the defection of Owen Coyle half way through. The heart and soul was torn from the club and fans, and the appointment of Brian Laws viewed as a mistake by many at the time, did little to lift the gloom. The mood at the end was almost one of relief that it was all over, and fans were apprehensive of what was to follow.

Contrast that to this season. We entered the fray after a magnificent promotion season, but with the knowledge from last time that the task ahead was immense if not impossible. We had a manager who commanded the respect of the board, his staff and players, the media, and almost impossibly all the fans. We exited the season despite relegation with a manager who I think it can be said enjoyed that same respect.

What we had in between was probably as good as we could realistically have hoped for, except the relegation. It was a magnificent effort by all at the club, not just management and players, but also by fans who backed the team to the hilt all the way. That backing was certainly repaid on the field with maximum effort and desire, and no little skill. It was a pleasure to see the Clarets go toe-to-toe with far more illustrious opponents and give as good as they got. None of the away day drubbings (West Bromwich apart) endured which marked our first season in the big time, no this time we were competitive in nearly every game.

Our competitiveness was down in no small part to the organisation and discipline to maintain the shape of the team, particularly defensively. The physical demands on the players to operate the system were exhaustive but everybody to a man produced the effort unstintingly. For that every man on the pitch, in the offices, and on the terraces, can HOLD THEIR HEADS HIGH.

We end this season disappointed, but in the words of Sean Dyche, bloodied but not broken. There is an optimism that providing the basis of the squad can be retained, and in my opinion more importantly our inspirational manager, then next season can see us challenging again. It's time now for everybody to take a short break (shorter than usual) and be ready to come back in July with the knowledge that we have done it before and can do it again. The club leaves the Premier League in a strong position both financially and in terms of personnel, and with good stewardship can return.

At this time I'm sure all concerned with the running of the club will sit down and review what was done and how it could have been done better. Of course football is very much a game of opinions and in the pubs and clubs of Burnley there will be no shortage of those amongst the fans.

Without doubt clubs of our size are at a massive financial disadvantage entering the Premier League. The comparatively massive budget afforded to us by the TV revenues is miniscule when compared to that available to the clubs who are the playthings of rich foreign backers. When a club can spend more on one transfer fee than Burnley have spent in their entire history, it leaves us on a very uneven playing field. But we have in some measure shown that organisation, commitment and belief, can on some occasions overcome this handicap. Who would have dreamt that four points would be taken off reigning Champions Manchester City, or a draw possible at this seasons Champions Chelsea. Unfortunately when every game is against a side with much bigger resources every week is a mountain to climb.

I think it's fair to say that most fans were pretty underwhelmed by the club's dealings in the transfer market during both windows. During the close season and with Sky TV £ signs blinding our eyes we waited for the major signings to start to roll in. Obviously our expectations didn't run to a Di Maria but we had anticipated one or two signings of players probably in the £3/4m category to appear. The McCormack move from Leeds to Fulham for a reported £11m obviously scuppered this. We were obviously also handicapped by the reluctance of major Championship clubs to sell their better players as they dreamt themselves of emulating our achievements. For whatever reasons the major signings didn't materialise, and most importantly the most needed area central midfield, did not get any cover.

Whether the board were unprepared to put sufficient funds up, or whether the market had moved too far away from our budget, or whether players used us to get better deals at their current clubs is academic now. The fact is that we went into the season without necessary cover for injuries in centre midfield, or without the morale boosting 'big name' signing. Promising England U21 youngsters were brought in on loan, Michael Keane from Manchester United, and Nathaniel Chalobah from Chelsea, but initially only used very sparingly. With Michael Duff's injury the former got his chance and was offered and took a permanent contract in the January window. Chalobah did not flourish and was returned to Chelsea at the end of the loan. Ahead of the summer window closing, George Boyd came in from Hull and performed creditably for the season after quickly establishing himself.

The feeling was that following the disappointments in the summer window, and in view of the fact that we were still in the mix, January would see a veritable by our standards spending spree. This again for whatever reasons didn't occur and a thin squad was stretched even thinner by the injury to Dean Marney. The loss of Marney one of only two senior centre midfielders was nothing short of a total disaster. Scott Arfield was moved from his wide position into the centre for the remainder of the season and did his best manfully. How could we have failed to bring in quality cover which was obviously needed in two windows? Many will point the transfer dealing failures as the major reason for our demise.

Precious points were lost at one stage of the season due to a catastrophic inability to defend corners. Others will point to two crucial missed penalties, Arfield's at Crystal Palace, and inexplicably Taylor's at home to Leicester as the reasons for our demise. However the inescapable fact is that the lack of goals ultimately doomed us. Chances at a premium in this division must be taken and unfortunately we were insufficiently clinical in that department.

What became increasingly apparent throughout the course of the season was that in the long term quality will always come out on top. All the positivity and hard running cannot ultimately overcome moments of sheer class. Every team in the league has several players with that class, which they allay with supreme fitness and physicality. A lesson to be learned there.

Of course all the above observations I am sure were contributory factors to our eventual downfall but to me not the major one. Without a doubt our relegation can be laid fairly and squarely at the feet of the 'unlucky charms'. Never in all my fifty plus years of supporting the Clarets have I suffered from such duff talismans as were entrusted with keeping us safe this season. The lucky wristbands, provided so thoughtfully by Judy W after scouring Europe, turned out to be hopeless bits of French tat. Not a patch on the Greek worry beads of the promotion season. Sean the Gnome I suspect was an impostor planted in my home by Steve C of Hull City infamy. He will be banished to the garden by August and made to face the fence till things improve. Even the expensive luxury Clarets Polo shirt has been committed to the wash basket in an attempt to 'cleanse' it of evil spirits.

So where do we go from here? Danny Ings is almost certainly an ex Claret and we wish him well. Question marks remain about Kieran Trippier, and Jason Shackell but we hope that we can retain them for at least one serious go at promotion. But without doubt most important of all is Sean Dyche. We have a blueprint in place for success, it may need a little tinkering with in terms of personnel but the framework is sound. A change of direction is now the last thing we need.

Finally can I just assure all my friends, some of whom are supporters of local rivals but friends nonetheless, that anything written here has been done in the spirit of good fun, and amicable rivalry. Indeed this is the essence of supporting one's team, the elation and the disappointment, the banter and one-upmanship amongst fans is what keeps us sane.

For supporters of clubs our size life is always going to be full of ups and downs. But would we have it any other way? How much more pleasurable it is for us when we achieve something by hard graft and merit, than by simply *'buying it'*.

In the words of the Calder Vale Claret, *"Keep The Faith"*.

UP THE CLARETS!

Printed in Great Britain
by Amazon